FOR PETE'S SAKE

A son reflects on his father's forty-seven year confinement with mental illness

By

Gene Gilbreath

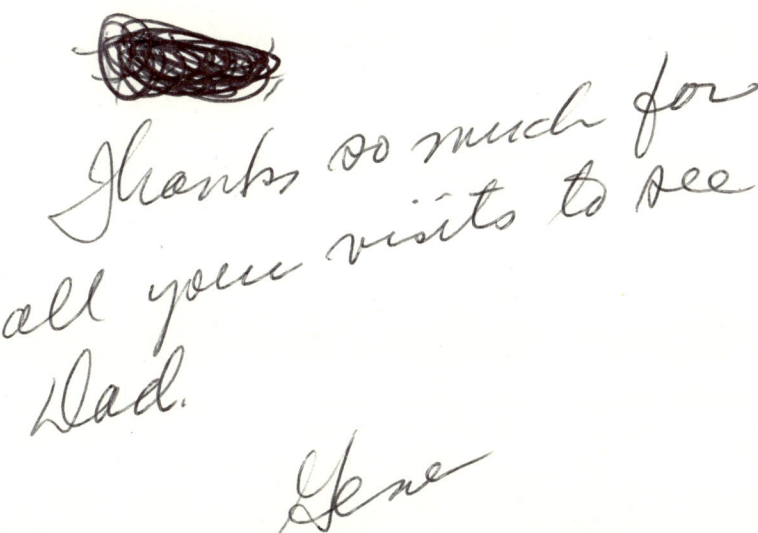

Thanks so much for
all your visits to see
Dad.

Gene

This book is a work of non-fiction. Names and places have not been changed to protect the privacy of all individuals. The events and situations are true.

ISBN: 1-4107-4480-9 (e-book)
ISBN: 1-4107-4481-7 (Paperback)

Library of Congress Control Number: 2003093043

This book is printed on acid free paper.

Printed in the United States of America
Bloomington, IN

1stBooks - rev. 08/29/03

DEDICATIONS

To the memory of my father, Pete, the subject of this book, whose suffering I now understand more fully.

Pete at nineteen, all dressed up, and ready for the world.

To the memory of my Mother, Fleda, (right) whose mental and physical strength were so admirable during Dad's long absence. For her assistance in providing records and pictures for this book, without which there would be no book. She passed away on January 20, 2003, at ninety-three years of age, as the final touches of this manuscript were being prepared.

To the memory of my only sister, Mary, (left) who was so encouraging in the early days of writing by purchasing a scanner for me. It is so regrettable that her ill health and now her death on December 21, 2002, prevented her from seeing this book.

ACKNOWLEDGMENTS

To the memory of Enid Shields Monk and Homer Arnett, my high school and junior high English and grammar teachers whose demand for excellence prepared me for this venture.

To the memory of Marge McCormick of the Vigo County Mental Health Association who lent invaluable assistance to my mother in her effort to make sense out of the state regulations.

To those caring volunteers especially people like Thelma Klatte, Floris Petty, Dale Phillips, and Dr. Betty Duke.

To all those in my lifetime who have let me share their troubles and thus have taught me to respect and respond to their need for understanding and caring.

To my wife, Stella, and my grandson, Jason, who coped valiantly with my stress on days when the word processor didn't allow smooth preparation for the publisher. They prayed for my mental health!

To all those others who assisted in many ways to bring this book to completion. To Lou and Bobbi for the initial review; to Riley, Marilyn, and Barbara for picture scanning; to Debbie for her invaluable review of the chapter on medical records; to Nancy for her honest evaluation of the chapter on Education; to the unnamed gourmet cook whose proof is not only in the pudding but in her proof reading; and to that other author, Naomi, who kept asking, "When will the book be done?"

To the administration of the Evansville State Hospital, the Macanell Nursing Home, and the Sullivan Convalescent Center for their cooperation in providing Dad's medical records.

To the Sullivan Daily Times and the Terre Haute Tribune who provided invaluable resources at a time when my incapacitation restricted my researching.

To the reader who by the very act of reading this reveals something of his/her desire to be better informed and to be a more faithful advocate for those who are mentally ill. Thanks for reading this from a nonprofessional who herein expresses his reaction, his response, and his ideas on this subject. This is written with no malice toward any of those who ministered to Dad in any way. It is written, however, hoping that caretakers, at all levels, will be more aware of how their actions and attitudes affect their patients.

TABLE OF CONTENTS

DEDICATIONS iii

ACKNOWLEDGMENTS v

THE PROLOGUE TRILOGY ix

      FOR THIS PETE'S SAKE xi

      FROM ONE AGE TO ANOTHER xii

      FROM UNDER THE CLOUD.. xiii

CHAPTER LETTERS TO DAD.. xvi

CHAPTER 1 LAYING OFF A LAND 1

CHAPTER 2 A BACKWARD OUTLOOK.. 33

CHAPTER 3 FROM GRANDMA'S TO GRADUATION 81

CHAPTER 4 SLATE BOARDS TO COMPUTERS.................................... 137

CHAPTER 5 WOODMERE TO WOODLAWN 179

CHAPTER 6 CONFIDENCE AND CENTS.. 230

CHAPTER 7 KNEELING TO DANCE... 285

FINAL TRIBUTE TO PETE.. 326

FINAL TRIBUTE TO FLEDA... 327

LINGERING QUESTIONS... 328

APPENDIX I 332

APPENDIX II 333

BIBLIOGRAPHY 334

THE PROLOGUE TRILOGY

FOR THIS PETE'S SAKE

FROM ONE AGE TO ANOTHER

FROM UNDER THE CLOUD

x

FOR THIS PETE'S SAKE

The key figure in this drama is Pete, the towering gentleman above who was felled by mental illness about fifteen years after this photo was taken.

His wife, Fleda, is the heroine, who at 36 was left to be the breadwinner for herself and four children.

The baby is their first-born son, the author, who reflects upon this family's ancestoral heritage, their early family life, the schools of their day, the common and separate struggles of Pete and Fleda, closing with a statement of faith that sustained them for a lifetime.

Throughout the story, the writer raises diverse mental health issues as he seeks to find meaning in this tragedy and triumph.

FROM ONE AGE TO ANOTHER

The Historical Perspective of <u>FOR PETE'S SAKE</u>

at a glance

EVERYONE IS A SEGMENT OF THE AGES,

A PART OF HUMANITY'S LARGER PICTURE,

ONE WHO SHARES OUR SPACE.

**2048	**HOW DIFFERENT WILL IT BE?**
2000	NEW CENTURY FOR CARING
1995	YEAR OF PETE'S DEATH
1993	MOVED TO WOODLAND
1976	MOVED TO MACANELL
**1948	**COMMITTED TO WOODMERE**
1944	FIRST HOSPITALIZATION
1935	CHILDREN
1929	WERE BORN
1929	MARRIED TO FLEDA
1907	YEAR OF PETE'S BIRTH
**1848	**1ST INDIANA PSYCHIATRIC HOSPITAL BUILT**
1800	EARLIEST TRACED FAMILY HISTORY

MAY IT NOT BE TRUE THAT THIS MAN WHO

SUFFERED SO MUCH MENTAL ANGUISH FOR A HALF

CENTURY LEAVES NO LEGACY TO SOCIETY.

FROM UNDER THE CLOUD[1]

One can only make sense out of the status of mental health treatment today by taking, at least, a peek at some very significant history. There is no match to the story from Indiana of one Anne Agnew, of Vincennes, one county below Sullivan.

As noted on the previous page, Indiana built its first psychiatric hospital in 1848. Agnew was a patient there from September, 1878, to April, 1885. Upon her dismissal, she lobbied the State Legislature for reforms and wrote her story, FROM UNDER THE CLOUD.

In her book she describes deplorable conditions at the Indianapolis institution. Others followed her example and sought drastic corrections to the abuses. Among the reformers was Dr. William B. Fletcher who became famous for the 1883 Christmas Eve burning of the mechanical restraints used to subdue patients. We still use restraints, but in this past century we traded the mechanical for psychotropics.

Fletcher was fired in 1887 amid a political storm focused on methods of treatment and costs. The reader will see that such issues are not absent in the mental health field today. The transfer of patients mid-century in Indiana to community based sites is a case in point.

---

[1] Agnew, Anna. *FROM UNDER THE CLOUD*. Cincinnati: Robert Clarke and Co., 1886

xiii

1946 aerial view of Central State, Indiana's first psychiatric hospital. Most
Victorian buildings were razed in the late 1970s.

In the year of Pete's birth the hospital changed its name from Indiana
Hospital for the Insane to Central State Hospital. Pete's first hospitalization
was at Central State in 1944. It was finally closed by Governor Evan Bayh in
1994 amid continuing controversies.2 The description of "Insane" is not
absent from our street vocabulary today.

What changes? We still get into heated debate over treatment and
costs. We see mental patients as lacking in individual worth, not deserving
dignity, and as to insurability, we have yet to fund their mental treatment on
a par with physical treatment. To make matters worse, doctors all too often

2 Boomhower, Ray E; King, Lucy Jane; Drenovsky, Rachael L. *Traces*, a Publication of
Indiana and Midwestern History, Spring 2001, Volume Thirteen, Number Two, (ISSN 1040-
788X), Indiana Historical Society, 420 West Ohio Street, Indianapolis, IN 46202-3269

use an emotional "diagnosis" to explain what they can't figure out on a physical basis. "It is all in your head" is yet today an all too common response to some kinds of symptoms. Take a tranquilizer or antidepressant! Pop a pill for every problem and demand that new ones keep coming online.

Thankfully, great strides have been made, but after reading Pete's story, the author hopes that the reader will not take too much for granted as we look ahead. Anna Agnew, a patient no less, made a difference in the 1800s. May the story of another patient, Pete, make a difference. May all of us make a difference in the Twenty First Century.

CHAPTER LETTERS TO DAD

Each chapter will begin with a note to my Dad. In that note you will get the gist of what the chapter holds.

My mother had saved Dad's letters to his young family.

Our communication with him was so meager during his absence.

Those two factors caused me to consider formatting this book originally in letter form.

Later it was decided that the present format would better serve our purpose.

So I use the letters at the beginning of the chapters as a way, posthumously, to bring Dad into the picture in a personal way. I hope you like this personal touch to this story.

LAYING OFF A LAND

Chapter 1

"The worst sin toward our fellow creature is not to hate them, but to be indifferent to them; that's the essence of inhumanity."

George Bernard Shaw, Irish-born playwright (1856-1950).

Hi Dad,

Writing to you now seems so strange, but, for many reasons, I must do it.

Yesterday was All Saints Day at church. Members who passed away this past year were remembered in a brief ritual.

Members were asked to turn in names of persons in their family, other than church members, who had died during the past year. I gave your name. It was listed in the bulletin with all the others. It was a touching moment of personal remembrance.

There is so much to say. These are very special circumstances, and it would take many letters to tell the story.

First of all, few of us write letters to our Dad after they are gone. You know you didn't get many letters during your long stay away from us. There were reasons for that which you may want us to explain. Sometime soon here we will do that.

1

Secondly, you were gone so very long. Our gap of knowledge about your world is huge. And your knowledge about us during those forty-seven years and more has been scant. You told me recently that you did wonder what happened to your children. We will tell you a little about them and the changes in the world that you once knew.

And, thirdly, in recent times you started coming out of that awful void. While you didn't recognize us as family, you had a keen interest in the family that you knew so many years ago. Remember one day when I was getting ready to leave your room? You shook my hand as always but with an unusually firm grip. You said, "Come back soon and stay longer. We have so much to talk about."

That day, Dad, we had talked about our family history. I had been studying it and had asked you questions. I was amazed that you could remember so much and yet not know the year was 1994. We had been unable to talk together for so long!

Do you remember the story of Rip Van Winkle? You were Rip II. And like him you were anxious to relate to those who at one time had been so precious to you. And like Rip's family we were just as anxious to fill you in on what you had missed.

We only got started on that exchange before your life was over. It seemed, as for anyone who has lost a loved one, that time had been too short. We had miles to go before retiring, and so many of those miles were never traveled. Your rest is well deserved, but there was so much for each of us to share; we were not ready.

I wonder if you understood anything about your condition? What happened to you? What did you understand and feel? We couldn't converse with you for about forty years. You talked about things in another world that we didn't understand. And apparently, you couldn't comprehend our world. What terrible years those were, for all of us.

Now, for all these reasons, I want to explore your world and that of ours, your family and community. Even though you are gone, there is a void in our life that can now be filled, and your life, that appeared so meaningless, can take on new importance as we bring together the pieces of our mutual story.

You were always a caring kind of guy, helping others as well as your young family. That I remember so keenly about you. You can rest in peace knowing that through this means you will be helping us all make some sense out of the life that we all have endured.

3

There's so much to say. And we will write again soon to bring you up-to-date about our search for understanding.

Love, Gene

As you read this, you are already very familiar with email. My father never heard of it in his lifetime. My niece just sent me an email story passed on by Doug McSchooler that is both an introduction and summary of what we intend to share here. Here is the first of five beautiful stories he relates. The original unknown author states: "During my second month of nursing school, our professor gave us a pop quiz. I was a conscientious student and had breezed through the questions, until I read the last one: 'What is the first name of the woman who cleans the school?'

"Surely this was some kind of joke. I had seen the cleaning woman several times. She was tall, dark-haired and in her 50s, but how would I know her name? I handed in my paper, leaving the last question blank. Before class ended, one student asked if the last question would count toward our quiz grade. 'Absolutely,' said the professor. In your careers you will meet many people. All are significant. They deserve your attention and care, even if all you do is smile and say 'Hello'. I've never forgotten that lesson. I also learned her name was Dorothy."

Mentally ill people, even now in such an enlightened age, are still shunned, misunderstood, and avoided. It seems at times that knowing their first names or saying a cheery "Hello" is more involvement than we care to have. Now we begin a new century and a new millennium, and we all have our own ideas about the significance of this event. By the time you read this you may be in the position to begin to evaluate some of the positive and

5

negative predictions engendered by the artificial chronology brought on by a man-made calendar. At least, this writer was optimistic and believed you would have survived and can now give your attention to the subject of mental health that is still with us.

We will not be expecting drastic changes toward the challenges in this field just because the calendar has turned over another day, month, or year. We are hopeful that changes will come, as they usually do, because there are people who will be dedicating their lives toward making great advances in all aspects of mental health. This writer is not a mental health expert but is one who, through this book, hopes to make a difference because he knows the first name of this man, Pete, his father. He would like for you to say "Hello" to him, get to know him, and be motivated to assist in the healing and comfort of those today who are suffering mental illness.

One night over fifty years ago, I was awakened by my mother. Being aroused from sleep in the middle of the night was not unexpected. I immediately knew what was wrong. My father had increasingly become mentally disturbed and difficult to handle at times. That night was one of those times, and my mother needed help. Please, pardon the use of first person on occasion in this book. This is a son's reflection, and the use of the third person does not always do justice to the personal nature of this writing.

Up until this point there had been denial on the part of his mother and brothers that their family member could be having such problems. That was

6

not an unusual response, and understandable, in the 1940s. In fact, until this point in time he could act quite normally for a brief visit from them. However, they would be enlightened this night as to the reality and extent of Dad's illness.

So I dressed quickly and shimmied out the bedroom window. I hurried down the gravel road to the neighbors, the Ferrees, about a quarter of a mile away to make a telephone call to my Uncle Ollie. He lived in Sullivan, the county seat, about six mile away. He reacted quickly and was out to our house within the half hour. That night Dad was disturbed enough that my uncle had no doubt about the seriousness of his illness. It was so difficult for all of us to come to grips with the gravity of his illness. In this book we want to tell you about our experience that is both our story and that of the patient, my father.

So here we "lay off a land" as has been the custom of farmers for as long as land has been plowed. With no-till farming and with the use of chisel plowing, farmers are not laying off lands like in the past. The phrase, "laying off a land," refers to the farmer's way of beginning the plowing process in a section of the field. In the desired section, the farmer engaged the plow and made a furrow the length of the field. Returning, plowing another furrow parallel and adjacent to the first, the farmer had laid off a land. Now the tractor or team of horses and plow would be steered down one furrow and

7

back up the next overturning the soil until the desired area, a "land," was created.

Laying off a land set the stage for plowing the field and eventually a harvest. "Effort and courage are not enough without purpose and direction," said John F. Kennedy.3 Laying off a land gave direction for the farmer, and for us it gives purpose for the task ahead. The field of mental health has been "plowed" many times and on this occasion with a different perspective and from a different experience.

On the left is Phillip Badger of Graysville, Indiana, helping the author break ground for a garden near Rockport, Indiana. This was in the Spring of 1950 at the parsonage of Rockport Parish, Gene's first pastoral assignment. The horses, Maude and Bert, were borrowed from neighbors, Fred and Ethel Boyd, whom we came to know affectionately as "Grandpa and Grandma".

From our vantage point we have come to view mental health issues as arising out of, and dependent upon, our total life experience. Everything we do, say, and are, affects our capacity to cope with life and to have some semblance of being mentally healthy. In reviewing my Dad's life and times, we will from time to time show how various everyday happenings influence us for good or ill. Out of our

3 *Tribune Star, The* Terre Haute, P O Box 149, Terre Haute, IN 47808, "Thought for Today"

experience we have come to the conclusion that mental health or illness permeates the entirety of our lives. Mental health is the mosaic of life, the tapestry that adds color to experience, and the thread which holds together life's quilt.

The dictionary definition of a mosaic expands on this idea. It is a picture made of small pieces of stone, glass, or whatever, of different colors which is made into a design. It is composed of diverse elements combined. The different elements that you will find emphasized in this book are those of everyday life in rural Sullivan County in the State of Indiana in the Twentieth Century. Indeed these elements form a mosaic that is not unlike that in any other county in this wonderful land of ours. Whatever your connection with rural America, hopefully as you read you will feel some linkage to this county and its people.

Sullivan County is located in the heartland of these United States. In fact, at one point in history, in the mid 1940s, one of the county's towns, Carlisle, was designated to be the center of population for the United States.[4] In this reference the newspaper editor quotes from the "C&EI Flyer" magazine stating that the corporate headquarters of the C&EI at that time were located in Carlisle. Both US 41 and the C&EI tracks carried the traffic from Chicago to Florida during that period.

---

[4] *Sullivan Daily Times*, The, 115 W. Jackson St, Sullivan, IN, July 7 through 13,1946

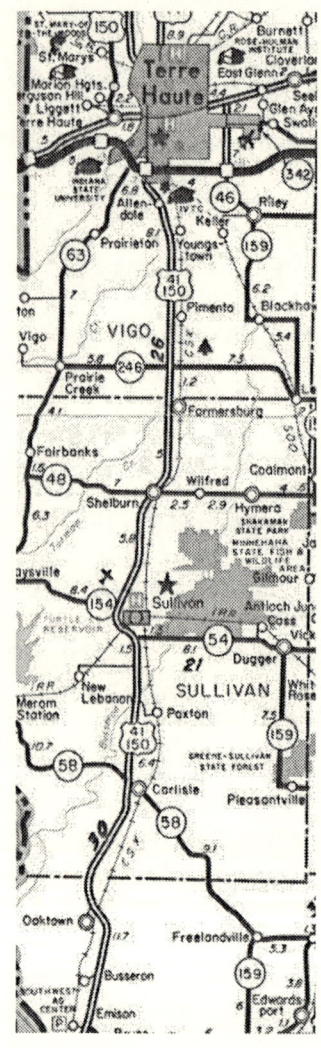

MAP OF CARLISLE-TERRE
HAUTE

Our neighboring Vigo County to the north is billed as the Crossroads of America where the Old National Highway, US 40, and now its parallel, Interstate 70, intersect US 41. We have been and are part of the mosaic of this nation by location and also, as we shall see, by the mix of experiences that are akin to the rest of the world.

One other definition of mosaic is helpful to note. The dictionary refers to a mosaic as a process of its production. We indeed are aware of this mosaic of mental health as a process. It is a process that engulfs all of life, and although it has a history with rather specific form, it is still in the making. May we in the Twenty-first Century see the day when we promote mental health as much as we have concealed mental illness in the Twentieth.

In one chapter we will examine the medical record of Dad who was diagnosed as schizophrenic and later as having an organic brain syndrome. But just as importantly, we will examine the setting, life as it was and is, in his native surroundings. We want to show

10

throughout this book how mental health is an issue regardless of life's expression. Whether we are talking about ancestry, family life, education, business, medicine, or religion, you will see little bits of color that give meaning and instruction for our present time.

In order to state my purpose more fully, we need to know more history about this man I am calling Dad. This is not fiction. This is, in fact, a real life story of my father and the world in which he lived. Further on we will see what life was like for him in his early world and in each succeeding stage. For now, a summary of the circumstances that brings us to this point is necessary.

His life as Clarence Homer Gilbreath began in 1907 in rural Sullivan County, Indiana. He was the youngest of five children. His oldest sibling was Sarah Jane. His brothers were Ollie and William James. He lost a sister, Grace, a handicapped youngster, when she was ten years of age, three weeks before the death of their father.

Dad was only six years old when he faced this loss of these two family members. Life was hard for the struggling family and this to be sixth grade dropout. They tried to keep their farms, one hundred acres where they lived and another twenty acres about two mile away. Much of his boyhood was spent as an uninformed, inexperienced farmer, forced too soon to do a man's work. During the Great Depression, the family lost the larger farm and then moved to the twenty acres. Soon they lost that, also.

11

In 1929 Dad and Mom were married and their first son, yours truly, was born. Then my brother, William, was born in 1930 and sister, Mary Kathleen,

"I can't change the loss of my Dad and sister but maybe I can ride this goat!" Pete got 'bruised' from that, too, when the goat threw him off and scarred his tail-end.

in 1932. Tommy Lee came to the scene in 1935. We lived with Grandma Gilbreath from 1930 until 1933, and then she lived with us until about 1940. We used her furniture, pieces of which are still within the family. She was a hard worker, co-partner with my mother in the home. Necessity demanded that we all work together.

That was a day and situation in which work was for survival but yet rewarding. Believe it or not, we did do chores that were fun. We all learned much about resourcefulness and adaptability from our mother and grandmother as well as our father.

From early 1936 to 1944 we rented a small acreage that had room for a large garden, some pasture land, and about five acres that were tillable. And the house? Would you call two rooms small? The house, an outside toilet, smokehouse, chicken house, a barn, and a well made up the setting for eight years of good and tough times. Yes, it was a two-bedroom, both rooms.

At this place Dad farmed for himself, raising hogs, cows, and chickens.

A couple of mules were used to till the five acre patch and the garden. We raised our own produce and canned and canned. Dad supplemented the income by working for other farmers, doing odd jobs, and working on the WPA. We survived but ate well because we all knew the source of our

The Bicknell Place as it looked several years later when the Monk family lived there. In the intervening time the large tree on the right grew. A pear tree on the left was the only tree we had when we lived there.

food, that being our labor and God's Providence.

Finally, in 1941 we bought twenty-five acres that had on it an old two-story house. Dad had acquired some skill as a carpenter on wartime construction projects and began remodeling this farm house. It was a major task, taking off the upper level and squaring up the building. He worked so diligently and was so happy for what he was doing for his family. We knew the meaning of "workfare," doing all possible for ourselves and being proud of our accomplishments.

This was in World War II, and near the close of the war Dad was called for duty. The house was not finished. He wanted it done for us. But a bad bout with the flu would change his life and ours drastically. He finished out the chimney sitting in the snow, while I warmed bricks and mortar. It turned out Dad didn't have to go to the service, but by now he was very ill with a setback of flu. It was all down hill after that. The flu had caused inflammation around the lining of the brain, our family doctor concluded, that could not be controlled with the medications of that day.

His brain had been damaged. He became difficult to get along with, withdrew, became suspicious, and finally became violent. No way could we handle this. A court order sent him to jail and finally to Evansville State Hospital in Evansville, Indiana. Various treatments made no significant change. He was there twenty-eight years. Then came the change in the way patients in State hospitals would be served. In Indiana that would mean a transfer of these patients to nursing homes for custodial care.

Apparently the nursing home atmosphere was so different that he began some slow improvement. He became more communicative with both family and nursing home caretakers. He had passed the violent stage for whatever reason and became very agreeable and cooperative. We will be investigating the role of medication in this perceptible change for the better.

Something was different for him after going to the Macanell Nursing Home in Clay County, Indiana, where the State had sent him. Besides having a better attitude, he started counting his age, always minus the twenty-eight spent at Evansville. He didn't know the day of the week, month, or calendar year, but when they told him it was birthday time, he added another year.

Pete and Fleda at Macanell Nursing Home in Clay County, Indiana, about 1990.

Strangely, he seemed to be "waking up" after a long and restless sleep.

In 1993 he broke his hip. When it was set, the family decided it was time to bring him closer home; Mom's fears of him coming home unexpected had subsided. The transfer was made to the Sullivan Convalescent Center at Sullivan. During his stay there, I began to discuss old times and family history with him. I had been studying our genealogy and knew when he responded accurately. He could not grasp that I was his son, a white-haired man standing beside his bed and leaning heavily on a cane. Truthfully, I looked older than he. A nurse thought so, too. Her notes state that his brother came to visit him! Yes, he had a son, Carl Eugene, his first-born, he told me and named all the others. But it was beyond his comprehension to believe I could be his son. He tried!

This is an effort to make some sense out of all this. How does a family deal with this situation? What goes on in the mind of these mental patients? What role does medication play, and what about certain environments that have negative or positive impact on a patient? There are all the treatment modes and their effectiveness to examine.

However this is not a classic scholarly discourse, well documented by mental illness/health studies, but one well supported by a lifetime of freelance study and personal experience. It is an effort to share in one family's and one patient's pain and triumph. It is a perception of things as we saw them and nothing more. Although it is anecdotal, it is not irrelevant. It hasn't been to us! Hopefully, you will say one of two things: "There by the grace of God go I" or "I know exactly what you are talking about; my family has been there." It is hoped that we will remember the Arab proverb, "Examine what is said, not him who speaks."

Neither you nor I need to know all about apples to enjoy and benefit from a big juicy bite. One doesn't have to be a horticulturist or nutritionist to explain the taste or recommend the experience to others. That is my position here. I do not have degrees in the subjects of this book, except a masters in counseling and divinity both of which included many courses in sociology and psychology. So these subjects having influence on mental health are not discussed by a mental health expert but from the experience of a common family who walk our streets or dusty roads.

In this case, there is the question about how Dad might have been brought nearer to the 1990s had this fledgling process of "waking up" been pursued. What were the changes that he would have encountered had he launched out on that perilous journey? Imagine the changes in the past 50 years and the adjustment, the re-education, that would have been necessary. And we want to take an imaginary journey with this man on the way back to civilization, back toward reality. It is a journey begun, but not one completed, as his family might have envisioned. We could do a play on the meaning of the Gilbreath (Galbraith, et al) name "foreigner" on this journey. How many of us find ourselves in "foreign" situations, sometimes set aside and overwhelmed by loneliness, whether institutionalized or not?

Legal questions and government regulations were imposed, sometimes as a welcomed service to the disadvantaged, but sometimes as a devastating intrusion. There were emotional stresses connected with appearances in court and dealing with the federal, state, and local assistance programs that took their toll on our family.

We will be attempting to understand the burden and challenge faced by a spouse. What is it like to be left alone all these years, but yet your spouse is somewhat always present? Are there things worse than death? Is this one of those times when there is no clean break? How do you alone,

17

increasingly a more common experience today, rear a family and provide the physical and emotional support necessary? How does this play itself out at different stages of the spouse's life, from the children at home to the empty nest? This is a success story, but one that was not without severe emotional and physical stress to a spouse. We will devote one chapter to these matters faced by my mother.

In our preparation for this writing we have seen that mental health is most often the prerogative and domain of the medical professionals. Be it noted here that this writer feels strongly that we are in this together. Mental health must become a vital concern and responsibility of each of us regardless of our expertise. As will be noted by the chapter on Dad's medical record, medical professionals have their invaluable role to play. However, the other chapters will reveal that we all have the responsibility to enhance our emotional environment for ourselves and those around us. We are emphasizing emotional health here as well as calling attention to mental illness as a clinical entity. All of us have an interest in emotional health whether we ever become mentally ill or not.

So we present you with glimpses of this century's history of Sullivan County, Indiana, my Dad's world in reality and memory. It is intended to serve two purposes. One of those is to explore in this historical context the relationship of all of life to mental health as suggested by the subjects of the chapters. That will lead us to another reason for writing which is to give recognition to ordinary people who walk our city streets and our country roads. Dad was one of those among many others whose lives were intertwined in the community.

The mere presence of ordinary local personalities in this story is testimony to the significance of every human being. In every chapter we will be taking everyday events and suggesting an implication for our mental health. I believe that every life deserves recognition, support, and affirmation. Dr. Robert Schuller, pastor of the Crystal Cathedral of Garden Grove, California, recently said in a sermon, "There are potentials within any one of us that are yet to be grasped. God looks at human beings and He does not see a single castaway. God has no wastebasket for hopeless people. No person is a discard."5 No name here is just another name, no event just another event, but rather each one is a touch of color in the mosaic of life in which we all search for meaning. There is no mental well-being without both receiving affirmation and giving recognition to others.

"Do you include the grayscale when you speak of color?" you ask. Yes, this introduction requires one further consideration. Another definition of mosaic refers to a virus on plants. A plant suffering from that virus has varicolored, mottled areas on its leaves. Mental illness has that effect like in the plant world. Our challenge is to develop varieties of experiences that resist the virus, or better yet, develop cures or at least palliatives. Mental

---

5 *Hour of Power*, The, Channel 10 TV, Terre Haute, IN, March 1997

health is the process of coming or staying alive. It holds the potential for us to be a productive member of society, making a future that improves on the past.

My father's story reminds me of the "virus" that incapacitated Rip Van Winkle. Rip's returning home was an experience that required something of him, his family, and the community. There are so many similarities, as well as points of departure, that we want to take you on a tour of that Catskill community to help you to get into the struggles and hopes of those who are mottled by mental conflicts. Let's begin there, and later, on to Sullivan County, Indiana.

About one hundred seventy-five years before Dad was born, another man, Washington Irving, began this human existence. Never in my widest imagination would I have ever made any connection between these two men. Washington was named after President George Washington. Dad, even as Clarence Homer, had no such name recognition. "Homer" probably came from his mother's side, the Robertsons, but the source of "Clarence" is not known.

Irving was born to well-to-do parents. While Dad's parents and grandparents were prosperous farmers by the standards of the day, they soon lost it all during the Great Depression. Irving spent much of his boyhood hours in his father's library laying the groundwork for a literary career. Dad only completed the fifth grade of elementary school and some of the sixth. In contrast to Irving, Dad had quite limited literary possibilities although he did write a few letters that we will examine later. Doing farm chores in isolated rural Indiana was far different than rustling the pages of books in a father's library.

Later Irving would develop a liking to social life and the ladies. He was the stylish man around town. He would, however, finish law school, but his desire to write won out. He started by writing essays which he and a friend published in *Salmagundi* in 1807, an imitation of the Addison's *Spectator*. Dad wrote only what the teacher assigned and probably did not do well at that.

The Great Depression moved the Gilbreath family from a prosperous home on St. Rd. 154 to the two rentals and then to the two room Bicknell Place that you just viewed. Pete had lost his father and sister, the farm, and now this, too.

Our well-known author began and continued much of his early life without financial want. Dad learned the hard facts of poverty especially following the death of his father in 1913. Yet, Irving would come to know hard times, too. There came the time when he was forced to earn his own living.

It was at that point in time that he wrote the familiar "Rip Van Winkle". That work is what brings our men of highly disparate ways of life into the same arena.

21

One might think it is an affront to the famous Washington Irving's reputation to bring these two men into the same room. Yes, from the literary stance, they are far apart. But we are not making that kind of association here. The connection has to do with life itself. We are speaking of human experience that transcends status, education, financial means, profession, or popularity. There seems something eternal about Irving, while the wind blows over Dad's grave and the world will soon know him no more. If the two had sat down together to chat, they would have been engaged in a congenial heartfelt chat about their commonality. Would they have discussed how both good and bad times can affect our mental outlook for either good or ill?

But wait! Isn't Irving remembered so well because he wrote about the life that we all know, about human experience itself? And doesn't that put us and him on the same plain of importance? So now for me to bring these stories together, is a much deserved compliment to the work of Washington Irving. His work lives on, not on the pages of the many books in which his story of Rip is recorded, but in the lives of us who experience the truth of his story anew in every generation.

The Rip Van Winkle story came home to its author himself. Irving had been to Spain. After a seventeen year absence from America, he returned to find his familiar world changed. He left the Hudson River at New York bordered with forests. On his return, he found a busy port filled with sailing vessels and steamships. The streets were filled with carts and many workers. The Erie Canal completed in 1825 had transformed the scene from rural solitude to hectic commercialization. As we move on, we could relate drastic changes that have taken place in this past century in rural Sullivan County, Indiana, only incomprehensible if you have been gone for forty-seven years!

There are two more essential elements in this comparison of Irving, Rip, and Dad. Irving wrote about native happenings, subjects close to home and heart. In the waning days of the eighteenth century, people along the Atlantic seaboard had gained enough free time to be interested in such pleasures as newspapers. It was through a newspaper that matters of local interests could be shared. Likewise, it will be through local newspapers that we will get a glimpse of life in the twentieth century in Sullivan County, Indiana.

So short stories held attention, especially if the writers were speaking of life as they saw it and if the writers themselves were natives. The native writers boosted the developing patriotism. There was demand for interpretations of life in the vigorous new nation. Irving's writings did this well. Dad knew very little about life outside his native county and especially outside the state. From morning till late at night any reading, when there was time and energy, would have been the newspaper, the *Prairie Farmer* magazine, and the short stories of the *Bible*.

23

The second element of Irving's is his romantic approach to life and his work, something more and different than the realism of his early *Salmagundi*. Beginning with *The Sketch Book* of which "Rip Van Winkle" is a part, Irving told stories of getting away from life as well as facing it, of the historical as well as the legendary. In *The Sketch Book* he goes beyond the familiar to the quaint. Probably his readers were beginning to have more time to delve into something other than realism, maybe to experience more fanciful dreams. Life for Dad will be shown as this mixture of realism and the romantic. It remains to be seen if his fancies went beyond the normal and in what way they became a part of his mental illness.

Washington Irving looked to Addison, Goldsmith, and others, imitating their works with great success. We now do some imitating of our own. We do not pretend to copy the great literary stature of a Washington Irving. We would defeat our purpose to even think along those lines. The imitation here has to do with reproducing one of life's experiences to which we can all relate. A man goes off into a far country, for whatever reasons, and returns to a changed scene with which he may, or may not, be able to cope.

Now the story of Rip Van Winkle himself and the similarities of his life with Dad's. Dad and Rip both knew of another time, place, and people, feeling the eerie tug of familiarity but seeing nothing that looked like home. Dad felt that tug in the spring and fall and made numerous attempts to find home once more.

Although Sullivan County, Indiana, is located many miles from the Catskill Mountains, there is not a passing similarity. The Catskills belong to the Appalachian family of mountains, but dismembered, Irving relates.6. My grandparents and their immediate family were somewhat disconnected from the other Gilbreaths. Dad had two cousins from Greene County, next door to Sullivan County, who came to visit occasionally. So it was that I grew up thinking of our Gilbreath family being detached from the main branch of the family. We will never know how unyoked Dad may have felt during his long stay in a wilderness of confusion.

My Mother's family, the Riggles, were somewhat different. There was a larger family on her side, and they visited each other quite often. There were connected and collateral families of which we will speak more later. The Chastains, Breedloves, Bells, and many others made me feel that I belonged to a family of many kin. When you add in the in-laws, Greggs, Houses, Brewers, Mizes, Jewells, Sparks, and Rooksberrys, there was never a time to think that we were on an isolated ridge of our own. Just the Gilbreath side remained a mystery.

Irving supplies us with these words that express so beautifully, but poignantly, the nature of the Catskills:

"When the weather is fair and settled, they are clothed in blue and purple, and print their bold outlines on the clear evening sky; but sometimes when the rest of the landscape is cloudless they will gather a hood of gray

25

vapors about their summits, which, in the last rays of the setting sun, will glow and light up like a crown of glory."6

And such was the nature of my Father's life. Gathered over it was "a hood of gray vapors." Also at this point it seems that the only time those vapors glowed and lit up was in his latter days when he could at least remember his early life. In death, then, he re-entered the cloudless landscape. In reference to the mosaic, even "gray vapors" can be tinged with glory for those who want to behold.

Irving describes his character, Rip Van Winkle, with many terms that unequivocally apply to my Dad. A good natured fellow, kind to his neighbors, liked by all. Dad had his way with children, doing with them the things children want their father or a neighborhood male model to do. That included assisting with sports and improvising a game when play got boring or even making something with which to play. Makeshift fishing poles actually were productive in catching those little bluegill. Kite flying needed some adult expertise, and children needed to know just how to hold the marble shooter. And there was time to tell the ghost, witch, and Indian stories.7

However there were differences when it came to work. Both tried their hand at farming. Dad's failure at that was not because he was allergic to

---

6. Witham, op.cit, p.434

7. Ibid. p 435

work. Both he and Rip had the misfortune of possessing pieces of land that were not the most productive. Rip gave up rather easily, preferring sometimes to be doing good deeds for his neighbors or hitting the jug. Since farming seemed so useless, Rip could find other things to do. If nothing else, he found refuge with town philosophers, exchanging opinions or heading off to the woods, rifle in hand.8 Neither of these outlets lack commendation, but Rip let some things go and failed to find an important balance in life.

Dad swigging the homebrew, a "fashionable" answer to the pressures of the time about 1929 and to the duress of an uncertain marriage and family. Thankfully for his family, he soon chose a better way to deal with the stresses.

Dad stuck to the task of mending fences, or building new ones when necessary, to hold the animals. Weeds would grow for only a short period, and then he would hoe them out or sickle them down. The crop might not produce much, but he made the best of it and used it wisely for added value. He, too, planted the corn and potatoes, but had enough for hominy and winter storage. He kept the barn stalls

---

8. Ibid.

clean, making sure the manure was scattered where it would enhance next year's crop. He taught his children the importance of maintaining what had been given to them or what had been earned. That concept is more difficult to teach in this day of throwaways. Are our youth any happier in our world of consumerism gone awry?

Only once Dad came home drunk during our early years. He knew enough to go on to the barn to do the milking, but not enough to know which end of the bucket was up. That episode is remembered yet with a smile. Mother didn't think it was funny, though. Another time, we kids found a jug hanging in the well, one of home-brew made by Elmer, his brother-in-law. Other than that one time, he stayed sober, and alcohol was not an escape as it came to be for Rip. It could have, in fact, been a different story since Dad did hit the bottle briefly the year before and after marriage.

If we look in the right direction we see the majestic Hudson River with its rich woodland resting near by. But Rip's emotional condition drew him in the opposite direction, overlooking the glen with its lonely, wild, and jutted landscape filled with the avalanches of yesterday's breakaways. It is a scene where we imagine that our friend is the jug or the friend is some kind of unreality.

Whether Rip or Dad, either would choose the forbidding side to find peace for the tormented self. While either had a disease by today's understanding of their conditions, does that preclude any personal responsibility? And in what sense would either make a conscious choice of a route to nowhere? What would seem to them to be an acceptable selection, one that would bring amusement, would in fact be the "most melancholy party of pleasure (they) had ever witnessed".9

But daylight would come. The birds would be heard chirping their happy song. An eagle soared majestically above. A fresh mountain breeze would soothe the face. Suddenly, there is the realization of morning. Here's a new world, something like most of us awaken to each morning. Sometimes we are a little dazed and must look around to get our bearings. Rip looked for his gun, only to find an old rusty looking object that hardly could be the remnants of his firearm. So many look for crutches of the past. Could so much time have elapsed or had one of his friends paid a trick on him? What about his dog? He was not in sight, but he surely had just gone hunting.10

But what about Dad? Did he awaken from a mental illness with anything like a rational thought? Did he wonder where he was? Did he remember home and where it was located? Did he ever regain a sense of the real world? Or did he remain unclear as to what had happened to him? Did he wonder where his family were? Would he have any concept of the time that had passed? Did he understand that he had out-slept Rip? The answers will

---

9 Ibid. P.437

10 Ibid

29

never be really clear, but there will be some indication as we struggle with these questions at a later time in this book. At this point we can only guess what it was like for either Rip or Dad to reawaken to this earthly life and find it so different. Assisting mental patients in returning to "normal" life must take into consideration today's rapid change during their incapacitation.

Irving does an excellent job of describing Rip Van Winkle's feelings as he re-enters the village after being gone twenty years. If you haven't read this story lately, you should do so soon. Let's point to just a few things that caused consternation as Rip came home. First of all, even the familiar landmarks of

He was trying to "come back" as he attempted a UNO game with his daughter-in-law and his g-grandson, Jason. He would say at this point that he remembered Stella's father. He would not say she was his son's wife but when she went to see him, he was always glad to see her. Taken about 1980 at Macanell.

nature were changed. The opening to the amphitheater was now closed, but he found another way and finally entered the village. There he met numerous strangers, dressed in changed fashion, who would pretend to stroke their imaginary beards in response to seeing his foot-long beard. The town's children harassed him, and the dogs barked at this strange sight.

Some houses were gone, and new ones had taken their place. Surely something was be-addling his head, maybe that jug again.

Rip finally found his own home. No dog with a warm welcome; no well-kept house. Turning to find the familiar Inn, he discovered it, too, was gone, replaced by the Union Hotel. No British signs now, just blue and buff, for the Revolutionary War had left telltale signs of changed allegiance. Trying valiantly at long last to tell the townspeople that he was a native and subject of the King, proved almost disastrous when mistaken for a Tory.

Then he began to inquire of his friends, and one by one they had been forgotten, were dead, some killed in the War. He would ask about Rip Van Winkle, and, in response, have his attention called to a dummy leaning against a tree. In a short time, a lady would appear with a child she called Rip. Yes, Rip's daughter and grandson. His wife, Dame Van Winkle, he asked with great hesitation? Yes, she had died also not long ago. Finally Rip was recognized by one old lady, and not long hence he retold his story finding eager listeners at the village hotel. 11

Dad had a similar "homecoming". For him there was a place called home, access to which he was prevented from entering. He never really physically came home and did not experience the drastic changes that would have awaited him. Yet, in his improved mental ability, he made continuous "trips" back into his pre-illness past. One can only imagine his

---

11 Ibid P. 437-440

consternation had he regained his consciousness as much as did Rip. Dad tried a mental trip home and only partially succeeded. Maybe his anguish, if it could have been measured, would have surpassed that of Rip Van Winkle.

To come to know that this is not your world, and seek to find the familiar one in vain, surely is the greatest of tortures. The details of this aspect of his life will be left for a more extensive exploration at a later time. Suffice it to say here that this author believes that the mental illness of his father produced a modern Rip Van Winkle. He was totally "gone" for some twenty-eight years and only was able to repossess significant portions of the past for another nineteen.

In the next chapter, we will make a trip that Rip Van Winkle didn't make. Irving's story centers in New York State and stops there except as our interpretation has lead us on to Dad's home territory. Dad's life didn't just begin in Sullivan County at the hour of his birth as is the case for us all. We will take him back on a genealogy trek to Pennsylvania and suggest that knowing our ancestry can be an enhancement to our emotional life. It was just such a discussion with my Dad towards the end of his life that caused me to begin to put together the outline of this book.

A BACKWARD OUTLOOK

Chapter 2

"In order to drive safely ahead, you must use the rearview mirror."

—-Gene Gilbreath

"The past is never dead. It's not even past" William Faukner

Dear Dad,

The most enjoyable visits I had with you during your illness were at the Sullivan Convalescent Center. In earlier years you were wrapped up in your world, a world that I didn't understand well enough to be able to communicate with you. By the time you got to the Center, you were able to speak about the past that you had known nearly fifty years earlier. For once I could go home and report that I really had appreciated our time together.

The delightful subject at the Center was genealogy. When I was growing up, we could usually find a subject that we both wanted to pursue. Over fifty years later we were once again on the same wave length. What a good feeling, Dad. It was that brief time of common interest that made it more difficult to let you go when death came. I wanted the opportunity to redeem our lost time, a blessing few people get to enjoy.

33

Remember back at home that we thought of the Gilbreath family as having very few relatives? Grandma Gilbreath would try to tell us something about the family; however, being just children, it went in one ear and out the other. I do remember her telling us that a Gilbreath married a Gilbreath and that they were two different nationalities. The latter idea appears not to be true. However, for her to have known something of a marriage between cousins, she had to have some grasp of the general history since she was referring to her husband's grandfather. Dad, if I had listened, maybe it would have saved myself a lot of research.

I remember so well the three or four times we spoke about the family. You knew some history about your grandfather and that helped to verify what I had learned. Those were the only times when you enthusiastically insisted I come back soon and stay longer. Anyhow, Dad, I learned from both Grandma and you that we ought to seize the moment. Belatedly, I have taken the opportunities to learn of our ancestry.

So, Dad, as I write this note, I think of our brief but delightful moments of discussing our past. I will always think of those times and be grateful that you were finally well enough to participate in that kind of discussion.

It sure would be nice if you were here to read about our history and to see how important I believe the topic is to our mental health. I doubt that, given your type of illness, you would have been able to appreciate this potential. However, I hope that my readers will grasp the connection.

Just a few days ago I heard from Yvonne, a Gilbreath in-law. No, I didn't know her either. She sent me an e-mail in response to an invitation to our reunion. Remember me explaining how you can get mail through a computer? Anyhow, she is Paul's daughter-in-law. You would remember your nephew. Yvonne sent me information about the Gilbreath history, some of which neither you nor I knew. It is nice to get to know more of our family. You were such a family-oriented guy that you would appreciate that thought.

Also, I just heard from Avis, a granddaughter of your Uncle Milt, telling me about the death of her brother Gerald. Their sister, Janice, had sent me information about your Uncle Milt's branch. Gerald had paid me a visit only a month after you left us. We had a good time talking about the family.

I had better get to writing this chapter. I hope you are enjoying your much deserved rest. See you later.

Love, Gene

Gene Gilbreath

"History must stay open, it is all humanity" —William Carlos Williams (1883-1963)[12]

"There is no point of our ancestors speaking to us unless we know how to listen." —Mortimer Adler

Connections and networking are such an intricate part of our lives today. Whatever position we may hold in society, we take advantage of our connections. To do so with an ulterior motive or for selfish reasons might not contribute to our mental well-being. Positive networking, however, can bring emotional satisfaction. When we use those terms we are usually speaking of the contemporary situation mostly in business. But in this context, I am speaking of an engagement that has a personal historical import. We will note Pete's and Fleda's connection to their history and in that way reveal more about their background.

Our family history becomes a way to make connections with our past. It seems to me that this is an important pursuit. In working with genealogy for awhile I have discovered many who do not share this interest. At one time I didn't give time to such a quest either. However, having experienced an ancestral search at a particular time in my life, I now realize heretofore unknown benefits. It is those that I want to share with you. And as we do, maybe you will come to appreciate the possibilities of a rewarding experience. It is hoped that the reader will substitute his/her own family

---

[12] *Tribune Star*, op.cit. "Thought for Today"

36

names in this part of our story and come to appreciate your own heritage and what it has to offer for your satsfaction.

To be sure, if genealogy is just an accumulation of facts gained from compulsive trips to cemeteries and searches of old moldy archives, then count me out, too. To be obsessed with exact information, for the sake of the information alone, does not contribute to my emotional health at all. There certainly is a place for such a search, and on a professional genealogist level that must be given its just recognition. In no way do I intend to say that exact dates, times, and places are not important. I am saying that for my purposes in this writing the enhancement of our emotional well-being does not lie in exactness of fact as much as in the process of satisfying some inner longings, curiosities, or achievement.

As a personal testimony, my enjoyment working in genealogy did not come from exactness as much as pursuing a hobby that brought a sense of achievement. Much is to be said for running whether the goal is reached or not. Much is to be said for playing whether we win the game or not. If your basic satisfaction is not in the pursuit, what victory is there when you lose? In ancestral searches, as in all of life, you will often fail to fill in all the blanks. It is rewarding to have participated in a journey and yet accept the fact that you missed a few sights along the way.

Finding a missing piece to the puzzle is the icing on the cake. The exploration is the cake. I will take cake without icing anytime rather than icing without cake. It was wonderful to learn that my great-great grandfather, John Gilbreath, was born in 1810 and that his date of death was 1883.[13] Finding the out-of-the-way cemetery, Calvin-Gilbreath, just east of Newberry in Greene County, Indiana, was a rewarding adventure in itself. When we located it, the stone was unreadable. It sure would not have done much for my emotional state if that trip was only to find those dates.

Let me use another analogy. A giant oak tree symbolizes most of our family records. It is fun to search for the acorn that started the tree. It is exhilarating to climb its branches. How comforting it is to sit under the tree and enjoy the shade. Some trees may look rather ragged if some branches have been marred by scandal. Some may be misshapen by some missing branches. Some oaks may appear to be a pencil drawing by an amateur. Others may seem to be the work of a professional artist.

In any case, the oak, however artistic or obviously lacking in sophistication, is indeed our own "family oak." It is our family, and it has some possibilities for appreciation. We simply do not have to know and understand every detail of the tree to appreciate it. Exploring the tree with what time, energy, and expertise we possess will surely bring us an emotional high. Such limitations and achievement I have experienced.

Now that you have a general idea of how I intend to approach this topic of emotional wellness as it relates to ancestral searches, let's go back to

---

[13] Gilbreath, Elmer C, *GILBREATH, GALBREATH, GALBRAITH*, publisher not known

investigate how and why I ever became interested in the subject. In the process of relating those beginnings and the continued search, we will be including some family history. That history will not be in forms like charts or some popular computer program familiar to genealogists. Rather it will be a narrative that gives you a glimpse of what I experienced as I searched and that may stimulate you to give it a try. By this means we hope you will see more clearly the connection between such a search and our emotional health.

Many searches begin as nudges. Over twenty years ago I officiated at a couple's wedding. An aunt of the bride introduced herself as a Galbraith. At that time I knew almost nothing about our history so that was the end to that. Sometime later I did buy one of those books that has a brief history of your surname and then a listing from the phone book of all the family in the United States. No, I didn't find that very helpful except it was another nudge.

About ten years before I really got serious about the subject, I received a letter from a Joyce Gilbreath in Missouri who was the wife of a fellow pastor of my denomination. Since confession is good for our mental well-being, I must tell you that I answered that letter nine years later. Her gracious forgiveness and helpfulness causes me to write this paragraph in her memory.

Another nudge came about the same time as that of Joyce's. A cousin from California on my mother's side, Brenda, stopped by to inquire about the

Riggle history. I gave her some recent history and referred her to my mother. Later a neighbor, Cecilia, was taking a course in genealogy at Indiana State University. She encouraged me to buy the book, *THE HANDY BOOK FOR GENEALOGISTS*, published by the Everton Publishers, Inc. The big shove came when the Sullivan County Historical Society decided to produce a 175th Anniversary edition. My mother helped with that process and in doing so encouraged me to write our individual living histories.

It was also interesting to compile the same for my wife's family, the Foutzes. By now I had been bitten by the bug. My curiosity had increased, and I wanted to know more about my family. Looking back, I must say "Thanks" to those who gave those nudges. Expressing that gratitude is always a good exercise in emotional enhancement.

I think of all the opportunities that I missed because I thought I was too busy to learn more about my family history. You, the reader, may be thinking the same. We live in a "rootless" time. That is to say, we act as if we are rootless, so involved in the present that we give little thought to the foundation that supports our very being. So many are physically rootless, living so far from family. When stresses come, family are not available to ease them.

At the same time many find themselves rootless in respect to values. Our sense of being disconnected could be eased for many of us by exploring our family history. And even if we discover something we would rather have not known, truth is the best road toward adjustment and must precede our moving on.

Such a quest tells us where we have been. Yes, we "were there" in the minds of our ancestors who struggled not only for their own survival but for their descendants who would follow. And it tells us how we ought to be going, at least in one important respect. Closely knit ties are just as important now for our well-being as they were a hundred or two ago. We may not seem to be as physically dependent as we once were, but that is a faulty perception. We are just as dependent now both physically and emotionally on others as we ever were. Grandma used to rock the babies, and now the daycare center personnel do.

We ought not be so busy as to overlook at least one source that will help us to be better anchored in today's hectic world. Lessons about relationships can be learned from our ancestors. In this chapter there will be many names that will not be familiar to you. Notice relationships as you read and mentally substitute your family names. In almost every paragraph you will be nudged by questions or comments that will help you to see the relationship of the names, places, and dates in an evaluation of your own family ties.

Over forty years ago I missed an opportunity that was right under my nose, so to speak. For four years my employment was in a county where my maternal great-great grandparents had lived. The adjoining county where

41

we shopped had been the home of my great-great grandfather, great grandfather and my grandfather. I did not know that then and might not have done anything about it if I had.

I think now, that surely I would have tried to find my great-great-grandmother's grave. She was buried at West Lebanon in Warren County, Indiana, only about fifteen mile north of where we lived at Perrysville. Just a few miles to the west was Danville, Illinois, where the various members of the family had lived for several years before moving south to Sullivan County, Indiana.

As we have said, all the pieces do not always fall in place, at least not readily. My maternal great-great grandfather was John Riggle who was born about 1803, the place variously reported in Pennsylvania and Ohio.[14] Since Ohio became a state in 1803, maybe the changing border between the states is a possible explanation of that confusion. The first real evidence of his existence is in the 1840 census, living in Wayne County, Ohio, with his wife, Catherine Swarts Riggle, and their eight children. Our sparse record stated that they came from Wayne County about 1848 and settled in Warren County, Indiana, near her family, the John Swartses. Catherine died at age 45 and is buried with other members of the Swarts family.[15] So this Riggle

---

[14] Wolfe, Thomas J., *HISTORY OF SULLIVAN COUNTY, INDIANA,* The Lewis Publishing Company, New York, 1909, Vol II, p. 399

[15] Schmidt, Jo Ann Brant, submitter, *Western Warren County, Indiana Cemeteries*, Vol II

family, as well as the Swartses, made their way from Pennsylvania straight across Ohio into Indiana and Illinois, Northeast to Midwest.

John Riggle moved on to Vermilion County, Illinois, and died there in Newell Township in May of 1872.16 Any information in Vermilion County was elusive. Neither the Historical Society, nor the library, nor the clerk's office knew anything about his existence there. Finally a separate probate office found a record of the administration of his estate. There are two lingering mysteries regarding John. Who were his parents and where was he born? And where is he buried? Some of us can

Did Dad think that he knew all he wanted to know of this beautiful next door neighbor gal of nineteen? The writer is glad he didn't learn too much too early and change his mind! He never appeared to be sorry, though.

live with unsolved mysteries and some can't. Some are patient and others are not. An understanding of our own makeup will help us to cope with this frustrating experience of not being able to put all the pieces together as

---

16 Wolfe, op.cit., p. 399 and "Petition for Letters of Administration", Vermilion Co, IL, June 7, 1872

quickly as we would like. This critical understanding is so valuable in any area of life.

Since we are on the topic of my mother's line, we will continue that discussion. Let's pause just a moment to make another point, though. Since Dad married into the Riggle family, their history must of necessity become of interest to him. A spouse's history is a part of who we are. To understand a spouse better, one might well get better acquainted with the family history. Could it be that a mutual search for each other's family records might possibly be good marital therapy? Maybe it would be better yet as a preventative to take the importance of family history seriously during courtship. Could it prevent a divorce later?

One of the interesting bits of information in my mother's family is the effort that some made to keep in touch. John's and Catherine's son, John Thomas Riggle, moved on to Sullivan County, Indiana, in 1887.[17] One of their sons, Wilbur, remained in Danville, and another, Henry Harrison, my grandfather, spent most of his time in Sullivan County. We have several postcards of early 1900s that indicate the close relationship of these two coal mining brothers separated by some seventy-five mile. That was a considerable distance in those days. Some of the travel was by train from Danville to Terre Haute and by Interurban on to Sullivan. Some trips were

---

[17] Wolfe, op.cit.

FOR PETE'S SAKE

made by horse and wagon. The train trip was on the same tracks that I

traveled over fifty years later between Chicago and Sullivan.

Such close relationships were apparently not always the case. Nothing

has been found to indicate that the elder John had any siblings, and if he

did, there is no record of communication that we have found. It appears that

there was no communication between John Thomas and his siblings. Susan

and Josephus, the two oldest, had died before their father in 1872 according

to the probate record. Elias married Susan Dormor in Warren County in

1860, but we haven't found anything else about him. Mary married William

Bird and we have no other information.18 Louisa married William Keister in

Warren County,19and the youngest, Rachel, married John Goodner.19 Both

of these last two couples have descendants in the Danville area, it appears.

Keeping in touch with one's family is not necessary for good mental

health, except in the case of unresolved malice; however, doing so opens

many doors for sharing of a common heritage. Jon, a former member of one

of my churches was a Riggle descendent. Interestingly enough, his ancestor

was a contemporary of John Thomas Riggle and lived close to him, but we

cannot make any connection yet.

Likewise, for various reasons, my great grandparent's children were not

close. John Thomas and Mary Susan were the parents of nine children, six

---

[18] Marriage License Abstracts, Vermilion Co, IL, on November 18, 1865
[19] Vermilion County, IL, Marriage Abstracts

of whom survived into adulthood. The distance of Sullivan from Danville made little difference with the two closest brothers, Wilbur and Henry mentioned above, who were also closest in age.

Henry named his first son William Albert, William being Wilbur's first given name, and named his youngest son Wilbur. The other children of John Thomas and Mary Susan, all at one time locating in Sullivan County, did not associate very much. We have no evidence of big-time arguments; apparently, they each pretty much did their own thing. Twenty-three years between the oldest and youngest surely made some difference.

Henry's brother Sylvester Augustus, the sixth in order, married Mary Elizabeth Wilkins in 1893.[20] He died only three years later, and their son, Otis, became the stepson of James Bell. Sister Rozella married James Milam and did not visit much with the rest of the family. They had one son, John, who was killed in a mine accident when he was only forty years old. Rozella lived to be eighty-one years of age, longer than any child in the family.

Rozella's sister, Minnie Viola, married Robert C. Miller, and they lived much of their married life in the Newman, Illinois, area where she is buried.

Minnie died at age 32, and the Miller family was split up when Robert had to go to the service in World War I. Dorothy Rich Boothe of Sullivan is a

---

[20] Sullivan County, IN Marriages 10-106

Benjamin on father, John Thomas Riggle's lap. Girl unknown but most likely daughter Rozella, Sylvester Augustus, Horace Greeley (Henry Harrison), and William Wilbur. Minnie not born yet. Taken c. 1885.

47

were placed for adoption.21 The other brother, Benjamin, died when he was about fifty-five years of age and left two sons, Melvin and Mervin, and twin daughters, Cornelia and Cordelia. So it appears that this generation also had little contact with their siblings for understandable reasons, like early death, as we have stated.22

The next generation tended to follow the same pattern but for a different reason. They were scattered more, and since they did not have an example of closeness in the preceding generation, it was easy to not prioritize a close relationship. This is borne out by several attempts to secure information about these families. Even grandchildren and cousins found it difficult to secure much data. This writer is beginning to think that the Riggles were very independent and private people.

Privacy is a person's rightful privilege and maybe does not deserve a criticism. This becomes a mental health issue only if these same people choose isolation from others as well. We all need balance in life between solitude and sociability. However this balance worked out in the Riggle family is a matter of history, but the reader may want to consider the importance of family closeness and association as a positive asset.

My grandfather whom John Thomas and Mary Susan named Horace Greeley Riggle, was the second child. He didn't like that name and soon

---

[21] Boothe, Dorothy, granddaughter of Minnie Viola, and daughter of Daisy, Minnie's second daughter

[22] Gilbreath, Gene, compiler of John Thomas Riggle Family Group Sheet

changed it to Henry Harrison Riggle. Many years later when the parents shared their family history with Thomas J. Wolfe for publication, they still reported his name to be Horace Greeley.23 According to my mother, her father Henry was only left a dollar from his parents' estate as punishment for not keeping his given name.

Their third child was named William Wilbur. He, too, didn't delight apparently in his name. A grandson, who lived with his grandfather Wilbur for some years, reports his name to have been Wilbur Watson Riggle25 Names in genealogical searches are quite fascinating. Generations removed, we think of some of the names as being quite unusual. These given names here were not among the most unusual but yet not treasured by the recipients for some unknown reason.

The changing of names is an emotional issue. A name is related closely with one's identification of self. Without a psychological analysis here, which we do not want to appear to do in this book, we simply point to the importance of a name with which we can be comfortable. When someone calls me "Carl," I automatically respond with some reservation as speaking with someone I do not know well. When someone addresses me as "Gene," I instinctively believe I am speaking probably with a friend. Excluding some devious motivation and purpose, people ought to be able to make whatever

---

23 Wolfe, op.cit.

adjustments are possible and reasonable to merge their names and their concept of self.

Bullerman,

Dau. Mabel on Henry's lap. Ena standing, Roy on mother Elizabeth's lap. William Albert, son from first marriage standing behind. Nora, Daisy, and Susan unborn. Taken 1896.

My grandfather Henry's family were a closer bound group than the preceding generations appeared to be. That happened in spite of children being born over a span of thirty-three years. Henry's first wife was Charlotte Frank of Danville, Illinois.24 Before their divorce about three years after marriage, a son William Albert was born in 1887. Although Henry was reported to be an abusive husband in an undated news article, Bert went to live with his father.

On December 24, 1892, Henry married Elizabeth Chastain Breedlove of Sullivan County, Indiana. She was the widow of Noah Breedlove, Jr., who had been crushed to death by a threshing machine. Noah and Elizabeth had a daughter, Ena. Son, Bert, was a miner and met an untimely death in the

------

24 Vermilion County Marriage License, dated February 20, 1887, groom 25 and bride 18

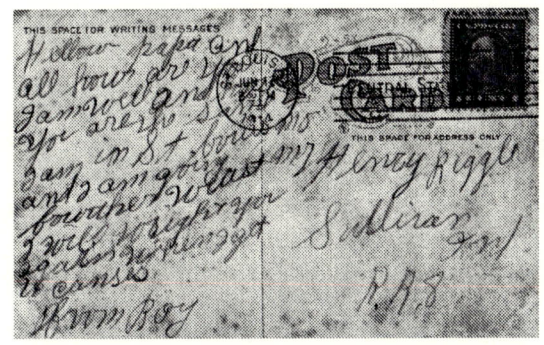

POSTCARD FROM ROY

mine at age 21, leaving his bride of two weeks, Frances Copple Riggle, who was only nineteen.[25]

Elizabeth and Henry had five children: Mabel Mae, Clarence Roy, Nora Estelle, Daisy Chloe, and Susan Idell. Susan died when she was only two. Roy left home at a young age and made his home in California and Nebraska, coming back home only a few times. He and his wife Velma had two daughters whom most of the Indiana cousins never met.

Also Daisy, childless, spent most of her life with her husbands; first, Cleo House and second, Leonard Smith, in Council, Idaho, and seldom came home. I remember seeing Aunt Daisy only once, and I do not recall seeing Uncle Roy although I am told I did once. Mabel lived in Sullivan County until her sudden death at age forty-eight. Although Mabel and Nora were half-sisters to my mother, we visited often with them. Nora and husband, James Gregg, with their five sons lived in downtown Terre Haute and came often to the country to hunt or just enjoy nature.

---

[25] *Sullivan Daily Times*, op. cit., August 14, 1909

Henry's second wife, Elizabeth, died from blood poisoning while all the above children were young. Elizabeth's daughter, Ena, had lived with the family, being older than the other children. At the death of her mother, Ena had her stepfather as guardian. She assumed the role of motherhood, and at the age of seventeen became the wife of her stepfather, two years after her mother's death.

The news article regarding the case states it this way, "Judge Harris of the Circuit Court was called upon this week to decide the puzzling question as to whether or not Henry Harrison Riggle, a well known miner of Shelburn, could give his consent for his ward, Ena Breedlove, to become his wife......on Tuesday Judge Harris decided that the application was sufficient and the

Vernia (left), Lillian, Amelia (3 yrs old), Fleda, with father Henry and mother Ena in the back. Wibur not born until 1920. Picture taken in 1918.

couple became husband and wife. She was almost 18, and he was 47 years of age."[26]

---

[26] *Sullivan Daily Times*, op.cit., October 30, 1906

Some people are afraid to pursue the past lest they find something they would rather not know. For the sake of our emotional well-being, it seems wise to face the facts as they are, rather than to ignore them. This is especially true here where family charts make the situation quite clear, except without the court record one might tend to read more into it than there may have been. Does that jumping to conclusions ever get you into trouble? At least in that day, people usually made sure that an unborn child had two parents to care for the child.

Today there is an outcry about sexual abuse and rightly so. However, there seems to be only a whimper about casual sex among teens who often have little thought of responsibility for bringing a child into the world. By today's standards, this situation with Henry and Ena should not have happened. Also, by today's practice little has changed. Anyhow, who would I be if I were not the grandson of Henry and Ena?

Five children were also born in this union. My mother was the second child, the only living one at this writing, and reports that this was a happy family that was void of any kind of abuse. The other children were Felix Vernia who with his wife, Oleta Sparks Riggle, had two daughters, Robertine and Thelma. Lillian Violet married Gordon Jewell, and they had two children who survived infancy, Twyla and Terrance.

Amelia was married to Hugh Mize, and they had one son, Jerome. Wilbur Wesley, named for his uncle "Wil," married my first cousin, Lora

Rooksberry, on my Dad's side, and they had five sons, Mark, Ronald, David, Lester, and Wilbur. These members of the family were all close, visiting often with each other, especially when the children were younger.

Another good reason to be informed about our ancestors and their families is to know about medical problems. This family has a history of heart and respiratory problems. Most of Henry's eleven children had one or the other and either was the major cause of death. The Chastains also often had weak lungs, and that may have contributed to so many related medical problems.[27]

Some of the earliest history that we have of the Riggles reveals a family conflict which is not that unusual. We have indicated that the Riggles and

Swartses came together from Ohio to Warren County, Indiana. When the father John Swarts died, his daughter, Catherine Swarts Riggle and her husband John went to court

Now that second child of Henry and Ena, Fleda, becomes of age, marries Pete, and they give birth to four children: Carl Eugene (upper right), William Homer (front center), Mary Kathleen (left front), Tommy Lee (upper left), and Mother Fleda on the right. On the screen behind one can see Mom/s g-grandfather, Noah Breedlove, Sr. as well as many others in her family of whom we have written. Mom was eighty seven when this picture was taken Christmas 1998.

---

[27] Bell, Virgil, interviewed at 97 years of age, whose mother was a Chastain, and whose half-brother was Otis Riggle, son of Sylvester.

to settle a dispute with Catherine's brothers and sisters over the administration of the estate. Catherine died before the suit was settled, and the case was eventually decided in favor of her siblings.28 The animosity was not sufficient to keep Catherine from being buried with her family.

Good comes from many unexpected sources. These documents gave us the first listing of Catherine's siblings and the affidavit of her death. It also led me to two Swarts cousins, descendants of John Swarts and his wife, Susannah: John, a namesake of his ancestor, of Shawnee Mission, Kansas, and Jo Ann of Texas. They both provided me with lots of Swarts history.

That was one family quarrel that did not leave lingering resentment for generations to come, at least not in the case of these two wonderful people. Now isn't that the way that all family problems should be resolved? Residual hostility serves no good purpose whether it extends for one or more generations or for whatever "good" reasons in any area of life.

Since we believe that emotional health includes showing appreciation, we want to honor one other person who has done so much footwork in this search for Riggle history. Donna of Florida has given invaluable assistance to me in this search. We met on the Internet when I was trying to discover what the relationship was between the Swartzes and the Riggles in Warren County. It did not take long for us to determine that we had no ancestral connection. Then the miracle of friendship happened that occurs so often

---

[28] Rigle, John, Probate Box #29, Warren County, Indiana, Case filed August, 1849

among researchers; one reaches out to help another, even though they have not met face to face, and strangers become friends.

About the same time and in the same manner, I found a Hoosier genealogist who also was generous. Audrey, of Northern Indiana, gave me the early Chastain history of my maternal great grandmother, Elizabeth Riggle's family. Looking back at my Riggle data disks, I see maybe fifty more people who answered my Riggle/Swartz inquiries. My wife's cousin, Chloe, lives in Nebraska and did the research for me regarding my mother's non-communicative brother, Roy. A recurring theme in this book will be how our mental health is advanced by helping others and by appreciation of that assistance. So read on to find out why I needed the help of others at that point in my life.

Before we move on to Dad's family, the Gilbreaths, who also had migrated from the Northeast to the Midwest, let's pick up my story of getting involved in genealogy. It truly was a mental health issue for me. In 1984 I had to take a disability leave. For the first few years I needed assistance with most personal needs. A neurological problem affected, among other things, my ability to walk and sit.

In 1988 we purchased a used Apple IIC computer for our grandson, Jason, who lived with us much of the time. While he was at school during the week, I learned how to use that computer, especially as a word processor. This opened the door for me to write letters seeking genealogical information. By having the computer elevated, I could stand and use it for short periods of time.

Not being able to sit, nor stand very long in one place, and not driving made library research quite unlikely. I had joined the Clan Galbraith Association of North America and through their library had found some important information about the Gilbreath family. However, for me to access it, I needed to go to the library to use the microfilm machine. My neighbor, Georgena, took me there and did the mechanics for me as I indicated what needed to be copied. Two trips gave me lots of data with which to work at home. Later, when uno grandson, Jason, received his driver's license, he, in similar fashion, copied census information for me to review at home.

Getting to the library was a physical chore, but it didn't equal the stress of trying to cope in a world where people are expected to sit. Emotionally I needed an outlet and diversion from the physical disability. Genealogy was providing that for me, and I was determined to find ways to get data about the family. Finally, in 1995 we managed to get enough money together to buy a new computer and to get online. That experience has taught me that there are any number of people out there who will help even a total stranger. Let us not let the negative in some of life's offerings prevent our accessing the positive.

If you would like to find a group of wonderful, caring, helpful people, try those who are searching for their roots. That common denominator brings birds of many feathers into a flock of watchful eyes looking for any tantalizing morsel. Can you imagine what this has meant to one who had a goal that would not be reached unless there were others who were willing to help reach that goal? Some other special people like my wife, Stella, and her sister, Fern, ran other errands that were necessary for me to reach my goal. Edith Ham, the Sullivan County Historical Society president at the time and Turman Township native, gave invaluable support in the early stages of my searching. Virgil Bell in his nineties was a delight to interview.

Some resources for mental health lie deep within oneself, but some other important ones may not be available except through the assistance of others. Accepting that help from others minimizes the tendency to think unduly about self. Genealogy teaches us so many lessons, and this one about the availability of assistance ranks high among them. I also must note that had I had the money to have hired a professional, my life would not have been so enriched with the associations which are herein listed.

Let's look for more mental health connections to genealogy as we take a quick glance at the Gilbreaths who, like the Riggles, traveled from Northeast to the Midwest. By common consent, the Gaelic word "Galbraith" means "foreigner, or stranger, a son of the Bretons." They had been pushed into Alba, later called Scotland, by the Angles. Our Clan later migrated to Ireland and from there to Pennsylvania, and elsewhere, in the early eighteenth century.

This writer has a special appreciation for the definition of the Galbraith name. Until I became seriously involved in genealogy, we Gilbreaths had lived in Sullivan County and were a small family. There were four of us children, and we had only twelve first cousins in the Gilbreath line. We knew of no history of Gilbreaths ever being present in the County except my father's grandparents and their unmarried son over in Jefferson Township. Genealogy is one way to broaden our outlook after feeling "disconnected" or being a "stranger" in the community in which we may live.

Researching our beginnings is a great way to see how we fit into the grand scheme of things. Now, music, scenery, personal interest stories, or politics of Pennsylvania, Ireland, and Scotland capture my attention. When Highland Games are scheduled close by, there is a desire to check them out. Ancient history is not so ancient anymore.

In the grand scheme what happened then is a part of my past and what occurs presently is of interest. Such connection of then and now must have significance in the totality of our being. In the grand scheme of things our past and present are intermingled and contribute to our emotional well-being. George Edward Woodberry stated it this way: "To feel that one has a place in life solves half the problem of contentment."[29]

Shortly after King David I assumed the throne in Alba in 1124 AD, Gilchrist Bhreatnach was born. When he grew up, he built a castle on

---

[29] *Tribune-Star*, op.cit., Thought for Today, August 15, 1997

Inchgalbraith (Galbraith Island) at Loch Lomond. He laid the foundations for the Galbraith Clan, being the First Chief, as well as building this man-made stronghold. Remains of the castle are still there. Gilchrist's son, Gillespic Galbraith, spent many years in Gaul, present day France, and later became his father's successor.32

Wouldn't it be wonderful if everyone researching their roots could find such tangible evidence of their family history in the ruins or in an extant castle. There were about seven Galbraith keeps and castles and one, Culcreuch, still stands. Maurice Galbraith owned and lived in this castle in 1320, and it was the abode of nine of the seventeen Chiefs of the Clan.30 It is located two-thirds of a mile N.N.E. of the town of Fintry in Stirlingshire, Scotland.

The Clan Galbraith Gathering was held here May 19-23, 2002. The main part of the castle is over 700 years old. It is one of the oldest castles in central Scotland which has been lived in continuously since it was built. You may go to this website and learn more about the Clan Galbraith: www.clangalbraith.org.

The Galbraiths were a warlike and oftentimes lawless people and used the Culcreuch Castle as a place from which to carry on their fighting. In about 1630, the last of the Galbraith Clan Chiefs, Robert, sold the castle to

---

30 Ibid

his brother-in-law, Sir Alexander Seton. Two years later the estate was sold to Robert Napier of Merchiston, the inventor of Logarithms. It stayed in the Napier family until 1778 when it was sold to Dadr Spiers from Glasgow. James Dunwaters and later Walter Menzies owned the castle after the Spiers family occupation of over a hundred years. In 1985 it was purchased by Hideaway Country Holidays, Ltd., who has turned it into a charming country inn.[31]

John Galbraith was among those who came to America, settling in Allegheny County, Pennsylvania. He and wife, Agnes, were the parents of fourteen children who in turn used the spelling "Galbreath." Most of the siblings traveled south into Shelby County, Kentucky, now Henry County, and on to Indiana. William, the eldest, came to Indiana via Shelby County, Kentucky, and has descendants in Orange, Wayne, Hendricks, and Davies Counties, Indiana.

The third child, David, married Margaret West and is listed in the Wayne County census of 1820. His descendants scattered to Cass, Pulaski, Fountain, and Henry Counties in this state of Indiana. The youngest, Rachel, married Abijah Price. Their daughter married Samuel F. Williams in Wayne County, Indiana, and later moved on to Pendleton in Madison County.[32]

---

[31] Paterson, Barbara, "Culcreuch Castle, a Synopsis of its History and Construction" *Red Tower*, Vol XVI, No 3, Summer 1995, p. 46

[32] Gilbreath, Elmer C., *Gilbreath, Galbreath, Galbraith, op.cit.*

John's and Agnes' second child, James, also came to Indiana via Shelby County, Kentucky. His descendants settled in Marion, Jasper, Bartholomew, Miami, as well as other counties in this state. Jean, the sixth, married Issac Williams and lived in Clinton County. Robert, the tenth, made his home in Wayne County as a farmer.

Some of the children may have stayed in Shelby County, Kentucky, which we are led to believe by lack of information indicating a trek to Indiana. Among those were Martha, the fourth, who married Elijah Sutton there in 1801. Elizabeth, the fifth child, may have married Samuel Long as hinted in the Henry County deeds of 1838 and 1845. Also there is no information about daughter Agnes, the eleventh; John, the seventh; and Rebecca, the thirteenth. The children's births ranged from the mid-1700s to about 1792. Father John died August 18, 1800.[33]

There are three others that we will discuss later. Let's pause for a moment and pay tribute to the man who spent years collecting information for us. He is Elmer C. Gilbreath who spent thirty years collecting, sorting, and indexing the data. His book found in the library of the Clan Galbraith Association contains 929 pages, including a 96 page index of names and a 23 page index of places. A very thorough work which is a must for review by anyone researching this family. We are indebted to those, like Elmer, who have given so much time in search of our history.

---

[33] Ibid

Elmer sometimes relied on interviews, and that opens the door for mistakes. However, here we reiterate the belief that the fun of this is in the process. So much can be gained from secondary information. If that were not true, I would not be writing this book. I have had to rely on secondary data and freely acknowledge it as such. I have not seen many original sources, limited as I was by physical restraints. In this chapter we mean to pave the way for you to do more work on your own, even making corrections in data as may need to be done.

No mistakes made by my grandmother in an interview with Elmer or his failure to copy it right, dampen my enthusiasm for a hobby that is good for my emotional satisfaction. Posthumously, Elmer, you are to be thanked! And may the reader find someone to thank for helping you understand your family history or for preparing the road for smoother travel in other areas of our lives. Gratitude has a healing, reconciling, and energizing effect.

The other three children are closer to my line. One, Thomas, the twelfth child and youngest son of John and Agnes may have followed my g-g-g-grandparents to Washington County, Indiana. We know nothing more than that he appears, after being married in Henry County in 1817, in the Washington County census when my ancestor, Samuel, was there. Samuel was the eighth child and born in Allegheny County in 1780. He married Mary Catherine Colglazure in 1799 in Shelby County. They moved from Kentucky to Washington County, Indiana, about 1810.

Samuel's sister Mary, the ninth child, married Daniel Colglazure, Mary Catherine's brother, in Shelby County. They also came to Washington County.[34] Is it important to come to appreciate the arduous and challenging travel which our ancestors endured? Is it important to appreciate one's heritage to enhance wholeness?

Samuel and Mary Catherine had seven children who were born between 1804 and 1823, all in Washington County. Catherine, the eldest, married Jesse Grace and lived in Washington and Greene Counties. Here again we can point out a benefit of being knowledgeable about our family history. When we lived at Clay City, Indiana, pastoring the Methodist Church, Chester Grace was the United Brethren minister just two blocks away. We had Sunday night services with that church as well as the United Church of Christ and the Church of the Brethren. We worked closely together for three years on so many activities including the proposed merger of our two churches.

Recently I made contact with his family, he now being deceased, to inquire about us possibly having a mutual ancestor in Samuel. Had I known that possibility thirty years ago, surely it would have made for a closer relationship. Genealogy does have present day application if we know our family history.

---

[34] Ibid

The second child, Mary, married Frederick Sapp. I have learned from one of their descendants, George Sapp of California, that they had ten children. Mary and Frederick moved to Spencer, Owen County, Indiana, from Washington County and were charter members about 1824 in the Methodist Society in Franklin Township. One of their sons, Willis, became a Methodist minister and served in the Missouri and Los Angeles churches. Mary died about 1851 leaving six children orphaned, five of them under twelve.35 Two children "bound over" to the Montgomerys, and two others to the Issac Barnes family. Since my wife's mother was a Montgomery and we have little information about that family, genealogy curiosity makes us wonder about a possible connection.

One thing is for sure: the thoughtful seeker cannot but notice how families are intertwined with each other. The more we expand our knowledge of families, the more we understand our common lot and responsibility to each other. Contrary to some extremists' views, we all are of the same human family, and there will be no peace on earth until we act on that fact. Samuel's first two children have supplied us with examples of our interconnectedness, an example so needed in our divisive society.

Nancy, the fourth child, married Ferdinand Memsing. They lived in Washington County and had no children. We have no information about

---

35 Sapp, George G., personal correspondence with this writer, July 26, 1995

Sally, the sixth, except she was born in 1817. The next child, Elizabeth, married Allen Smith in Washington County and moved later to Iowa.36

David Colglazure Galbreath, the youngest of the children of Samuel and Mary Catherine, was married to Eleanor Stafford in Greene County, Indiana, in 1848. David had come to Greene County along with his brother John, the third child, my g-g-grandfather. John used the "Gilbreath" variation of our family name. He was born June 14, 1810, most likely in Washington County. His first marriage was to Mary "Polly" Hoke in September of 1831. They had two children: Cynthia A. and William H. who married Eleanor Hale in Greene County in 1858. (Elmer does not record this first marriage but records these two births in the time frame of this marriage in 1831) Apparently there was a second marriage, recorded by Elmer as being March 17, 1836. The third child, Samuel, whose birth is recorded as being about 1837 must be the child of the second unnamed wife who apparently died, maybe in childbirth. Samuel and his wife, Addie Hansen Gilbreath, moved to Kansas in 1870.37

If the above sequence is accepted, then the third wife was Mary "Polly" Galbreath whom my g-g-grandfather married December 20, 1838, in Washington County. She was the daughter of John's first cousin, David, son of William Galbreath, grandson of John Galbraith. This is probably the Galbreath marrying a Gilbreath of which my grandmother had spoken. The

36 Gilbreath, Elmer C., op.cit.
37 Ibid

variation in spelling did not indicate different nationalities but simply different spellings within the same family. John's fourth child, and the first one of his marriage to his cousin, was Mary Ann. She married John Tibbett in 1874 and later took a claim in Kansas following their son, John, there. Their sixth child was Francis M. who married Mary J. Chaney in 1871 in Greene County. They may have also gone to Kansas.38

Elizabeth Jane was born a cripple in 1849 and only lived to be twenty years of age. She lived with her Aunt Nancy Memsing, mentioned above as John's sister. The two younger children stayed in Greene County. Barbara Ellen married William Heitman and was still living in Linton, Indiana, in 1934.39 My Dad and his brothers spoke of Uncle Milt. Milton Austin, the youngest, designated as the administrator of John's estate in 1883, lived at the home place next to the Calvin-Gilbreath Cemetery east of Newberry, Indiana. They also spoke of Uncle Henry who may have been William H.

Uncle Milt and his wife, Ellen Thomas, were the parents of seven children, some descendants of which remain in Indiana. A granddaughter, Joanna, lives not far from us and attended business school with my wife in the late Forties. I am now in touch with other of Milton's grandchildren and doing so broadens my concept of family. Milton and Ellen's family consisted of Francis William (m. Verna McDonald) who used to visit us; Anna (m.

---

38 Gilbreath, Elmer C., op.cit.
39 Ibid

Emerson Goad); Wayne (m. Tillie Daniels); Agnes (m. Alonzo Jolliff); Alva (m. Pearl Simpson); Edith (m, Elvan Martin); and Elsie (m. Ned Spinks). Elsie, the mother of Joanna, also came to visit us.[40]

My g-g-grandfather and his wives had one other child, the fifth in the family, my g-grandfather, David James. He was born in 1844 and married Sarah A. Jowette in Sullivan County in 1866. The Jowette and Gilbreath farms were adjoining each other separated by the Sullivan-Greene County line south of Dugger, Indiana. They lived near the Ripley's Believe It or Not Four-Way Bridge, a continued novelty in bridge construction. The couple are buried alongside her parents, James and Susan Jowette, in the Morris Chapel Cemetery on the western Greene County line.[41]

Buried there also at Morris Chapel is my great uncle, James' and Sarah's son, John David. G-uncle Johnnie was never married but fathered a daughter whose mother was Arlie Smith also of Sullivan County. The elder Gilbreaths raised the daughter, Gladys, who later married Lawrence McKinley.[42] G-uncle Johnnie, a cripple, would come to our house and stay for several days. He had few possessions, mostly the clothes on his back, and would walk across the county to see us, some twenty mile. Walking that distance was common for both Johnnie's father and brother. Walking, out of necessity or whatever, was also a trait of my Dad.

---

[40] Hasler, Janice and Metzger, Joanna, correspondence and interviews variously

[41] Gilbreath, Elmer C., and writer's own personal files

[42] Sullivan County marriage records, Bk 16, p. 443

I will always remember G-uncle Johnnie's funeral and burial. I was only twelve years old and had experienced only one close family member's death preceding G-uncle Johnnie's. I had been so much closer to my Aunt Sarah whom we will speak about later. This time the issue was the starkness of death. It seems that there were only seven of us there: my father, his brother Ollie, two friends of G-uncle Johnnie, my brother Bill and I, and the minister. Better recalled is

This bridge is located south of Dugger, Indiana, on the Sullivan-Greene County line close to the Gilbreath-Jowette properties in the late 1880s and into the early 1900s.

seeing for the first time a "welfare" casket being inserted into a wooden box. Just the very nature of genealogical research brings us to face our own mortality.

When the process of searching becomes a healthy part of our life, being integrated into our interpretation of the present and the future, then we are engaged in finding meaning and purpose in life. Genealogy can be one way of taking out the fear of death. The more we know about those who have gone before us, the better we understand the endings and the beginnings of life. In fact, we can come to see that those beginnings and endings are blended as we see the past of our ancestors and the future of our

descendants as being a prominent thread in the total tapestry of life.

James' and Sarah's other son, James Francis, was my grandfather.

"Jimmie" as he was called by his friends, was born in 1867, married in 1893,

and died in 1913 when Dad was only six. His wife was Susan Martha

Robertson, daughter of William and Helen Jane Turner Robertson, who

lived close to him in Jefferson Township. In 1902 they purchased 100 acres

in Northeast Turman Township and 20 more acres in 1911 on State Road

154 about a mile and a half east of Graysville.

Jimmie, the walker, had walked back to his parents a few days before his death seeking assistance with his last illness. Genealogical searches sometimes give a glimpse of people who would have been close to us had we had the privilege of knowing them. An interview with Virgil Bell, seven years

James Francis Gilbreath and Susan Martha Robertson Gilbreath, wedding picture, May 6, 1893.

Dad's senior, gave a little more insight into the Grandpa that I never knew.

Before we say more about Jimmie's

and Susan's family, let me tell you a little about the Robertson family. Since

Grandma, mother of Pete, lived with us for so many years, we children were saturated with stories about her family. They came to Sullivan County in 1866 when my Grandmother was only six weeks old according to her. They had traveled from Mercer County, Kentucky, in a covered wagon. Here is an example of how the exact dates are not as important as the story. I can hear her yet telling about the trip that her parents made with her older brothers and sisters when she was only six weeks old. However, when I wrote the article for the *Sullivan County 175th Anniversary History Book,* I accidentally wrote "six months" rather than "six weeks."

The Farmers' Directory of Sullivan County, Indiana, 1896, records that the Robertsons came to the county in 1865. But the discrepancies are not something to get hung-up on. Since Grandma was born on September 12, it seems that such a journey might not have been wisely made that late in the year. Her Grandpa, James Robertson, born in Maryland, apparently came with them, or preceded them, and resided in Cass Township in the same household in 1870. So give or take a year, or month, or day, my Robertson line came to Sullivan County from Kentucky by covered wagon. They purchased 120 acres southwest of Pleasantville. They were devoted Christians and donated land for the building of the Hickory Methodist Protestant Church in 1870.[43] Like others in that era, they found time to find sustenance for the soul as well as the body.

---

[43] Archives of Indiana United Methodism, The, Depauw University, Greencastle, IN 46135, Church Survey

A casual walk through the Hickory Cemetery tells the tale, in part, of generations of descendants of William and Helen Jane. William's father is buried there. It is not known by this writer if any of Helen Jane's family came to Indiana. The eldest of the Robertson children was Georganne. She is recorded as "George A. 'm'" in the 1870 Census of Sullivan County. If my grandmother had not shared stories about her siblings, that part of the history might be more difficult to unravel.

The cemetery record has Georgeanne's birth date as 1854, but the same census indicates that it was about 1850. Discrepancy in commonly used documents is all the more reason for us to find meaning beyond dates. Georganne first married a Parks, then a Norris. Names of Parks and Norris siblings that we know about were Silas Parks, Ann Parks (Wools), Ruth Parks (Harris), and Tony Norris.

The Robertson's second child was Nancy Lucretia, "Lute," who married George Deckard. Their children, Dulcee (m. George Boone), and Floyd (m. Ivy Boone), Ina (Frank Creager), Ann (Ora Wolfe), Tilda (Cornelius Willis), and Alice (Elisha Bedwell) along with their families were regulars at the family reunions at the Sullivan City Park. Also remembered are Lute's brother Joe's children, Grover (Flossie Wilkins), Faye (Herman Samm), Bess (Lawrence Pittman), Maude (Ferry Harris), Lola (George Daye, et al), William and Alf (twins), and Arista. Several descendants of these people still reside in Sullivan County.

The fourth and sixth sons, John "Fudd" and Robert T., are remembered well. My Grandmother was the fifth child, and, thus, the three were very close. G-uncle John and his wife, Minerva Gambill Robertson, had seven children. They were Frank, Earl, Lex, Minnie, Robert, Ethel and Florence. G-aunt 'Nerv' was blind, and what an inspiration she was as she maneuvered around her house. The daughters operated a restaurant on Court Street across from the old Index store. In those days our family didn't eat out, but it was a treat to enter the business and observe the happenings. Robert was a door-to-door salesman of Whitmer products manufactured in Columbus, Indiana. We always enjoyed his visits and admired his sales pitch.

To visit G-uncle Bob and G-aunt Cora was also a very special event. It was usually on a Sunday with a late dinner since we all went to church first.

Robert Thomas Robertson (left), his sister, Susan Martha Robertson Gilbreath, and their brother, John "Fudd" Robertson. Taken at the annual reunion about 1940 st Sullivan Park.

Before and after dinner the men sat out on the north porch facing the barn and the well in the yard with its "old oaken bucket." In the barn was a buggy which the couple had used in much earlier days. The women spent

73

their time in the kitchen preparing, serving, and cleaning up after the meal, as well as no small amount of chatting.

The children would be out playing until called. A child was to be seen and not heard and was served dinner after the adults had eaten. That was different than we were accustomed to, but we said little, making our adjustments to another of life's perceived unfair practices. In fact, we learned that you can't have everything you want when you want it, a lesson that goes begging today in our age of instant gratification.

G-uncle Bob had two sons, Hallie and Homer, by his first wife, Myrtle McClung. G-aunt Cora's two daughters, Ada (Stanton-Goodman) and LuEmma (Benefiel-Walters-Perigo), were always present with their children. Genealogy has put me back in touch with some of this family. Recently, I heard from Dillard Stanton and have received information indirectly from LuEmma's Deloris Sexton.

Also, I have heard from two of G-uncle John's grandchildren, Ruel Robertson and his sister, Beulah Walters, as well as Uncle Joe's granddaughter, Lucille Johnson. Ruel, I discovered, only lived down the road over a mile or so from me, and we got to visit several times before his death. Getting back in touch with cousins who attended the reunions over fifty years ago is a heartwarming experience of reconnection with the extended family. William and Helen Robertson had one other daughter,

Mary who married an Alumbaugh, and we have no information yet on that branch.

Now just a brief word about the family of "Jimmie," James Francis and Susan Robertson Gilbreath. Jimmie died in 1913 leaving Susan with nearly forty years of widowhood. His picture hung on the wall always whether at her house after his death, or at our house, or at his

James Francis Gilbreath

son's where Grandma lived out her last years. This picture, beautifully framed, of this handsome man who never became a grandpa, served as a constant reminder of a relationship that might have been. It now graces the walls of a g-grandson's home in Florida.

Michael William Gilbreath, son of William Homer with his G-uncle William James Gilbreath, posing by Grandfather Gilbreath's picture that hung on our walls at home and now at Michael's home in Florida.

Sarah, born May 14, 1894, was the oldest child of Jimmie and Susan. She married Francis Elmer Rooksberry and gave birth to eight children. She died at the age of forty-four from an auto accident complication.

75

The second child was Ollie, born January 3, 1897. He married Ethel Lee Williams, and they had four children. Ollie was a coal miner, a Sullivan city policeman, and a correction officer. William was the third child, born January 2, 1901, and was an auto

Sarah Jane Gilbreath Rooksberry shown here as a student at the Bell School, 18 yrs of age. At this very hour, 8:00 pm, February 26, 2003, visitation for her youngest daughter, Barbara, is being held, leaving only one of her children, Lora Mae, living out of eight.

factory worker in Munice, Indiana. He was married to Nellie Brown and secondly to Vivian Hall. There were no children.

The fourth child was Grace, a handicapped child who died when she was ten years old. Pete was the last child born to Jimmie and Susan.

Genealogy awakens memories of family associations in the past of which we were a part and had forgotten. The search beyond our more prominent memories gives us inklings of what might have transpired in previous generations. A family by any other name is still a family, given, of course, space for lots of variation

on the kind of activities that held it together. These names above help me to

Ollie Gilbreath married Ethel Lee Williams. They had four children: Marjorie, Paul (Deceased), James, and Le Anne.

remember the good times we had together. Also, they nudge me to make contact with those living in order that we may revive the associations. For instance, I just saw Donald Willis, G-aunt Lute's grandson, recently when he was hospitalized where my mother was confined.

Such memories help the individual not only to find their place in the larger scheme of humanity but also in the extended family of their line or branch. Since beginning this book, I have now found descendants of my g-grandfather William's brothers, James Robert and Henry right close to home. No one need be alone if they can and will discover their extended family through family research. I submit again that such study can enhance our emotional well-being.

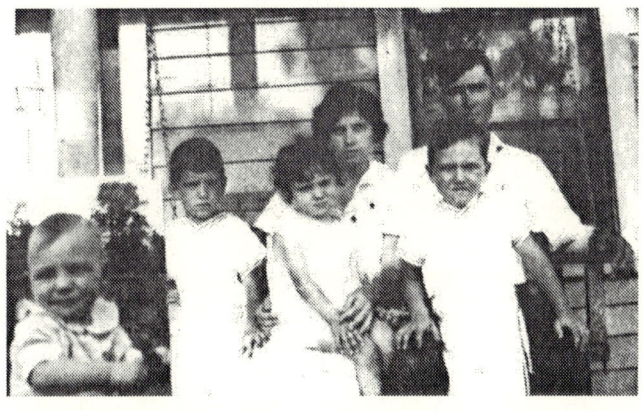

1935 Pete and Fleda with Gene 6 yrs old (left in swing), Mary 3yrs old (middle), and Bill 5 years old. At that time we lived on the Homer Ray Place west of the Poplar Cemetery. Tom was born later that year (insert)

Another mental health issue in regard to genealogy is found among many adoptees. According to an Associated Press story run in our local paper, Bob Mulvehill of Pennsylvania operates a nonprofit organization called "Lost Loved Ones."

77

An unidentified adoptee shares that she doesn't know who she is and that the emotions are tearing her apart. "I don't know how to bond," she confesses. "I don't feel I can be the person I was meant to be."[44] Granted, there are many other factors beside adoption that can make any of us experience the same emotions. However, when an adoptee feels this way, they might want to engage in a family search.

Engaging in such a search is not free of pitfalls. Some find their birth family easily and the experience is all positive. Others may continue to search, never finding them, or if they do, they might wish they hadn't looked. Is the risk then a reason not to try? Surely not, given the searcher's healthy capability of tolerating disappointment. There appears to be something in our blood, so to speak, that drives us to know to whom we belong. Whether in more general searches like we have been describing or in the case of adoptions, maybe that urge needs to be acted upon.

The "Lost Loved Ones" organization, although maybe not intentionally, seems to hold out for a positive experience for anyone who pursues it. More accurately, adoptees are looking for their birth family who may or may not turn out to be lovable ones. And it must be said that ofttimes adoptees already have loved ones within their adoptive family. That fact does not preclude the search, however.

---

[44] *Tribune Star* op.cit., September 9, 1997

Our two children are adopted. Our daughter engaged in such a search and with the assistance of information which we gave to her. Her brother has chosen not to seek his birth family. Either one has made the right decision because it is his or her own decision as a means of dealing with that urge to examine their past history. There are many mental health issues related to adoptions, and searching for biological parents or children might be one avenue toward emotional wholeness for some people.

We have shared some of our experience regarding our search for our ancestors. Some of the important ways we believe that mental health is accentuated by the process have been given. They include using genealogy as a process of satisfying some inner longings, curiosities, or achievement. Your world becomes enlarged as you meet new friends and as you rediscover relatives that you have not contacted for a long time.

It is an opportunity to understand more of what your ancestors endured and enjoyed in their day. The search helps us to see the importance of family yesterday and yet today for support, respect, and love. An understanding of our own makeup will help us to cope with this frustrating experience of not being able to put all the pieces together as quickly as we would like.

A search gives us a chance to study human nature over a period of time. We all continue to have frustrating and impatient moments as did our ancestors. The lesson of the moment for us is to find ways to deal with

79

frustrations realizing that much of our life does not fall into place when, where, and how we would want it. I met so many generous people who as strangers were ready and willing to be of assistance. For me, the process itself came to be good therapy when I could not continue in my usual occupation and was in the need of a good hobby.

Genealogy is an encouragement to make the most of the present situation, for you may be entertaining unawares someone with whom you share a common ancestor. Researching our beginnings is a great way to see how we fit into the grand scheme of things and the importance of an extended family. It can be a wonderful opportunity to deal with the imperfections of our humanity, the skeletons in the closet that need not reflect upon our own character. Also, it is a good opportunity to come to terms with our own demise as well as our legacy to future generations.

Genealogy is like driving down the road. It is important to keep your eyes focused on the road ahead. Family searches teach us that it is also important to take a look in the rear view mirror occasionally, an experience that is absolutely necessary for a safe trip. Looking ahead and at once glancing back gives one a satisfactory journey. Rear view mirrors are for the using.

FROM GRANDMA'S TO GRADUATION

Chapter 3

"The only good in pretending is the fun we get out of fooling ourselves that we fool somebody"—-Booth Tarkington

Dear Dad,

This is another one of those chapters you would really enjoy. In fact, if you were here, you could tell me lots of stories that I have forgotten. We all seem to remember different things about our past depending on our perspective. A father certainly would have different memories of his children growing up than the children themselves. Since you aren't here, I'll have to do the best I can remembering episodes that come to mind rather easily.

You may never have heard the above statement by Booth Tarkington, but you sure knew the truth of it. How often we thought we were fooling you or Mom, only to discover that we hadn't. But it was fun to try to outwit you, fruitless as that effort usually was.

This is a part of your life that you came to remember quite well after you came back from that "wilderness" of Woodmere that we will write about in a later chapter. Gosh, how I wish we had taken

81

more time to think together about those days of my childhood when you were well. I hope that others reading this will take every opportunity possible to treasure childhood days with their parents.

As we noted in the last chapter, our reflection upon the past must have purpose. We hope that is true as we recall the good and bad of our childhood days. You will remember that the purpose of my book is to do just that, adding meaning to the past so that we can secure a better emotional future for ourselves and others.

So here is some of the story of being a child and youth in the Gilbreath family from 1929 to young adulthood. We will talk about such common things as food, games, chores, school, cars, and more. Woven into this childhood mosaic will be hindsight reflections on those times and their influence on our emotional health.

And, Dad, we certainly will talk about your illness that comes at the end of this period. It is that experience that continues to motivate us to examine its relevance to our own mental health and that of our readers.

Well, Dad, I had better get with it. It's a chore that must be done, you would say! Make hay while the sun shines!

So long for now,

Gene

"There are periods when the principles of experience need to be modified, when hope and trust and instinct claim a share with prudence in the guidance of affairs, when, in truth, to dare is the highest wisdom." — William Ellery Channing, American clergyman (1780-1842).[45]

COUNTRY BOY
Pearl D. Anderson

"Little man of the soil
Yet to know of work and toil,
Laughing in the summer rain,
Playing with the golden grain,

Wondering at the seeds that grow,
Fruit and flowers for to show.
Work and pride await you here—
God and love and none to fear.

Lend to me for one small while
Sunshine of your freckled smile.
Through your laughing eyes so clear,
Show me my own yesteryear.[46]

One time when I went to a well-known clinic for a physical examination, I was given, as are all patients, the Minnesota Multiphasic Personality

---

[45] *Tribune Star*, op.cit., "Thought for Today," Associated Press, January 12, 1996

[46] Anderson, Pearl D., "Country Boy", printed in the *Woodland News*, Sullivan Convalescent Center, Vol 9, No 26, June, 1997

Inventory. It was reported to me that one phase of the test raised some questions. According to that test, I was not honest about how I felt regarding my childhood. I had painted a more rosy picture of that period in my life than the test designers considered normal, they reported to me.

Now who am I to argue with the standard in psychological testing, the MMPI, as it is commonly called? Since this book is not meant to represent the technical side of the psychological field, I won't delve further into that except to say that an evaluation of that test did not escape my study.

The test, in its own right, can continue to wave that flag, and I will continue on with my story of what childhood meant to me. Lest there be misunderstanding, this test can be helpful to anyone, and it should not be avoided. However, in this chapter the MMPI and I may part company as an attempt is made to tell you the best I know how what my childhood and youthful days were like.

Indeed in the process, the "principles of experience" mentioned above may need modification. What has appeared to me to be a time of hope, trust, and instinct may well face some moderation. As I dare to submit to that process, hopefully truth will overrule where necessary. It is hoped that you, the reader, will also be open to an honest examination of this period in your own life and arrive at the same sense of peace.

As we begin this chapter, it might be helpful to make comments about what I consider to be a serious distortion of what is otherwise a helpful process. In the counseling process where childhood is often examined, there is sometimes an encouragement by counselors to involve the hurting person in a blame game. I cannot conceive of a therapist doing this intentionally; nonetheless, there have been reports of such experiences. Hopefully the counselor does not have some residual anger towards his/her own parents who were less than they might have been and believe that it must be a universal experience for others.

Often there is anger about what has happened in childhood, and that may be resolved with the help of a therapist. However, parents need not be blamed for what are often unintentional mistakes. Some gross expressions of behavior may be another matter. Someone who is angry about childhood is not well-served unless there is some kind of reconciliation as opposed to further estrangement. Reconciliation, it seems to me, is preferable to estrangement in good mental health.

Certainly, taking responsibility for one's emotional state is taking the high road, rather than settling for blame. My parents did so well under the circumstances of their day. While never perfect, except in their love, my parents are not blamed for shortcomings that were not intentional. Now, being a parent and grandparent and having experienced the usual stresses of parenting, I judge that my parents did quite well.

My journey began at my Grandmother Riggle's home in Sullivan County. The day was August 5, 1929. It was a moderate summer day between seven and eight o'clock in the morning. My arrival had been expected all night. Bill Wade had brought his wife, Gertie, over to Grandmother Riggle's the evening before to be the midwife. A healthy, eight and one-fourth pound boy was the first child for my mother and father.

My Grandmother Gilbreath already had nine grandchildren, but I was the first grandson for Grandma Riggle. I didn't lack for attention with so many uncles and aunts around. If I had any competition, it was from my cousin, Robertine, who was just six months and two days my senior. Robertine and I would hold center stage for about a year and a half in and out of the Riggle homestead.

Gertie's presence was typical of that era. Most children in that county were born at home in those days. Dr. James Maple, the well-respected physician of the county, did the actual delivery as he had done for my mother's birth. However, women helping women was the norm. If not in a midwife role, neighbors and friends would help each other following the birthing. After being discredited for about fifty years, the practice of midwifery is slowing finding a place in today's society. The ready-made support was soothing to the emotions during the stress of birthing.

We hear of stories such as that of Margaret Dorroh who was serving in Rincon, Georgia, in 1996. "Today's midwifery is a balance between the human touch and the latest in technology, and many women prefer a nurse-midwife because of the holistic focus on the healthy woman and her newborn", states Ken Wibecan. The ancient practice of midwifery is now gaining acceptance, this time assisted by the best of both worlds. There are about fifty programs and close to five thousand nurse-midwives in practice, and such centers are licensed in thirty-four states.47

My father was not physically present for my birth. He was working in Muncie about 140 mile away. The road was longer seventy years ago! His departure had been quite disturbing to my mother. Dad had just taken leave to go back to Muncie without telling my mother he was going. Mom tells that story best, and we will hear it from her in the chapter, "Confidence and Cents." Suffice it to say here that all went well after just a few weeks as we can detect from the letters that he wrote.

I was named after two of Dad's best friends, Carl "Bud" Plew and Eugene "Pete" Woodard. These were the names Dad had picked for me if I turned out to be a boy. As Mom relays that name tidbit, she also states that Dad "was a good (underlined) husband, family man, and father. After he settled in, he was crazy about his family."48

Dad wrote several letters from Muncie during those early days of my life. His secretive departure had not kept him from writing and expressing his obvious concern about his first-born. Here are some excerpts from a couple

---

47 *Modern Maturity*, AARP, 601 E St NW, Washington, DC 20049, article by Ken Wibecan, Nov-Dec. 1996

48 Gilbreath, Fleda H. Riggle, "Memorable Notes in the Life of Fleda Helen Riggle Gilbreath", January,1996

of his letters in 1929 when postage was only two cents. From the New Home Hotel on South Walnut Street, he writes on August 22: "Dear Fleda and Boy, How are you and the boy by this time? We just got here in time to go to work Monday. Are you feeling better than you did Sunday? Well, I have to close, it is time to go to work. It's work and sleep. Ha! Write and tell me all about the baby and yourself. Goodbye xoxo, Clarence."49

On September 1, he wrote: "Dear wife and Boy, How are you this morning? I am fine. Did you go to the doctor Friday? I have been looking at some furniture. Good stuff is high...we can get the rooms we had for $6.50 a week if you want them. But I can't get a letter from you till Friday or Saturday so I will rent them. We can stay a week anyhow and get the furniture. I wish you would go down home (to my mother's). If you do, take your clothes. We will come back Sunday. We will start early and I want to stay at home for I will just have one night to stay. Will close and write more next time. To my dear and baby, Clarence."50 Remember that we don't just marry a wife. This husband was also committed to his mother. Maybe the reader has felt that same division or conflict of loyalties. What a temptation for the have-nots to try for what they can't afford.

Earlier in May, he wrote two letters that indicate he was in the habit of sending money home to his pregnant wife. On May 12, he wrote: "They had

---

49 Gilbreath, Clarence Homer, "Collection of Letters to my Family", 1929-1940
50 Ibid

a shortage in my check so I told them about it. I bet you will be disappointed but I can't help it. I was mad myself. I will send it to you when they get my check straightened out. So be good, Clarence" And the next week he sends the money in a letter, willing to risk not getting a money order. He tells Mom: "if you want some more you can tell me. Goodbye xoxoxo Clarence"[51]

The stresses of an unplanned family, unstable livelihood, limited transportation, and physical separation are well-known elements in many of today's families as well. It is a wonder that any marriage survives under such negative circumstances. While there are many more resources available now to encourage success in the family, all too many are failing. There is no panacea, no short course, yet general awareness of the pitfalls might help many young couples.

We must rely on all of society to hold before our youth the available resources for survival of the family. When about half of our children are from broken families, there is an obvious shortage of role models for successful marriages. Believing that all must enter family life void of the accumulated wisdom of others is folly. We owe those entering family life both a caring heart and training so that they may experience emotional health.

We are paying a terrible price for thinking and acting as if it is "every couple for themselves" or "they will just have to live and learn." Schools, churches, civic organizations, employers, and government must accept the

---

[51] Ibid

responsibility to do more than decry the breakdown of the family. If we could see the above stresses as being a mental health concern, we might then devise a united approach to ease the burdens and strengthen the family.

In our family there was never much money. Mom and Dad learned early that there had to be more going for them than the material side of life. They taught us children that love, communication, respect, and responsibility will go a long way in making a successful family. Those families who had to live with financial deprivation in the Depression days might well have had secrets of success that we seem to have forgotten or are ignoring.

Along came my siblings in rapid succession. William Homer came along just fifteen months after me when we lived with Grandma Gilbreath on State Road 154. We were quite different in personality and often clashed as brothers sometimes will do. He was more aggressive than I in many ways, yet I always felt a real satisfaction with a more-like-Dad laid-back approach. The competition continues to this day, he in his field of endeavor and I in mine.

Never did the rivalry keep us from remembering who we were and are, brothers who grew up with the same set of family experiences. The positive side of his fighting nature is recognized and appreciated when I recall his contribution to our nation in the Korean War. In like manner I salute my youngest brother Tom for his service in the Armed Forces. They fought for my freedom. I fought in a different way to help us see the rightness of brotherhood. Together we make a better world.

William's birth was preceded as mine with Dad working at Muncie. His letters reveal his concern for me and for Mom and their unborn child. In August of 1930, he gets a job but wanted to work nights thinking he would get to work longer. He is very concerned about Mom not feeling well and insists she go to the doctor. Money would be on its way to pay for it. On eighteen dollars a week he can not have us up there, too. He will send ten dollars and try to get by on five or six and still be able to keep the furniture.

In September of 1930 he writes in part: "I sure would like to see you and (Gene). It has been a long time. How many beans did you get canned? You want to can all you can for we will need it this winter. I don't look to have a job very long. I sure wish I was making enough for you to come up. I know you feel like I don't want you but I do but I am not making enough to. I just got $14.40 Saturday. That is not very much is it? And I will have to pay house rent next week. I will close and go to bed. It is so lonesome to set up. I go to bed as soon as I get the work done so it won't be so lonesome. Write every day this week. I sure like to read them when I get in from work. Goodbye, Clarence xoxoxo to Fleda and Gene"52 He handled the aloneness one way, and we will see later that Mom handled it another. It is surprising that he did not choose Rip's jug to ease the pain.

---

52 Ibid

91

His last two letters of September contained the bad news that work would soon end. Planning for that, he said: "I got a letter from Sarah (his sister) and Mamma this week. Sarah said if I got layed off she would give me a job getting the corn out. I am glad you got your things before I did get laid off." He had been back for a check up at the dentist's office and reports: "I have four teeth that need filled but I can't have that done now. It would cost $8.00 and that is lots of money now days, isn't it sweetheart?"

As time goes on, he expresses more and more love and concern for his family. He is coming of age as a father of one with another one about to be born. But losing a job in the Depression days with only the prospect of a few days work from his sister at a dollar a day caused him to close his September 23, 1930, letter by saying, "Goodbye, Clarence. I have the blues. Be good. I love Fleda and Gene."[53] This son is not the "boy" any more; I have a name and Dad uses it now.

And as if being timed just right to make up for not being there for my birth, he is home for brother Bill's entrance into this world in November. Mom was proud to have Dad there when, assisted by Hazel Davis, Dr. Maple delivered their second son. The same circumstances would be the case for the birth of Mary Kathleen in May of 1932, also at Grandma Gilbreath's about five and a half mile west of Sullivan. I would revisit that property some nine years later to mow the yard for the occupants, Lyman

---

[53] Ibid

and Lois Ormiston. My recollections of that place are only two. The Gilbreath's of Greene County came to visit, although they were just some visitors to me at that time. It was there that I learned not to put paper wads up my nose.

I'm sure I enjoyed the attention of older neighbor children such as Murry and Jeanette Frakes and my first new overalls given me by their father. Preceding Christmas of 1998, I visited this brother and sister who were near eighty, alone and Murry ill and with no close family to attend to the needs. With the gift of a basket of fruit, I symbolically said "thank you" for their friendship of over sixty-five years. My parents taught me by example to be appreciative, but I only gave a token to the Frakeses.

In the spring of 1933, the sparse belongings were loaded up and moved about two mile east and then south off of State Road 154 (450S) to property owned by Roy and Nellie Kelley. Grandma moved with us. "We would all move together," said Dad, and Mom agreed.[54] Each needed the other. Grandma had the furniture, and everyone had to have a place to stay.

The Kelley house stood on what seemed like a big hill. The house still is occupied but at another location in Graysville. A newer home now graces the top of that hill on the west side of the road. I remember trying to catch the Easter bunny there (just an ordinary rabbit, of course) and looked closely to see where the bunny's eggs were being laid. In the Turtle Creek

---

[54] Gilbreath, Fleda, op.cit

bottom just in front of the house, there was an abundant growth of peppermint. To this day, I love it and have it growing in my garden. As I would walk to the gate at the road, I would break off a leaf and enjoy its refreshing flavor.

Very early we were taught to sample and enjoy nature's plenty, with Grandma's or Mom's approval, of course. It was here that I learned that you could go out in the fields and gather wild greens that were delicious to eat. There is something emotionally refreshing about eating directly off the land. City dwellers could have window boxes of lettuce or herbs or grow a tomato in the flower bed.

We were renters, of course, at the Kelley Place. We lived there only about one year. I recall the huckster wagon that came. It was a traveling grocery store and was driven by Gene Medsker. His was the first death that I recall, a sudden one. Local stores either in Sullivan or Graysville would sponsor these stores-on-wheels for the sake of a population far less mobile than now. One of those driven by John Kirton of Graysville was still active in the late forties. And like the Frakes family, what wonderful neighbors were Orland and Florence Stanley. Years later she would give us newlyweds a kitchen table and chairs. Some friends are forever.

It was here at the Kelley Place that I remember hearing my first radio. Cousin Hallie Robertson, nephew of Grandma Gilbreath, came and hooked up a radio by running wires back outside to his car battery. He had a

Terraplane car with front doors that were hinged just opposite of today's cars. We had a Model T Ford, and I would pull down the spark lever so it would start when Dad cranked it. There was no radio!

Other memories include some anxiety. A problem developed with the payment of rent. I remember the tension, and not the conversation, the day that Mr. Kelley came to discuss this with Grandma and Mom. No satisfactory agreement was reached, and the road gate leading to the house was padlocked. So that Model T sat out on the road. When the padlock was not sufficient to force the necessary action, the owner removed the pump handle.

Gene (5), Bill (4), Mary (3) Sailor suits were handed down from Gregg cousins. Mom made Mary a blue burgandy outfit. 1935

Dad could park out on the road, no big deal, but could we do without water?

No, we didn't. Dad owned a pair of fence pliers so designed to pull staples as well as hammer them into the fence posts. That pulling part of the pliers fit just right into the eye of the pump suck-rod. Now you could pull the rod up and down the same as it would go if it had a handle. How long we did that I don't recall, but it was long enough to be remembered quite vividly.

What a desperate father won't do for his family. How does a welfare agency view the emotional dynamics of disadvantaged parents today? Try jumping through the hoops to get Medicaid or SSI today, and the reaction of a landlord sixty-five years ago seems very mild. Condescension, mistrust, disrespect, and misunderstanding are frequently hallmarks of the system as they try to cope with those who would cheat. It is quite all right for the state to do it all the wrong way in order to prevent clients from doing it wrong?

At this young age of four to five, I took in the wonders of the world around me and sensed that which caused my parents great pain. Mr. Kelley, no first name basis in those days, must have had his problems in the Depression, too. Mutual understanding is a great basis for resolution of a problem. Dad did work out some of the rent with Mr. Kelley and did some logging with Arlie Spoonmore up around Scott City on State Road 48.

Bill, Mary, and Gene at Uncle Vernia's in Sullivan. 1935

For a child, these surroundings were not issues of dollars and cents. The issue of rent, I did not understand. I did learn that we do what we have to do to survive and that process can contain joys, too. "The life of a man is a journey: A journey that must be traveled, however bad the roads or the accommodations," said

96

Oliver Goldsmith55 The Depression was such a journey, but it also had its inherent delights and pleasures. One need not underestimate the transmission of adult feeling, both good and bad, to our children.

Now we moved again, this time not quite a half mile northwest down the lane west of the Poplar Cemetery on the Homer Ray Place in the spring of 1934. During this time of residence, Dad worked for Ray Ferree who had contracted the job of providing gravel for the State Road 63 street running through Graysville. That as well as a short term job a time or two at Muncie didn't help a whole lot. He received $12 for driving the team, and Ray got $24 for furnishing the team and wagon. Again Dad worked out some of the rent at this place, too. And like the last place, there would be disagreement about their agreement.

Our stay at the Ray Place was interrupted by a tornado on May 2, 1935. That was the first recollection of understanding the destructive forces of nature. It was also the time for me to see how other people worked at their occupation. I watched every move that Orville Sebring made as he repaired the damaged house and rebuilt the barn. Carpentering still holds great interest for me. Dad and John Eaton assisted with the repair. Dad's work became a matter of dispute with the home owner when Dad insisted on being paid the same for a day's work as the others in lieu of rent. That unresolved problem led to another move by late November of that year.

---

55 *Tribune Star*, op.cit., "Cryptoquote," date not known

I remember the day Tommy Lee was born at the Ray Place. Florence Stanley had come over to stay that day. The three of us children were taken to another neighbor's, Naomi and Wilbur Kelley, to stay most of the day. The Kelleys lived on what was known as the Kelley Landing, the home of Wilbur's parents, John Kelley and wife, just south of the Poplar Cemetery. This was a different line of Kelleys than those who lived on the west side of Turman Township. It was an enjoyable day and one remembered well for a lifetime. What significant memories can be made in the life of a child when an adult outside the family demonstrates concern as did these neighbors.

School had already started when Tommy was born in September. Although the circumstances surrounding his birth seem to have been exciting, I never told my teacher that I had a new baby brother. When my mother visited school at Christmas time, it was she who divulged this little bit of important information to my teacher. My silence must have had much to do with my own attitude and decorum in the classroom. In the first place, I was not very happy going to school. In fact, my first day was spent crying all day long. It is doubtful that my participation in the first grade with Miss Helen Willis was any different than my later experience. I was not real talkative in school anytime, not even in later times when I thoroughly enjoyed any learning experience in the classroom.

I suspect that not wanting to go to school precipitated this following event. It seems that the lane down to the bus stop was about a quarter of a mile. Trees lined the lane on both sides, and about half way to the road was a low place in the lane. It was just low enough that a first grader could not see the end of the lane. Tie that physical stage with my unhappiness with school, and you have the setting for some wild imagination.

Sure, there was a bear at the end of that lane! My, how I tried to convince my mother when I quickly retreated to her safety. I must go to school, she insisted, and taking me by the hand walked me back through the low area until we could see the end of the lane. "There", she said, "see the bear is gone, and there is the bus waiting." I had conquered the bear and would enjoy education henceforth. That was a turning point in my educational endeavor, made possible by a mother who knew how to make imaginary bears vanish.

Tommy was about nine weeks old when we moved to the Homer Bicknell Place which was only a quarter of a mile straight south of the Ray Place, and about three-fourths of a mile around the road. There we paid $15 a month for rent for about fifteen acres and did that faithfully for nine years. The earlier squabbles over rent seemed to be related to the aftermath of the Depression, affecting owner and renter alike. The most memorable times of childhood transpired in this location.

My first grade of school continued from this home but on a different bus route. Jess Canary drove the last horse-drawn school hack of the school corporation, and that was the "downer" for moving. My parents got me up before daylight, sometimes helping me to dress while the driver waited. It was dark when I came home since I was the first person on and the last one off the hack. The route took us nearly three mile, the long way, to where we would meet the driver of a motorized bus who had hauled me earlier. There was a kerosene heater in the middle of the wagon. There were benches on each side. Sometimes it was better to get out and walk if one wanted to keep warm.56

We lived far enough from school, and, having no other transportation,

My wife's father's school hack looked like this. No doubt the last one being used in which the writer rode looked similar to this one parked at the old 1903 Graysville School.

we always rode the bus after that first year. That was an education in itself. I do not recall anyone ever being thrown off the bus—no, not literally. Discipline then was much less of a problem than now. Early-on the bus still had benches on the side. You could take a seat where there was an opening. Sometimes it was clear that a student was not wanted in a certain spot and

---

56 An article that appeared in the local newspaper indicates that some children in the nation might have ridden in those wagons as late as 1928. So we were behind the times by still having one operating as late as 1935-1936 school year. The first school bus built in 1914 with a motor was a Model T truck. By 1935 all buses were built with metal bodies to enhance the safety factor, except this one in our school district which was still drawn by horses. Now twenty-three million children ride in nearly 400,000 buses.

ranks would be closed. Bashful kids or ones disliked for whatever reason were sometimes systematically refused a seat by certain people. One rider insisted on spreading his legs as far as possible so he would not be crowded.

Here was much opportunity to learn what it was like to find your place, when to hold your own, and how to respect others. We were lucky to have a driver like Earl McElwain, better known as Buddy, who took interest in the total welfare of his riders. I was permitted to sit on the toolbox beside the driver and operate the stop sign. A learning experience it was for me; one, no doubt, that would not be permitted today.

The outdoors was our domain and sanctuary. Every child today should have fifteen acres to roam freely, as well as a few mile of roads that can be traveled safely. Everyone can't have that; however, there may well be substitutes that will serve the same purpose. Children should have some space in which to try out their wings of creativity. There should be some spot of privacy where life has a chance to be pondered, where we consider our inter-relatedness to the world. Youth today may have to learn to accomplish the same purpose within greater spatial confines.

It was mentioned earlier that work can be fun. Maybe the chores themselves may not always be fun, but the sense of accomplishment and contribution to the family is highly rewarding. Our disconnectedness in today's world is a source of much discontent among our youth, as well as

101

the expectation for instant gratification. It is everyone for himself, and that is destructive to the formation of character and responsibility.

We had farm animals to feed and water. There was no garden hose. If a lot of water needed to be moved, it was done sometimes by placing a stick through the bucket handle and two children shared the load. Sharing loads is about to be a lost art. In order to get some chores done expeditiously, the work was often divided so as to hasten the completion and reap rich rewards.

If the animal that needed water happened to be a pony, we were happy to take a ride. We understood that there are no free rides. If the animal was a cow, we knew that the proper feed would make for a

Four year old Tom on our pony, Laddie, at the Bicknell Place. 1939

wonderful glass of milk. It didn't take money to buy eggs; they came from chickens for which we had provided food and water. When we enjoyed a steak, bacon, or ham, we understood that as a cause and effect lesson. We always enjoyed having the horse pull the double shovel to cultivate the garden. It saved a lot of hoeing, but the horse needed nourishment in order to do that.

When we sat down to the table, we did not only know the source of the meat but also the vegetables. We always had a large garden. Early and late in the season we enjoyed its production. Grandma Gilbreath would go out to the garden when the potatoes were just small in size and do a procedure she called "graveling." She took a small instrument of some kind, sometimes only a stick or a table fork, and dug very carefully into the hill of potatoes.

Gene and Tom on work break from gardening.

The vine must not be damaged and only slightly disturbed in order to "steal" a few small potatoes that would be served with the early peas. Only Grandma could do that chore so the vines would never wither until their due time.

Gardening taught us about the principles of growth. It is so much better to learn them firsthand than from a book. We came to understand the whole process of preparing soil, planting seeds properly, cultivating with care, and harvesting with pride. Those are lessons that apply to all of life. There is a sequence to achievement, doing one thing before another is a significant finding. Maybe every child can not have a large plot as we did, but everyone surely has some kind of container in which they can grow a flower or maybe a tomato. Here we note the therapeutic effects of such activity, highlighting the potential of sequential seed time, cultivation, and harvest as components of good mental health.

At the end of the season, Dad would dig a hole in the middle of the garden in which to bury potatoes, carrots, cabbage, and apples. Dirt would be piled high over the vegetables that had been covered with straw. In midwinter, Dad had the chore of going out there to open a hole in the side, pulling out a fruit or vegetable, and resealing the hole. We did not have apple trees, but we would go to the Rickard Orchard north of Sullivan and buy enough to have all winter. I can taste the apples yet, sometimes partially frozen if the winter had been very cold. When we were small, Grandma Gilbreath scraped an apple in the evening. She did this because she had no teeth. We had teeth, but sometimes Grandma didn't get any apple because we gathered around and took turns getting our little scraping.

What great moments of reflection can happen on a cold wintry night as you find a warm spot around the fire, play guessing games or checkers, or better yet make taffy. In an old cookbook, there is a recipe that was most likely the one Mom and Grandma used. Take 2 cups granulated sugar, 1 tablespoon butter, 1 cup water, and a tablespoon of vinegar, placing all ingredients in a pan and cooking without stirring until a small amount of mixture hardens when dropped in cold water. Then the candy was poured onto a well buttered plate and allowed to cool enough to handle. We took turns, two at a time opposite each other, pulling until the taffy was white.

When it had been stretched into the desired size strips, it would be cut into pieces.57 The remainder of the evening was pure bliss. How much better candy tastes if you have helped to make it. This was another of our family fun times. What does

Grandma Gilbreath standing tall, confident, and ready to help with any chore. c1938

the modern family do together?

The Home Comfort Cookbook was the only other cookbook in our home, but the two were sufficient for great meals and in-between snacks. Mom made divinity candy quite often, Seafoam, we also called it. There were so many other special foods that I remember, all cooked over that Home Comfort cook stove in our kitchen. We had the best homemade donuts made with potatoes. The jam cake that we took to the Robertson reunions was delicious. For old-times sake, I recently made a jam cake to take to my mother's eighty-seventh birthday party.

Homemade mincemeat made the best pies especially in the winter time. Molasses or vinegar pie was hard to beat anytime. The bread bowl of

---

57 *The People's Home Library,* Culinary section, The R C Barnum Company, Cleveland, OH 1919, P 122

Grandma's, sitting on the ledge in the dining room here, reminds me of the aroma and taste of bread she made. It was always better than the sliced bread from the store. On a hot summer day when Uncle Ollie's came with their children, Marjorie, Paul, LeAnn, and Jim, homemade ice cream would top off any meal. Again, our turn cranking the freezer by hand made it taste all the better. A side benefit was stealing a chip of ice to cool our mouth or to put down the neck of some unsuspecting cousin. It was a common treat for any of the Riggle/Gilbreath uncles and aunts and their families whose visit was planned or unexpected.

We butchered as many as five hogs for the winter. The meat was sugar-cured and delicious no matter how you chose to cook it. The butchered calf would be hung in the smoke house, as well as the pork. The beef cured itself as it hung there, and what delicious pan-fried steak and gravy we had, accompanied by Grandma's biscuits, even for breakfast. Some of the pork was made into sausage that was formed in a cloth casing that Mom and Grandma would make. The outside of that casing would be rubbed with seasonings to preserve it. If there was any question about either the pork or beef keeping due to a warm winter, we would fry down the sausage and boil the beef and can them.

These foods and so many others that were special are comfort foods to us now. We are reminded of what O. W. Holmes said, "The true essentials of a feast are only fun and feed."[58] The two did go together at our house because we had all been involved in the growing of the food and often in the preparation of the food for the table. Children who learn to work together while understanding the source of their food, will be children who appreciate what is on their table and will also share with those less fortunate. While times have changed greatly since my childhood, the need for children to learn to appreciate good nutrition will not cease. Mental health and such appreciation are vitally intertwined.

There was more to learn from nature. Each new day was a testimony about the stability of the universe. We learned to go to sleep trusting that the sun would rise and that the new day would hold more opportunities for us. "Goodnight,

The four Gilbreath kids and cousin Jerome Mize. The garden is in the background where we all did our part to provide food for the table.

sleep tight, wake up bright, in the morning light, to do what's right, with all your might (and don't let the bedbugs bite)" was no superficial saying for us at the close of the day.

---

[58] Source unknown

We discovered that we could get hurt if we did not respect the forces of nature. Just how high up can you be and not get bruises or breaks when you jump? Just how unforgiving is a large oak tree when you bump into it? What happens when you get your feet too close to the fire? Matches were to start authorized fires, like burning trash or lighting the fire in the stove, not ever a play thing. Your unprotected skin would freeze instantly on the pump handle in zero weather. Unfamiliar waters were not for swimming. And the list goes on.

We have spoken of work being fun sometimes, but we did have free time and games, too. Those also were times of learning to get along. How many times someone became angry and went home. It usually didn't take long for that person to choose to be back in the game rather than sitting at home alone pouting. Even if there were only two playing, there was the opportunity to show respect for your opponent. Learning to lose was just as important as winning. That simple lesson of childhood is too soon lost in the competitive and the me-first-and-always world of today. A child must have this opportunity to develop a cooperative attitude if there is to be satisfaction in later life. Even if you won every high school or college basketball game, where does satisfaction come from after that?

Our games were almost never purchased in a store. Here in the nineties, store-bought party games are in vogue. Games like Jenga, Outburst, Pictionary, Scattegories, Taboo, and Gestures are popular choices. We probably would have played those if they had been available. However, the imagination developed and the creativity stimulated by making up your own games are vital to a child's development. I didn't have toy tractors and plows so I sneaked a spoon and fork out of the kitchen to use as implements to prepare my little "acre" of soil. My mother just reminded me a few days ago of my imaginary vehicle. I took her wash stand, turned it upside down, and, using two of the legs, I pushed it around. She told me that I had even driven nails in those legs to be used as my throttle, gears, lights, and horn.

The evening hours in summer were also significant times for us. Since there was only God's air conditioning, we spent evenings, after work and supper, in the front yard. Sometimes the neighbor children, the Huffs, would be there. Maybe the Harden twins, Lois and Louise, would drop by with their string instruments and sing us a song or two. Often our cousins, the Rooksberrys, who stayed with us a lot, would join in the evening fun. These cousins were the children of Dad's sister, Sarah, who had died at forty-four years of age leaving eight children. They were Noble, Jim, Bob, Junior, Lora, Audrey, Eddie, and Barb. There were also neighbors to whom we will refer when we talk about the support of our community.

During those evenings we played tag and other games mostly in the front yard where there was grass. Grandma sat in a chair along the front of the house. Dad and Mom often occupied the front steps, often taking turns resting their heads in each other's laps. What a great way to end a hard day's work, supporting each other, watching their growing family, and exchanging chitchat with Grandma. That sounds so boring to most today who require outside stimulation to find peace.

Those were nights when I developed a keen interest in the heavens. Knowing so little about the skies compared with today, I would wonder how it all came to be, what held it together, and what was really out there beyond our sight. My mother liked to sing, and often we heard the music from her lips;

"Twinkle, twinkle, little star, how I wonder what you are.

Up above the world so high, like a diamond in the sky.

When the glorious sun is set and the grass with dew is wet, then you show your little light."

Never did I seriously think then that in my lifetime I would be a part of something called the space age. We dreamed of getting a radio but never thought of such a thing as television on which we would see men walking on the moon about three decades later. One night there was more than the usual twinkling of the stars. An unusual glow in the northern skies caught our attention. It was so fascinating to see the movement, the variation of color, and the increasing brightness.

The longer we observed, the more the mystery developed as to the explanation of this awesome sight. It seemed that our parents and Grandma took their time in telling us about this baffling display. They had seen such an event back in 1918 when nearly all of Sullivan had been out to view this phenomena in the northern sky one night during the second week of March. It was the most brilliant display of the Aurora Borealis in several years. Many observers claimed to see the likeness of the American flag.59

One other memorable event of the nights under the country sky was the chasing and catching of fireflies. By now, the firefly may be our state insect. Early in 1997, the Indiana House approved a measure to that effect.60 Waiting for the yellowish abdomen to flash and being close enough to catch it when it did was just as exciting as making a conquering move in checkers. It seemed a little cruel the next morning when we examined the jar with our bounty and we found some of them dead. We couldn't reach the stars, but we could be more in control of our world with the lightening bugs on those warm summer nights. We sat in awe of that which was beyond our reach and gloried in the little brilliance of creation that we could hold in our hands.

One night was also memorable during World War II. The first county wide blackout was held on Wednesday, March 24, 1943, from 9 to 9:30 p.m. under authority of the U.S. Army.61 Flights were made over the county from nearby George Field to test the effectiveness of the drill. I remember sitting in the darkened kitchen around the table and waiting for the eternal-like half-

59 *Sullivan Daily Times*, "In Times Past," op cit., March 7-13, 1918

60 *Tribune Star*, op.cit., February, 1997

61 *Sullivan Daily Times*, op.cit, March 7 through 13, 1943

111

hour to pass. We had been attending church faithfully and used some of the time to offer up prayers for our soldiers. Our special concern was for our cousin, Robert Rooksberry, who had enlisted on my birthday, August 5, 1940, and who later lost his life in Korea while serving in the same unit with my brother Bill.

And the skies held our attention in the daytime as well. We were not under a regular flight path so we saw only an occasional airplane flying over. Always we ran outside to see the planes when we heard the roar of their engines. One day two of our Gregg cousins from Terre Haute were riders in one of those planes. An airplane that circled over our house at low altitude did not escape our notice. The mystery was solved when they called our neighbors after returning home.

Storms that brewed day or night were both fascinating and scary. The tornado that hit our home left a lasting anxiety in our minds about storms. Those that we watched from afar were, like the Aurora Borealis, beautiful to behold. I learned that it was not so wonderful to be knocked down by lightning. Neither was it a picnic when the winds would blow, window panes would break, and we felt the rain pelting us inside our home which was supposed to have been a safe haven. We learned that some forces are out of our control and that those are governed by Someone whose wisdom we do not always understand. Trusting His Providential care, we sang "A

Shelter in the Time of Storm" as the wind roared; a comforting thought yet today.

Our home at the Bicknell Place (now CR 150 N, about five mile west of Sullivan) was an "Embassy Suite," "Twice the hotel" says the Embassy ad on television. There were only two rooms. The West room was the kitchen and our parents' bedroom. Little Tom slept in that room, also. There was a large dining table where we all could eat, play table games, enjoy an after-school snack, or study our school lessons. The Home Comfort wood/coal stove cooked our food, heated water, provided heat in the winter, and "het" the irons for ironing our clothes.

In the northwest corner of the room stood the three-cornered cupboard that Great-grandpa William Robertson had made for my grandmother when she married. Next to the back door sat the kerosene burner that we often used to cook our meals in the summer. Behind the cook stove was a wood box sometimes used for a cradle for a newborn farm animal that was having a difficult time adjusting to life in this world. To the right of the cook stove was a smaller table that served as a counter for food preparation and under which lard and other staples were stored. Near that table was a built-in cupboard where other foodstuff and medicine could be stored including a bottle of whiskey on the top shelf to make hot toddy for ailing adult stomachs.

The East room, the same size, about 18'X24', served as the living room where we could gather around the wood/coal Florence stove for warmth and socialization. At one time we used the fireplace originally intended to be the source of heat for that room. The stove was adorned with beautiful chrome-plated guards that served as a foot-rest for those who knew just when to withdraw! In the summer the stovepipe was removed, the stove set back against the wall, and the flue hole covered with a decorative stopper. Sometimes the stove was taken out to the smokehouse to make more room for summer activities.

Along the east wall were two beds, one for Bill and me, and the other for Mary and Grandma. In the unused back doorway, sat Grandma's old pump organ. My only accomplishment as a musician was to learn to play by memory two hymns and "Peter, Peter, Pumpkin Eater." While there were no other musical instruments, music was always abundant as Grandma played and sang, and my mother whistled gospel tunes as she went about her chores. I could carry water to the chickens, but I never was able to carry a tune. Music is a matter of the heart, but I always wanted to play the piano or organ and sing. I wanted that so much that a few times my dreams have included quite impressive renditions.

The East room also included a dresser that Grandma had saved after the Depression had taken the farms. That dresser holds special significance to me since it served as my desk. By the light of the kerosene lamp, I

114

prepared my school lessons for the next time in class. That was the spot, too, where I stood later to learn how to shave and how to tie my necktie. Believe it or not, provision was made for company who might want to stay over. That was usually my Uncle Bill from Muncie or some of the Rooksberry or Gregg cousins. A cot was placed on the south side of the room and used for these visitors.

Looks like we just got home from church. There were not many other times to dress up a bit and put on our shoes in the summer. You can get a better view of this "two room mansion" and of the old 28 Chevrolet. c1939

We learned early how to take care of the kerosene lamps, more commonly called coal oil lamps. Cleaning the globe took care. Trimming the wick was a technical procedure.

Filling the base was a challenge so that oil was not spilled. Most of all, we learned to respect the possibility of an explosion when we turned down the light. Like the torches of Biblical times, ceramic jars filled with oil and several kinds of oil-burning lamps took away the feeling of total darkness. Most industry, however, stopped at dusk, so the invention of the kerosene lamp with a brightness of seven times that of any light before it, was a wonderful accomplishment.62 I would be gone to college at Taylor University in 1948 before my family would experience the incandescent lights in the home.

One of the vehicles best remembered at the Bicknell Place was a 1928 Chevrolet. Our parents had better control over us when we were put in the back seat of this two-door. Memories of standing up behind the front seat observing how this machine operated are quite vivid. When I tried to operate it alone one day, I found that observing was not the same thing as actual hands-on experience. It did not crash, but my heart did a big leap when the clutch engaged quicker than I expected. I only backed it up a few feet, but that was enough to tell me that I wasn't quite ready to get a driver's license.

Cars of those days had an inner structure of wood for the frame of the door. Naturally, it would not be long before that frame would begin to rot, letting the door sag. A reach out the window and a grasp of the door handle with an upward thrust would bring the door closed just right. There came a time when the door didn't stay latched securely, and the farmer's friend, baling wire, came to the rescue. Sometimes we had to haul water, and the old faithful Chevy pulled the sled with the barrel on it.

I do not remember a time when the old car had brakes. Slow driving, even around the Square at Sullivan, anticipating stops ahead, and sometimes using the reverse gear, always got us stopped. Much of the time we used the Washington Street Road from just south of us to enter the city

---

62 *Tribune Star*, op.cit., Helen Mitchell, April 9, 1995

of Sullivan more safely. Most often we would park on Washington Street, two blocks off the Square, to avoid the congestion.

I remember well the day my mother learned to drive. We loaded in the car without Dad and took off northeast through the country to Grandma Riggle's. I think it was soon after Grandma had married David Albert Worth. She had written on October 17, 1937, telling us of her wedding that had occurred in Vincennes. They were now at home on R.R. 2, Jasonville, Indiana. We could go across country and avoid most traffic. Mom did very well, although I, at eight years of age, had some anxiety about how well she might do. She proved herself adequately, and from that date I had no concern about her being under the wheel. In fact we could go a few more places now when Dad wasn't available.

One day we had gone out east of Sullivan to the feed mill, made our purchase, and were ready to go home. Sometimes the car had to be cranked, and that was one of those times. I was in the car waiting for Dad to start it. This day, he had inadvertently left it in a forward gear, and when it started, so did I and the car. I had often steered it, and, startled, I tried to put into practice what I had learned. I first had to dodge a corner post and then head it back west toward home. If the car was going to go anywhere then it might as well be headed home. Dad had jumped out of the way and finally caught up with me, at what seemed to me to be miles, but only a few feet down the road.

117

These were my driver formation years. I remember one time the motor had an oil pressure problem and had to be torn down. I learned to hand Dad the right wrenches when he requested them. Dad's labor was free and a little spring that cost only three cents put the car back on the road. Our next car was a 1931 four-door Chevrolet sedan, and it had a rather uneventful history. I can remember appreciating the back doors. It performed the same chores as the 1928 did including trucking. One of those was to haul a newborn calf that Dad had purchased. The calf would be fed by the bottle and finally end up as our beef for the winter months.

These old cars that are being described here always got us to town, to church, to school activities, and each summer to the Merom Chautauqua. This was a community event somewhat like a festival but also filled with positive learning experiences. While we children were too young to appreciate the potential, we did get the notion that Dad and Mom were taking us to a significant event where we would have fun and learn. The plaque that stands on the Merom Bluff tells the purpose of the events best. We would also go to Merom on Wednesday nights in the summer to attend free movies projected on the side of a grocery.

The Family Circus cartoon in today's paper reminds me of the next vehicle. The father is driving and son, tucked in by his suitability, is riding in the back seat. The only suitability that I had ever known was the belt that was applied just a few times to my seat when I had done

A local festival is still held on this beautiful Merom Bluff each year on the first weekend in June.

something quite out-of-line. And that procedure was tough love and not child abuse. So in the cartoon, son says to Daddy, "Daddy, could you buy a better looking car before I'm 16?"[63]

The 1932 International truck that Dad had purchased from a gentleman in Sullivan had been used by the dogcatcher. The first time we drove into Sullivan the metal cage was still on the truck. We children had chosen to ride in the back. Riding down Main Street, some kids yelled at us and barked like dogs. The sides came off that night when we arrived back at home.

And again, we had a vehicle that had a brake problem. This truck, however, had an emergency brake that worked. My chore was to sit close to the dash astride the brake lever that was off center towards the passenger

---

[63] Ibid, "The Family Circus", Bil Keane, Inc, 1997, Dist by Cowles Synd., Inc.

side and be the brakeman. Mother sat to my right holding Tom. Mary stood

behind me since I sat on the edge of the seat to work the brake. Bill sat between Dad and me. Seat belts? Never heard of them. Who went fast enough to get seriously hurt?

Again with this vehicle, I discovered that experience was an effective teacher. When I was about twelve, I was scheduled to mow the yard at the Ormiston's,

Dad was the mechanic who kept these vehicles running. Here you see the smokehouse where we cured our meat. This was taken about 1938 before Dad's onset of illness.

Grandma Gilbreath's on St. Rd. 154. It was about three

mile, and I was balking at walking to do the job in order to gain permission to drive the old truck. Finally Dad gave in, maybe remembering the long distance he used to walk to do the farming at the hundred acres.

I rounded a curve and started down a hill toward a one-lane bridge at the bottom. Stalled in the middle of that bridge was a tractor. I reached over and yanked hard on the brake. It worked, throwing me into a skid down the graveled hill. I was as scared as when the '28 Chevy ran away at the feed mill. Luckily, I stopped at the edge of the bridge, not over six feet from the tractor. That experience caused me to have great respect for unexpected dangers that may emerge as we drive.

It is firmly believed by this writer that all these experiences learned as a child are important in our later mental and emotional development. A child who has the opportunity to learn valuable lessons as a child is one who feels much more confident as the adult world is entered. As an adult, there have been so many different tasks that I would try to do without hesitation because of some training that gave me a head start on similar missions.

While chores may be different today, the responsibility of parents to teach their children basic skills cannot be evaded. Some children, all too many today, do not have a parent who will or can teach these skills. It is then that others such as schools, churches, business, must take up that slack so that we have children entering into the adult world who have had some affirming and successful experiences.

In my experience as a child and teenager, there were others who took responsibility in providing those positive opportunities for expression. One was the church. More will be said about the life of the church in the community in the chapter, "Kneeling to Dance." At my small home church I was given many occasions to develop various skills. Those ranged from firing the stove, pressurizing the gas lights, mowing the yard, fixing the roof, soliciting money to paint the church, to teaching a class, being secretary, acting as superintendent, and developing skills of public prayers and speaking. The church was a vital part of our family life and was the source of our strength and comfort when Dad became ill. That support will be outlined in the chapter on "Kneeling to Dance."

The school was another positive force in my life. Our teachers were mostly local people who had a real interest in the community. Their being "one of us" did much to help us feel connected to a significant happening in our growing up years. As in the church, I learned skills that have been most helpful to me both in everyday occurrences and in my chosen occupation. Being allowed to help paint the school one summer, carrying the school mail, raising and lowering the flag, popping corn for the

Front: L-R Jackie Riggs, Elizabeth Thompson, Frances Wilson. Back: Frank Parsons, Lloyd Huff, and Tom Gilbreath. Taught by Jeanette Frakes. c.1941

games, working on the school yearbook, doing personal chores for the teachers, all these and more were just as important as the facts learned in class.

In 1940 Dad spent some time in late summer working again in Muncie. During that time we tried to take care of the farm animals. Dad wrote often showing interest in what we were doing and how much he missed us. Each child would get a note from him. I had gotten new glasses, had missed school for some reason, but it was not the quarantine for scarlet fever this time. Something had happened to our pigs. Dad was consoling and made it clear that it was not our fault. He wished he had been back home to have seen a show with us. He was concerned about brother Billy's sore throat. Billy had asthma a lot, and that prompted the concern.

Dad was not happy away from his family. He had gotten a job with the Indiana Bridge Company but was going to try to find something else. We had Cousin Don Gregg who was with us part of the time and also Dad's Uncle Johnny stayed awhile. Grandma Gilbreath had gone to Muncie to live with her son, Bill, on Grant Street, where Dad also stayed during this job venture.[64]

Dad's various jobs served as my classroom. There were always interesting things shared about his day. We were always glad to see him come home, from the September stint in Muncie or each evening. The Bicknell house sat on a knoll so the yard was higher than the road. We would sit there on that bank awaiting his return. An unknown source quotes Herbert V. Prochnow on this subject. He says, "You can't trust a man who

---

[64] Gilbreath, Clarence Homer, "Collection of Letters to my Family", 1929-1940

has no music in his soul. A banker will ask how much security a man can give before he will trust him. But here's a new test of a man's character that is very good: He may have on a greasy hat, or the seat of his trousers may be shiny, but if his children have their noses flattened against the windowpane a half hour before he is due home for supper, he can be trusted."[65] My father fit that description of a man to be trusted.

We got to visit him on some of his jobs, and that was an opportunity to explore how various tasks were completed. If the job that day was a farming chore, we were always there, learning how to plow with the team of mules or

The building of a seven acre pond on the Bryon Foutz property with the labor of these WPA workers. Dad is the seventh from the left. Years later I fished there.

how to build and mend fences. Sure, we don't do it that way now, but there were techniques that are used yet today. Plowing was more complex than it sounds. You guided the mules, engaged the plow in the ground, kept it going straight at the right depth, and learned how to bring it out of the ground at the end of the field. You learned how to lay off a land, mentioned in the first chapter, and how to

---

[65] Prochnow, Herbert V., *A Treasure Chest of Quotations*

finish out a dead furrow, where two completed lands meet. You also came to understand the value of those mules. In 1943 a team of mules were advertised by Rush McCammon for one hundred and fifty dollars, a respected amount of money for that day.66

Other job sites were visited. Dad helped to build a seven acre lake about 1939, a WPA project, on the Byron Foutz property northwest of Graysville. That wasn't as complicated as building Hoover Dam but very interesting to see how little by little dirt was moved from one place to another by hand shovel and four-legged horsepower. Dad was the timekeeper there, and he would prepare reports in the evenings at home.

My later interest in bookkeeping, building a pond of my own, and interest in fishing maybe had nothing to do with those visits, yet I expect such experiences are the forerunners of adult interests. For sure, I see no connection with those visits and my marriage to Stella, daughter of Byron and Fern Montgomery Foutz. During that employment, however, we did develop a lasting relationship with the Vernard Wilson family. The daughter, Mary K., remained a lifetime friend of my sister.

Probably the most significant experience for me was the remodeling job that Dad did at the Lon Davis Place which we had purchased in 1941. We would spend three years getting the house ready, taking time to work when Dad was not on another job. There I learned a lot about carpentering. There

---

66 *Sullivan Daily Times*, op cit., March 7-13, 1943

was no electricity so hand tools were all that we had. Basic skills in house building would serve me well all my life. Twenty-five years later when I began reconstructing a log home, I recalled often that Dad had taught me how to do so many things. There, also without electricity, I would remember that the lack of that convenience was not an insurmountable obstacle. When there is a vision, there will be a way to get it fulfilled.

We all have some variation in memories of World War II. As has been expressed, we were rather self-sufficient in many ways. Rationing didn't affect us like it would have those who in the city did not have farm products readily available. We missed the sugar but discovered we could live without that also. Dad just looked more intently for bee trees when out cutting wood. We participated in the various drives for the war effort which included milkweed pods, scrap metal, tin cans, and paper. Most of that was done through the school which served as the organizer of the various efforts. We have a certificate signed by Clair E. Merrill of the County U.S.D.A. War Board that states that in 1943 we were enlisted in the all-out farm war production.

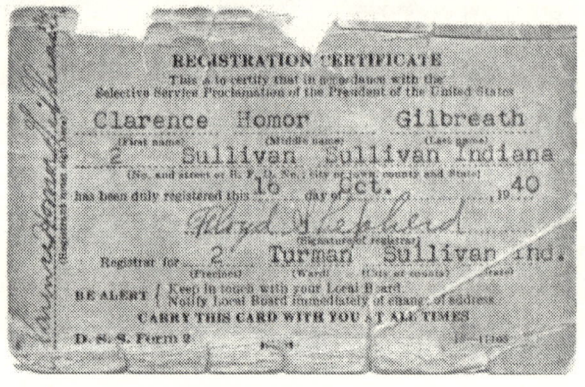

registration certificate

Memories of that period of time took on a different meaning for us. In October of 1940, Dad had to register for the service. I was only eleven years of age at the time but old enough to realize what it might mean if he had to leave us. However, before he would be called, he worked in the construction of the Wabash River Ordnance Works located near Newport, Indiana. He had applied for membership in the United Brotherhood of Carpenters and Joiners of America in August, 1940.

I remember him making a toolbox for his tools, a toolbox which brother Tom has in his possession. Also, I recall his learning to read a square, especially how to cut rafters at different

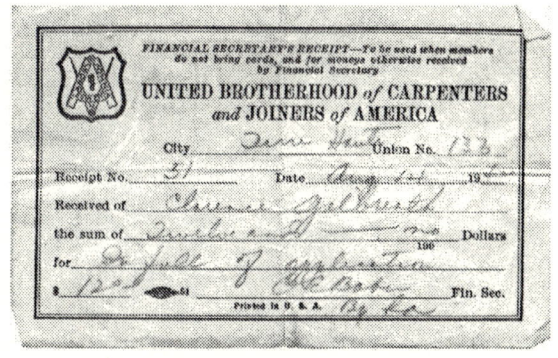

U Brotherhood of Carpenters

pitches. Never would we have known that the plant at Newport would be the storage place for the deadly VX gas. He also worked as a guard, as did his brother, Ollie, for the Concan Ordinance Company in Vigo County in the first part of 1943.

Paul Snow, local chair of the Selective Service Board, signed his notice to appear for a physical examination on December 15, 1943. As with other families, the Christmas plans were put on hold. But our anxiety was not different than other families who already had a father, husband, son or

127

daughter serving their country. This examination would turn out to be our first clue that something was wrong. We will continue this subject of his deterioration in the next chapter.

There is so much more that makes up the mosaic of childhood and youth and so little space. Before I sketch with the big brush some other significant memories, let me encourage you again to think of your own growing up and its influence on your later life. Maybe you are still a teenager and curious enough about the subject of mental health to take a good look at your present behavior. The greatest benefit here is not my family story, but how sharing it with you may cause you to reflect upon your own life at whatever stage you may be experiencing.

It's the little things in life that add up and later fit into a pattern that we call our life. My mother designing and sewing clothes is one of those events. She used the old treadle sewing machine to make shirts for us boys and dresses for Mary. Sometimes cloth was hard to come by, and she used the feed sacks to make many clothes including dresses for herself and Grandma. Later we will hear about her using her sewing talents to make a living for herself when she was left alone.

Utilities that we take for granted now came along late at our house. It was about 1943 before we got a telephone. Before that we had to go the neighbors to send or receive a call, like the arrangements for the funerals of my mother's sister, Mabel, and at another time of her brother-in-law, Cleo

House. The first day the phone was installed someone called at supper time, and I grabbed the receiver. I was so excited that someone had called that I thanked them profusely for calling us.

Wash day was a chore in which we all participated. In the summer an iron kettle of water would be placed over the fire early in the day. Dad made sure there was enough wood on the premise, and Grandma started the fire early in the day. The night before, we boys gathered the wood at the fireside. While Mom and Grandma did much of the washing, we children took our turn rocking the cradle of the old washer, scrubbing on the washboard, or wringing out the clothes.

The clothes were extra clean because we used lye soap that Grandma had made. Such soap sure took out the stains of Dad's work pants or the extra dirty clothes of us children. Team work and sharing responsibility makes for good emotional health. How many people are attempting to go it alone today and wondering why life is so stressful. Parents, too, are stressed out and cannot find ways to involve their children in sharing the load.

Pets were an important part of our life. They were outside pets and did well sharing their burden of survival. The many cats, one time twenty-one counting the newborn kittens, kept down the mice population. Their reward was warm milk shared at milking time. The smarter ones learned to open their mouths and receive a squirt straight from the cow's teat. Old Pal, our

129

German Police dog, preferred a rabbit and some scraps from the table. He was a good companion as we boys often took long walks through the countryside usually within about a three mile radius of our home.

The recent emphasis on pets giving solace to nursing home patients is very much understood. I wonder if my Dad would have been more communicative while confined if he could have cuddled a pet. Since 1978, Sullivan County has a Protective Animal League, Inc. operated by Shirley Cox. The League is dedicated to taking in strays and finding them a good home.[67]

One most important pet was a pony that Dad bought from Raymond Ferree. This creature had a mind of his own. The first day we had him, ole Laddie decided he was going back home with me astride, and no turning of his head made any difference. Passing the Huffs, I yelled for help. What else are neighbors for? They called the next neighbors, the Stewarts, and they intercepted him. He soon learned to like us and didn't do that anymore.

He did have the upper hand though about being caught to ride. If he didn't want to be ridden that day, he stayed his distance, once snickering as if he were making fun of our failure to corner him. I first sat down and cried but soon realized I must find a way to conquer him. He could also be ridden without a bridle sometimes when he was in the mood. One day when riding without the bridle, I was taken unwillingly across a brook and under a tree

---

[67] *Tribune Star*, op.cit.,"Sullivan County Today", Michelle Hudson, April 1, 1995

branch. He got away from me one day when I had ridden him to see my Aunt Lillian and was found a couple hours later at a neighbor's house. Every child needs a non-human friend who is faithful like the dog or challenging like this pony.

The list of little things goes on. From watching Gene Autry, Roy Rogers, and Shirley Temple at the movies to playing games of imagination that were fed by these movies. Dont' let the industry of violence kid you, children do mimic what they see. From selling cloverine salve to picking our five-acre patch of tomatoes for the canning factory at Terre Haute and participating in 4-H projects. From practicing slang words of our day to smoking grapevines,

rolling our own cigarettes, or trying Five Brothers chewing tobacco. One little bit of that chewing tobacco was enough for me, and the cigarettes didn't appeal either. Given the now recognized dangers involved, that is one habit that I am grateful not to have to break.

Look carefully and the rationing stickers from WWII can be seen on the windshield. Last good picture of Dad when he was healthy.

Attending a Democratic Rally was a stirring time.

131

Equally impressive was the get-out-the-vote effort of local committeemen. Someone provided transportation making sure Mom and Grandma got to vote if Dad had to work. Those who participate in the process feel better than those who use less productive tactics to show their agreement or disagreement.

And speaking of getting somewhere, the 1936 Chevy was quite a step up when we bought it about 1943. During the war we learned how to keep rebooting a tire to keep our wheels going. Later, I would also learn more about mechanics as I overhauled the engine. No happening was really insignificant during those days of growing up.

We never complained about the former two-room house when we moved into the Davis Place. The Bicknell Place was what had been available, and the important thing was that it had become home. We doubled our square footage at the Davis Place, and we were grateful. However, the addition of space had little to do with our feeling about life itself. We live in a time when so much importance is placed on material possessions.

Our family gave priority to relationships instead. It isn't what we have, or don't have, that counts; it is our attitude toward the plenty or the want. I wonder if I would be writing that statement if I lived in an inner city housing project today. A few more possessions would be nice, I'm sure. Yet, what is critical to our emotional satisfaction is how we feel about these external things and how important we perceive relationships to be.

Satisfaction and emotional contentment cannot be based on external elements. If that were the foundation of happiness, so much of the world would never hope to find any solace. Society must take some responsibility for the discontent that leads to behavioral problems. Democrats have thought of money as the source of a better life for those in poverty. Republicans now would redirect and reduce much of that kind of support believing anyone can make it on their own if they are so inclined.

Neither approach deals with the real problem nor should we expect politicians to provide the basic remedy. Student loans are an appropriate assistance for those wanting an education, but the money is a waste without the commitment and desire of the student to succeed. The student's success depends upon the inner motivation. Schools, churches, the media, and family can be crucial contributors in teaching our children and youth the importance of inner direction and purpose.

While I grew up in a different time when such instruction was taken for granted, society must take another look at a different set of reasons for being. We will discuss this further in the chapters on education and religion. However, let it be said here that my experience in childhood and days of youth convince me that there is something more intrinsic about life than economic and material issues.

133

Yes, it would have been nice to have had more, but that would have not guaranteed that I could look back and say it was good. Jane Austen, a British novelist, born two centuries ago, said, "One does not love a place the less for having suffered in it unless it has been all suffering, nothing but suffering."[68] I agree with her thought at the turn of the century. Others will not agree, thinking that one so long ago could not have anything significant to say to today's world.

Some ideas and approaches to life are applicable to any generation. Life is more about what we are and not what we consume. The choice is ours as to which has priority in our lives. We are the architect and builder of our own mental and emotional health, responding with hope and faith in the most difficult circumstances of our life. The building materials include one's own God-given abilities and are supplemented by society's respect and support for the right of everyone to develop those abilities to their fullest potential.

Elizabeth Cady Stanton, an American feminist of the nineteenth century said, "Nothing strengthens the judgment and quickens the conscience like individual responsibility."[69] This sounds like today's conservative message. Learning to cope with what life offers, good or bad, is enhanced by the opportunity to learn individual responsibility. Hopefully, that has been an

---

[68] Ibid, op.cit.,"Thought for Today," May 31, 1997

[69] Ibid, September 12, 1996

important factor in whatever judgment and conscience that I have exercised. We also learned to save and make do, being good stewards of what was at our disposal. That was no "throwaway" day and time. An old adage reminds us, "For age and want save while you may; no morning sun lasts a whole day."[70] A cliché? Refute it if you can.

For the emotional well-being of our children, all of us must ask, "Whose child is this?" In my experience a number of people, the school, governmental entities, and the church, along with my parents, answered that question in the affirmative, saying, "That child belongs to us." There is no doubt that my parents did what they could and doing what you can is commendable. I grew up in a community who placed a high priority on education

Enid Shields Monk

and provided committed teachers to guide me in my search for knowledge. Just today I received a note from one of my high school teachers, Enid Monk, thanking us for sharing her grief in the loss of her son, Dwight. In her nineties now, she is still the thoughtful, supportive person she was fifty years ago.

Government programs, especially the Works Progress Administration with a job, the U.S. Department of Agriculture with surplus food, and the local township trustees, William Watson and James Kinnett (Republican and

---

[70] Ibid, op.cit.,"Yesterday's Cryptoquote," June 6, 1996

Democrat), kept body and soul together. Not least of the supports came from our home church and local community. Education, the church and the community will be discussed in later chapters. It is instructive and somewhat overwhelming to think of all those who helped me to become what I am. I belong to all of them.

For the mental health of every child everywhere, I pray that we all together will get serious about providing the support system necessary for raising children to healthy adulthood. How can anyone deny that "It Takes a Village" unless one just wants to be partisan. Deny our common responsibility if you will, but who got where they are by the help of parents alone? Mental health requires us to put our formative years into focus both as a gift and as a personal responsibility, what was done for us and what we will now do for others.

SLATE BOARDS TO COMPUTERS

Chapter 4

Nothing you can't spell will ever work."— Will Rogers

American humorist (1879-1935)

Dear Dad,

I've been thinking about school days. The years went by so fast while you were sick, and now your children have been graduated long ago. That would be difficult for you to understand if you were here.

In fact your grandchildren and great-grandchildren are out of high school now. You have three great-grandchildren in college at this time. Ole Rip Van Winkle never felt this overwhelmed, eh?

I wish we had talked more about your school days. There is a picture of the old Bell school house with the students in front of the building. It was taken in 1907, the year you were born. In that picture are your brothers, Bill, Ollie, and sister, Sarah. Sarah is standing proudly there by the teacher, Mr. Turman. So many in that picture I knew when I was a kid. Virgil Bell, the only

137

survivor, just died in 1998. That was District Number Eleven, wasn't it?

Did you begin school in 1913? Mom says you went to Graysville for the fifth grade and then quit sometime during the sixth. I wonder why you did that? I guess school didn't seem as important as it does now. It would have been over three mile to do the chores and then over four mile back to school. I guess that would have been a little too much walking to expect of a kid, right?

Well, the Bell School is long gone and Graysville still stands as it did when you saw your kids off to school. It has been remodeled and looks real nice. Only the first six grades are there now.

I'm not sure if you remember this or not, but I helped paint the inside of the school one summer. You were still at home but not feeling well. I worked with Mr. Weir, the trustee, and his son-in-law, Ted Coppage.

You would not believe the changes that have taken place on the school scene. I'll write about some of those in this chapter. Changes can be difficult. Rapid changes in your life at that early stage must have been difficult for you. We have counselors now who try to help students adjust to the problems facing them, but you had good caring teachers back then, too. I wonder if counselors would have kept you in school any longer.

I think I know now why you didn't help us with much of our homework. You may not have known how to help us when we got beyond the fifth grade. Of course, by the time you worked somewhere, came home and did the chores, we already had our homework done. But I know this: you thought we ought to do our best, and we needed that encouragement from our parents, as do all kids. Our world today is changing so fast that parents have trouble helping for lack of expertise in some subjects.

Those old abandoned schools in our community always stood as a testimony to the importance of education. Within two mile of us there were the Concord, Providence, Ogle, Hayden, Thornberry, and Graysville District Schools. Our ancestors must have thought highly about education at that time to have put a brick school within a mile of everyone!

Maybe we need them that close again so we will get our much needed walking exercise. We don't have those farm chores to do like we used to do. Yet, schools today have a lot of extra activities to keep students busy and in shape. Despite that, we have so many who are dropouts, for different reasons than in your day. There's more serious trouble to get into nowadays.

Well, Dad, I wish you were here to read this chapter. But there are many others who are interested in what happens in our

139

schools. It's encouraging that people still care and provide for education as they always have.

So, I'll write again to let you know what I'm doing. You would like some of the chapters coming up.

Oh, I want to tell you that we just had company. You always remembered Byron Foutz. His grandson, Rudy Nichols and wife, Nancy, stopped in. They are music teachers in the Sullivan County schools. Hmmm, remember how good you and I were at music! Ha!

See you later.

Love, Gene

"Invest in the human soul, Who knows, it might be a diamond in the rough." Mary McLeod Bethune, American educator and reformer (1875-1955)

An earnest debate across the country highlights the seriousness of educational problems in our nation. Helpful or not, some of the debate engages the political conservatives and liberals. Discussions will continue regarding small vs. large, moral values within the curriculum, qualifications of teachers, the place of extracurricular activities, national testing, local control, and other subjects for dialogue. It seems that another topic ought to be added to this mix. The emotional side of the student, like the intellectual and physical, deserves critical attention.

Many are now promoting getting back to the basics. That is not a bad idea if one will also consider the importance of how well the student will learn if there are emotional blocks to the learning process. The whole person needs our attention so let's add to the mix mental health and do it in nonpartisan fashion. We agree to feed the kid who is hungry, but argue about what to do for the troubled one.

Since this book honors Dad, a sixth grade dropout, I would hope that this presentation can be understood by most sixth graders today. All our students know the emotional side of life and how it affects their studies. It will be great when we take that fact seriously and assist in the emotional well-being of our students.

141

This is the work of one who has spent seventy years in the school of life and twenty years in a classroom as a student. Either I was a slow learner or had an insatiable appetite for learning! We will insist that professionalism is not the key word here, but rather how the teachers and administrators feel about assisting with this task.

Let us see if we can indeed be nonpartisan and take note of this national concern. On March 5, 1997, Tipper Gore, Mental Health Advisor, and Donna Shalala, U.S. Health and Human Services Secretary, introduced the nation to the CARING FOR EVERY CHILD'S MENTAL HEALTH: Communities Together initiative. Tipper Gore said, "Today, we inaugurate a new era of awareness that mental health problems among the nation's children are real, painful, and severe. As a society, we can't afford to let our children's mental health needs go unmet. Not when one in five children has a mental, emotional or behavioral problem; not when one in 20 children has serious mental health problems and are not even getting the help they need."[71]

"Communities Together is a national public education campaign emphasizing the need for attention to children's and adolescents' mental health. It supports the Comprehensive Community Mental Health Services

---

[71] U.S. Department of Health and Human Services, Substance Abuse and Mental Health Services Administration, Center for Mental Health Services, CARING FOR EVERY CHILD'S MENTAL HEALTH: Communities Together. Internet http://www.infoseek.mentalhealth. April 1997

Program with 29 sites in 18 States demonstrating effective services. This public/private sector campaign is managed by the Center for Mental Health Services, Substance Abuse and Mental Health Services Administration."[72]

The above is one example of a national concern about the emotional well-being of our children and youth. Sometime Sullivan County, and the local county of the reader, may be involved in that campaign. Let it be said here in straightforward fashion, we must never wait to be given direction from our government in this matter.

There is a role that the government can play and should, but it is not the beginning nor the end of the matter. However, when there is authentic leadership, why not follow it or at least be stimulated by it? Isn't it sad that we have turned national standards into a political debate? Doesn't every group in society have a set of standards by which the individuals are judged? Why can't the American "group," the nation, have guidelines by which we all are assisted in our common task of educating?

A teacher, well-informed about the emotional lives of students and one who isn't afraid to care and be vulnerable, is one who is ready to deal with the total life of the student. A teacher, well prepared in the lesson material and just as well prepared in how to relate that to productive living given the emotional state of the student, truly deserves the "Golden Apple."[73]

---

[72] Ibid

Early in this chapter I want to share with you a portion of a statement made by a local teacher after she read the first draft of this chapter. I empathize with teachers of today. Never let that thought get lost as we become intense at times here stressing the responsibility of teachers and administrators to deal with emotional issues of the students.

"It would do us all justice as an educator" she says," to have a background in counseling. I find myself so inadequate as do my other colleagues...kids just aren't like 'they used to be.' And we really are not equipped to deal with their problems...and they are certainly overwhelming when you are trying to 'teach' something. We not

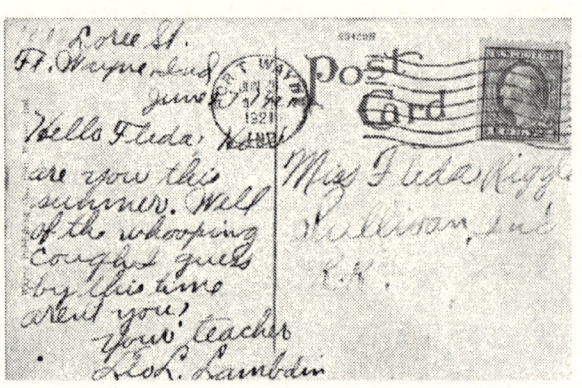

A card from a teacher to my mother after school was out in 1921, showing concern for her welfare. I recently asked my mother about this, and she replied, "Oh, he sent cards to everyone." Teacher, when school is out, does interest continue for your students?

only have to deal with emotional and home life problems, but now, it's the drug and alcohol babies. And I most certainly LOVED the part about teachers and administration contributing to our mental health......as a group working together! If they did, I believe I would have a much better attitude!!!

---

[73] Reference to WTHI TV Channel's award program for Terre Haute, IN area teachers. Sullivan County recipients have been: Harold Medsker, Russell Riley Nichols, Charlotte Dikowski and Erich Blevins.

Truthfully, teaching is one of those professions that you truly do become involved in and are vulnerable in what you are doing." [74]

Yes, it would be helpful if all teachers had a background in counseling. Yet nothing written here is meant to indicate the necessity of such training. The emphasis here has a simplicity that probably will be disturbing to the professionals in the mental health field. This writer does not feel that training, while important, is the main issue in this particular discussion. Caring enough to respect the inner life of the student is the issue. Seeing that student as one with emotional issues, not just one that should pass your particular subject matter, is the point here. This chapter is being written to encourage each of us, whether we have children in school or not, whether educators or not, to take personal responsibility in giving the mental health of our children top consideration as a means of fulfilling their learning potential. Teachers are in a strategic position to effect this hope of mine. We all can't be counselors, but we all must consider such responsibility to be our concern.

While I have already written a little about my own school days, there is much more to write about the larger picture of education and its partner, mental health, as it unfolds before us. Stories about the big cry the first day, the big bear between me and the bus, and the long ride on the horse-drawn school hack, just do not tell much about the experience of schooling for this

---

[74] Thanks to this teacher's sharing of her thoughts and emotions on this subject.

century in my native county. So there is much more to be said that has more universal application.

One important aspect has to do with change. Slate boards and slate pencils were the predecessors to note pads and pencils. Students had their own individual boards on which they would do their writing, spelling, and math lessons. What a contrast to today's computers was this method of communicating or recording your lessons for either the review of the teacher or for your own practice. How difficult today for teachers to exude

confidence before their students when rapid change has brought them face to face with the fact that sometimes students can do some things better than the teachers.78 This is one emotional health issue that can be solved.

The Bell School was one of the thirteen district one-room schools of the township and located in the NE corner of it. Dad is the second one on the first row from the left. This picture reminds us of obvious changes.

We can switch from the concept of education as something handed to the students by the teacher to the teacher being the facilitator.

Change has always been with us in education. Sullivan County and your own school district have seen these changes and felt their impact. Some of them have been physical changes. Consolidations have been among those.

Regardless of the pros and cons, such changes have their effect upon our students emotionally. Going to a larger school where you tend to get lost in the mob is a frightening experience for many. A wider choice of subjects is an advantage mostly to the better student. The loss of a

The old brick Thornberry School located West on 300 North, the last one of its kind. At least two other district schools are now incorporated into residences: The Island School at Robert Monroe's near the Wabash and the Graysville one in the Thurman Monroe house east of the present school.

school by fire has been more of an issue than just a long holiday. One only has to see the home town school torn down to get a feel of the attachment to a building and to experience memories of those student days.75

---

[75] *Sullivan Daily Times*, "In Times Past" June 23-29, 1906, These were times for new buildings, consolidations, and mergers, and damaged buildings. Therewere 23 graduates of the Jackson township schools at the annual commencement exercises in 1906, the second highest in the county. County Superintendent Richard Park urged those in attendance to secure a commissioned high school for the community. June 16-22, 1906, In the same year, 1906, just before the close of the Haddon Township school commencement which was held at the Providence Church near Paxton, the public school building in the middle of Paxton caught fire and burned down to its brick walls. So the end of the school year and the school building's demise came together. December 5, 1917, the Gobin schoolhouse northwest of Carlisle was damaged to a considerable extent by a fire started by a heater. Others met similar fates, such as Graysville in 1927, my mother's junior year. June 16-22, 1926, A merger was proposed between the schools of the city of Sullivan and of Hamilton township through a petition filed with the school board and signed by 25 residents of the city and 25 residents of the township. May 16-22, 1918, In accordance with a ruling of the Supreme Court of Indiana in 1918, Haddon township trustee, Tarleton C. Woodward was compelled to abandon a

As we experience this time of rootlessness, we need to help our students understand something of the local history wherever they may be residing at the moment. This is one way for us to help them find some kind of emotional anchoring. This writer knew something of the places, people, and activities that you will see as a footnote as we proceed through this chapter. Unfamiliar names and activities do not diminish the worth of these people to you the reader. They are symbolic of others who are a part of your own educational history. Yours and mine are threads in the tapestry of education and in their composite represent our past. Let the footnotes evoke your own emotion of school days and may they spark questions of how we may best serve this generation and tomorrow's.

If sometimes our students seem stressed out with the problems of today, we might help them put today's school situation in perspective. The majority of us never had it so good. That is not to say there is not room for improvement. If that were true, this chapter would not be written. In our county there was a classroom called the Island School on the west side of Turman Township along the Wabash River. This settlement encountered hard times in the 1800s. There were the usual Indian raids, then cholera.

---

township schoolhouse and consolidate with the schools of Carlisle. A number of voters petitioned for consolidation soon after the big new school was built at Carlisle; the trustee said the petition was insufficiently signed.

The 1903 building still standing close to the present school. It was used for years by the Masonic Lodge. This was replaced in 1915 by a new building which burned later in 1927.

The cemetery there contains eight Brenton children and four Halls, all infants and elementary school children.

Another hard fact of life there was the subjection of the site to floods. So when a formal school was built about the turn of the century, it was built on stilts. There had always been school, however. Thomas Turman, of the Turman pioneer family, was elected to the Indiana legislature, and he introduced in 1843 the first bill for free education. That goal would be realized in 1847.[76] We cite this to show both the hardships of some of our ancestors and their unwavering belief in public education for all. Gaining perspective is a good method

Thomas Turman, name sake of the Legislator Turman, with Sarah Gilbreath in 1911 when he was a teacher at the Bell School.

---

[76] *SULLIVAN COUNTY, IN, 175TH ANNIVERSARY,* Turner Publishing Company, P.O. Box 3101, Paducah, KY 42002-3101, 1991, Ham, Edith, P 66

of aligning our negative emotions with a healthy reality. History assists us in that process. The images of old schools has helped you to see the progress of more than a century and a half.

It would be helpful also for us to examine just how effective some of these schools were and how some things do not change, Now we are trying to swing the pendulum back to more basics. Certainly the schools were good at basics. Knowing how to spell was a common expectation.77 Many received an intellectual foundation for higher education as did Frank Aydelotte, who in 1905 was the first winner of the Rhodes Scholarship from Indiana.78 Do you suppose that the Ordinance of 1787 for education in the Northwest Territory had anything to do with past successes? Article III reads in part: "Religion, morality, and knowledge being necessary to good government and the happiness of mankind, schools and the means of education shall always be encouraged."79 History helps us to put important issues in perspective.

Those same schools had extracurricular activities such as Leap Year dances, musical nights, wiener roasts, and lots more. Even then our

---

[77] *Sullivan Daily Times*, May 5-18, 1926, Monette Springer bested Jack Butterworth for the honor of being the best speller in the Sullivan Junior High School.

[78] Ibid September 17-23, 1905, Frank Aydelotte left for Philadelphia and then set sail for Oxford, England to begin his three years' course Mr. Aydelotte was in Oxford's Brasenose College.

[79] Harrison Burns, *Indiana Statutes*, (Indianapolis: Bobbs-Merrill company, 1955), p. 375.

educational system while emphasizing the basics was not unaware of the need to consider the whole person.[80]

The story about the musical night at Shelburn[81] raises the question whether prominence and notoriety affect mental health and are they ever confused with excellence in performance. Always, regardless of the size of a school, there has been competition among schools. We have already indicated that is good if we are thinking about competing intellectually, desiring to perform as well as those in other schools. Our students ought not be led to believe they are better in any way simply because they attend the more prominent, the more wealthy, or the larger school. We encourage an unhealthy attitude when we take the competition so far as to confuse prominence with excellence.

Fun and games, musicals, and class plays all contributed to the emotional health of these students as do the extracurricular activities of today. These all help to broaden life's experience for the student. Often they

---

[80] March 26-April 1, 1920, Members of the Sullivan High School sophomore class attending a Leap Year Dance at the W.O.W. Hall, chaperoned by Tom Brown and Anna Hunt, were Pauline Medsker, Elizabeth Crowder, Monette Knotts, Josephine Bedwell, Hester Eaton, Anna Allen, Sylvia Hunter of Dugger, Helena Stewart, Melvin Hawkins, Joe Stratton, Paul Thixton. Ken Wiltsie, Willard Wolfe, Price Lindley, Joe Douthitt, John Neff and William Henderson.

[81] Ibid., June 23-29, 1906, And what a musical night in Shelburn when 149 citizens of Sullivan jammed into the trolley car that left the Davis Hotel there at 7 o'clock for the band concert on Thursday night in 1906!

Ibid.,February 14-20, 1918, Jessie Kinder and Bessie Booker, teachers at Bucktown school, arranged for a gala patriotic celebration on a Friday evening in February,1918.

Ibid.,July 16-22, 1945, Marilyn Hoesman and Naomi Ruth Hedrick were winners in 1945 of the Sherman Scholarships, given annually since 1926 except for 1932, 1934-35, and 1942.

are tension relievers. Sometimes they may even increase stress, a good

kind, that needs a positive response. Working in a play may bring one face

to face with stage fright, an opportunity to develop skills for speaking in

public.

A relatively new activity promoted by schools in our area is chess which does more than teach

strategy, but just as importantly, the game teaches staying calm under

The present Graysville School built in 1927, the last of a long line of schools serving the area. Only Elementary classes have been held since 1961 when the high school and junior high were transferred to Sullivan. High maintenance costs and policy will soon close this one, too. My mother and I were both graduated here.

the stress. This is a good example of bringing intellectual skills and

emotional ones into the same arena.82

---

82 Ibid April 9-15, 1945,Three high schools had Senior Class plays on Friday, April 13th, 1945. Players in the New Lebanon High School Senior Class drama "Her Emergency Husband" were John Meng, Barbara Willis, Betty McKain, Hope Hoesman, Mary Nell Cole, Roy Christy, John Pirtle, Alice Irvin, Eugene Volk, Juanita and Doris Garrard, and John Unger as the Wild Man of Borneo. Appearing in Graysville High's "Comin' Thru the Rye" were Lowell Badger, Anna Lois Patton, Norman Clark, Jeannette Burton, Judy Gettinger, Ralph Shake, Emery Ransford, Carol Canary, Norma Dean Padgett, Sylvia Walters, Darrel Monroe, Margaret Payne, Ernestine Kasinger and "Fuzzy" Unger as Bubbles, Mother's precious baby. Merom's players were Dorothy Bogard. Roscoe Bogard, Pat Frederick, Robert Brown, Bill Raley, Betty Brown. Pat Copeland, Eugene Sparks, Paul Gettinger, Patsy McNabb, Bob Jones and Norma Daugherty.Ibid April 13, 1995, The Hymera Chess Club participated in a national competition in Little Rock, Ark., on April 5, 1995, and came home with a 23rd-place trophy. Participating were Sarah Dix, Shannon Shidler, Ben Jacob, Toby Woodburn, Justin Shidler, Michial Jacob, Tyler Dix, Devin Jones, Steven Woodburn, Josh Shidler and Ethan Jones.

It should be noted that extracurricular activities should serve the academically poor student as well as the best. So many of those activities are constructed in such a way as to favor the top student or the athletes. How often is there a structured activity that costs little and is open to anyone?

Whether we are assisting the honor student or the learning disadvantaged, computers are a welcome new way to make learning easier and more comprehensive. In the footnote is a story at the elementary and secondary levels about upgrading the school equipment so as to take advantage of this new technology. If teaching some kind of values has ever been needed, such is imperative now. The controversy continues about what is appropriate for students to encounter on the Internet. With the overwhelming availability of all kinds of knowledge at their finger tips, is it not critical that students be given some guidance in how to choose that which is best for them?

I suggest that this Information Age reinforces the need for students to develop ways to determine what will add meaning to their lives. It seems that they can not do that alone. For the student who has parents who do not accept some responsibility for that guidance, the school must. Society will suffer at the hands of those who do not learn to handle the information for the good of all. We do not need only money for a new technology which is here to stay, but we need guidelines to handle what it gives us.83 How many

adults are up until the wee hours of the morning surfing the net? Do we

expect children and youth to be more disciplined? In education we want to

protect our free speech rights.84 When we talk of putting some kind of

guidelines on Internet searches, we open up that whole burning debate.

Without doubt, we must protect our speech rights. There is also the right of

a vulnerable student to be protected against that which may well mar his/her

emotional and intellectual development. If input encourages the student to

do that which is not acceptable in society, then obviously we have some

obligation to assist the student in finding acceptable material. Simply stated,

there are many ways that we protect our children and youth and never give

such a second thought. It is like driving on a permit, they do not have full

access to the road without restrictions. Suggesting some restrictions, to this

writer, is certainly not censorship. Let's save that debate for adults.

---

[83] *Sullivan Daily Times*, op cit., According to the news release in 1996, Central Elementary School will catch up with the Southwest School Corporation's other two elementary schools after Southwest's trustees approved $75,000 in start-up funding for new computers and $42,200 for a portable computer lab as part of the proposed $730,173 Capital Projects Plan for 1996. Trustees plan to lease a 60-foot by 24-foot portable classroom to be placed on site at Central. With no space for a lab at the school, this provided a feasible alternative, said Jerry Miller, SWSC superintendent. The plan also calls for an upgrade of computer technology at the rest of the schools, providing Sullivan High School $49,800 for new technology; Sullivan Junior High School $24,525; Carlisle Elementary $28,350; and Graysville $10,500.

[84] Ibid May 5-18, 1946, Mr. Eugene C. Pulliam, editor and publisher of *The Indianapolis Star*, gave a strong speech in May, 1946, emphasizing the need for full protection of the constitutional guarantees of free speech and a free press before the Sullivan Teacher's Federation at the Davis Hotel. A trombone quartet of Joe Scully, Charlotte Ingersoll, Ben Wernz and John McCammon entertained the gathering of over 100. The Pulliams were weekend guests of Mr. and Mrs. Hinkle Hays.

We have a long tradition of giving honors. Excellence should be noted and rewarded. The rewards of M&Ms, to award night dinners, to scholarships is an important part of the school program. These comments have nothing to do with the rightness of such honors. They are psychologically and intellectually efficient means of stimulating achievement. One of the problems is that they don't help those students who have less ability in proportion to those who could achieve even without them.

Lately, some schools have begun to honor the intellectually and emotionally disadvantaged in some specific ways. Would it not be good if we could honor students based on how well they achieved their potential? I am greatly concerned about what happens to the student who has done his best and is never good enough to get that scholarship, or that plaque, or a write-up in the local paper. It is difficult to deny that the best get noticed, and those who can't make the grade notice that they aren't noticed. It is also difficult to deny that all of us like recognition, and it is as important to our emotional maturity as food is to the body. It may be worth noting that those who do not receive awards are the majority of our students. There is not room to list their names in the footnotes. I would this once list them in the headlines if I could.

Where is there a monument to mental health within the educational system? No, it is not any one subject that warrants a monument any more than any other one. When I was in elementary and high school between

1935 and 1947, there was no course on psychology. I wonder if there was a book in the library on such a topic. Closest to it was Dale Carnegie's book, *HOW TO WIN FRIENDS AND INFLUENCE PEOPLE.* When Dad first became ill in 1944, there was so little information available about mental health, and there was nothing in our school library about the subject.

My first reaction to his illness was one of fear, fear of the unknown. "We fear things in proportion to our ignorance of them," said Livy, the Roman historian whose life spanned B.C 64 to A.D. 17.[85] A nine year old did not in my day and in that place have much access to information. At that point in time, a lifelong interest in mental health began. It is a wonder that what has been an avocational interest did not become instead a vocation.

That fear of what I didn't understand, motivated me to study anything I could find since that day. This is also the stimulus that moves me to discuss with you some inescapable connections of mental health and education. To me, education is the key to being able to cope with life, standing side by side with religion, my chosen vocation. Religion and mental health will be discussed later and holds a central position also but in a different way. There is so much we need to understand about our world that comes from diligent study of people, places, and things. That is what we receive in a good educational system.

---

[85] *Tribune-Star*, op.cit., "Thought for Today", March 13, 1996

There are people who cruise the streets or the countryside each day who are looking for a way to deal with their emotional life. It is suggested for those people who are reading this chapter that they give education their best effort. Start by studying how the world turns, what are the rules, what works for my good, and how can I make the most of my potential. A dropout or a graduate who needs continuing education needs to know that his community provides this option of extended education for him. And the youth of today need to know wherein there is hope.

This writer did not become a psychiatrist, psychologist, or professional educator. Neither have I done scientific research; I have read much of it but not done it, on either of these disciplines. The reader might be advised again that this is a human interest story and not a research document. A master's degree in agency counseling comes the closest to such formal training. However, what I have learned through the years is so compelling that I must share it. If, like giving a thirsty man a drink, I can share, then I must.

There need not be a debate about my qualifications, nor if the "water" has had just exactly the right amount of chlorine, and if the "cup" has been sterilized. I am the first to recognize those shortcomings, if indeed, they are. If there be any truth here coming from this consumer, then let it stand. Hopefully, the educational profession has not forgotten that students and

157

consumers are a part of the mix that makes a school and will be willing to listen to nonprofessionals; not necessarily agree, but listen.

We must, however, go beyond the facts that are learned in the classroom. Education for education's sake is not adequate. Learning facts for fact's sake will not help us in times of emotional turmoil. Educators who teach only facts and give no direction as to what is appropriate to do with the knowledge are shortchanging the student. I know of a "gifted" student who wrote unprintable words on the side of a building where all students could see. The words were derogatory words regarding a "special education" student. That "gifted" student needed to learn more than facts. One fact remains: neither student was receiving the emotional support necessary in the school for either one to be productive. How do I know that? That "special education' student was my son. The proficient math teacher who expects students to get it or forget it the first time around is short on understanding that speed does not guarantee retention. A slower student who is so happy that he learned the formula will remember it just as long as the student who got it the first time around.

Therefore, we believe that given the amount of time students spend in the classroom, they should be given the best. The best includes a discussion of what to do with the knowledge gained. This does not mean a teacher's dictatorial statement of what ought to be, but rather an open discussion of the possibilities that hold lasting promise. "What do you want to do with your life" ought to be a question that encompasses purpose and meaning as well as what you do to make a living. "How" and "why" are just as important questions as the "what."

We are suggesting that mental health be integrated into every aspect of the educational scene. Psychology courses in modern day curriculum are fine as far as they go. If they were a required course, the experience would nearer accomplish my goal. Then again, it would depend on how it were taught. Technical jargon and labeling are detrimental and will remain so until a more enlightened society appears.

Psychology courses can be taught just factually, without application to the student's life. It seems that the ideal is to have teachers who are aware of mental and emotional issues that concern students whether they are teaching math,

The Junior Class of 1946: 1st row (L-R) Virgilene Donaldson, Mary Lou Shyrock, Virginia Brenton, Nellie Foutz, Stella Foutz (later the author's wife). 2nd row: Marjorie Hayden, Joyce Murdock, Dorothy Harris, Ann Osburn, Carla Ann Hunt, Ms. Irma Gray (Sponsor). Top Row: Dwight Burton, Billy Joe Burnett. Karl Heidenreich, Gene Easter, Dale Cox, and Gene Gilbreath (Author).

English, psychology, or whatever the subject. Another good example of teaching just facts is that of sex education. It is understood that facts are not sufficient so condoms are distributed. What a confessional act.

159

Students bring with them to class a whole array of emotional issues. To ignore these regardless of the subject matter is to leave the students with less than they deserve. In my case, the teachers were aware of my father's illness, and just often enough, inquired about the matter and so gave me support. With that support, I functioned better as a student. Administratively, there should not be so many students in a class that a teacher would never be aware of their emotional needs. Space economics that produces large classes threatens the potential to educate our students for the whole of life. The emotional well-being of students can not flourish where a student is a number and not a face with capabilities of smiles and frowns.

Yes, such an involvement with students places a heavy burden upon the teachers. What kind of life, though, do we live if we are not considerate of the pain of others? We are saying that the mental outlook and purpose of a teacher's own life is a relevant issue, too. Is this occupation just a job that is done for only a paycheck? Speaking as a mental health advocate, important as a job and money are, is there not more if we want real satisfaction? Teachers and administrators who see emotional issues as irrelevant in the classroom, surely consider them unmanageable in their own personal lives. The proper integration of mental health and education begins with the teacher examining his or her own emotional health. Try out this question: "Why is it that I just can't stand this particular student?"

We acknowledge the services that are available for those emotionally needy students through mental health facilities. Some teachers or administrators who feel inadequate in this area may think that the issue should be left up to the experts. An example is the complementary and complimentary work that the Katherine Hamilton Center of Terre Haute does for education by providing at-risk counseling for the school corporations of Sullivan County.

A satellite branch is located conveniently for county residents at the Mary Sherman Hospital in Sullivan. They have also various other programs that support the educational process. Sullivan County is serviced by this branch of Katherine Hamilton Center located in Vigo County that serves a larger geographical area. That kind of service was not available back in the 1940s. Its presence today, while supportive, does not relieve school personnel of the necessity of a constant awareness of this issue. Understanding is essential for proper referral, awareness being a first step.

Society has given the school today more and more responsibilities regarding what may appear to be non-educational matters. Burnout happens and a great amount of empathy is due to the classroom teacher in that circumstance. Yet none of these new responsibilities are a justifiable retreat from the importance of integrating emotional life as a necessary factor in the educational process. It seems to me that an ever-present awareness of these issues is as vital as the air we breath. For that reason, it

161

is imperative that school personnel have enough of an understanding of their own mental states so as to know when to seek assistance for their own health as well as that of their students. We would feel sorry for the teacher who does not have a good friend or two with whom they may confide. Most helpful would be a peer who understands, but when one is not available, seek a reputable counselor.

An administration who is also aware of these issues would do well to provide more formal support groups for its workers. We have focused on teachers because they are the ones closer to the students. Yet, corporation superintendents down to classroom assistants, even the janitors, need to think of themselves as a team devoted to the total well-being of the students and each other. Yes, mishandled conflicts between teachers, teachers and administration, unions and administrations, do not enhance a conducive environment for emotional health for students or personnel. Thinking that we are all in this together is a positive approach that is sure to bring good results rather than the adversarial position too often taken.

A familiar and justifiable complaint of teachers nowadays is the lack of positive involvement of the parents. The disintegration of the family unit is a sure culprit. This problem, though, will take more than just talking about family values alone. Society has a serious problem in this regard, and it is not one that will be solved by blaming or "preaching." From the school perspective, we must come to understand what it is like for a student to

162

leave a dysfunctional home and be expected to arrive at school ready to learn. It is just as critical as coming to school without proper nourishment. Sure, breakfast is easier to fix.

On the side of families, a re-evaluation of priorities is necessary. Materialism and self-centered activity of parents and the consequential neglect of our children, whether we are rich or poor, will bring devastating consequences to our flesh and blood. Being obsessed with more possessions as a means to happiness, being bitter at our losses, or complaining that we live on the "wrong side of the tracks" are equally inappropriate ways to promote our own mental health or that of our children. Also, the teacher who does not understand the potential for stress of a child in either situation will miss an opportunity to give a helpful response to the emotional side of the student.

Lots of students early in the century went to school and were well-behaved and good students regardless of whether they lived with only one parent or with a stepparent. Death broke up a lot of homes. Now, we have much more divorce and other negative factors than we had earlier. There is no argument about that. Yet we must ask if it is mentally healthy to think that we have it so bad that our behavior is excusable?

We now have so many more mental health facilities and yet our students are too much out of control. Even something about mental health delivery isn't working sufficiently well, either. It might be suggested that a professional approach might be only a part of the solution, like going to a doctor is not all the solution. That is why I keep trying to say that emotional

health must be a "household word" and more than something professionals do to someone who is already out of control. Prevention must be the key word activated by us all, everyone from the psychiatrist's office, to the classroom, to the dinner table. The level of awareness must be equal in either of the places.

And from society's vantage point, we, too, are all in this together. Building more and more prisons without dealing with root causes is a mental health issue of gigantic

Earl Huffman, a disciplinarian, admired teacher of my mother, and a member of my congregation some 25 years later.

proportions for all of us. The burden of the solving is upon the educational system supported by parents and all citizens. Maybe we would rather it wasn't that way, but the schools have the children in the years when much can be done to help them reach their potential. This doesn't let parents, churches, businesses, or judges off the hook. Schools must have, however, support to accomplish their goal, the making of well-balanced and productive citizens fitted with facts accompanied with behavioral and emotional control. Yes, our task is to help to keep our youth out of prisons tomorrow.

Since we are talking about education, to speak about language is a natural. To talk of mental health itself is to conjure up words ranging from the professionals who treat mental illness to the nonprofessional who boosts another's self-esteem with a kind word. Teachers need not get caught up in the technical language and especially not use that language to label a student. I would go so far to say that the mental health professionals should not include technical diagnosis in their reports to the school. For one thing, psychology is not an exact science, and five years from now we might see that we were wrong or the problem will be called by some other name. Understanding the ramifications of a problem and what are possible solutions will enhance a professional's reputation more than the ability to toss around the technical language. Labeling is a cultural pastime which teachers and mental health professionals, as well as all of us, ought to avoid.

One way for teachers to promote mental health is to deal seriously with children's degrading language toward other students. A beginning point would be to make sure that the teacher's own language was free of such remarks. To excuse such talk as that coming from those who are just being kids, is quite unacceptable. If we accept their language learned at the TV as being OK, then we have in effect admitted who is the best and appropriate teacher. If you will, this problem is "treatable" and ways need to be devised to help the students know how hurtful it is to be on the receiving end of that language. It is also hurtful for anyone to go through life verbally attacking others, hurtful to the attacker, too.

What teacher wouldn't say that their desire would be for students to be kind to one another? If that is a goal, then the route there should not be considered impassable. Name calling is insidious, appearing in places where not expected. The categorizing of students as "A" and "B" is a simple illustration. Who can deny that "B" is second? Labeling of children "gifted" or "learning disadvantaged" is accompanied by an inevitable judgment of one being better or lesser than the other.

The truth is that the "learning disadvantaged" label hasn't lowered the name-calling anymore than "special education" did. We still have an attitude problem that transcends the label. Teachers must look deep within to begin a solution. My bet is that the majority of prisoners are "B" and "LD" students. Why don't we use initials for "gifted"?? Who else is more likely than the school to hold the solution? Who will take this production of second class citizens seriously? Alfred North Whitehead said, "Ideas won't keep; something must be done about them."[86]

---

[86] *Tribune Star*, op.cit., "Thought for Today," May 16, 1996

How many teachers do whatever to avoid being given the task of teaching one of those groups—which one being obvious? Teachers also sometimes feel they are less successful if they don't get a job at the school where the upper or middle class students attend. Hopefully educators will, first, not be caught up in labeling, and second, do all they can to help students overcome the tricky prejudices that accompany that practice.

There would be less obvious labeling if we were back in multi grade classrooms, right? There the honor student would receive rewards for extra assignments in assisting others. Who will make the best leader of tomorrow, one who has a goal of service or self-aggrandizement? Which approach to life will make for the most long lasting satisfaction?

Mental health issues encompasses how we feel about ourselves and our world, including the school. Certainly, I wouldn't be suggesting that educators become obsessed with this subject. However, it seems important to examine more of the breeding ground where emotional issues take their toll. A word about fashions further suggests a concern. There must be a balance between personal freedom and sense of community.

Some schools are trying uniforms. Maybe that is not necessary, while it certainly has some merit. There are more rewarding ways of showing our individuality other than dress. When those who can't afford designer clothes are adversely affected emotionally by those who do, then it is time for school administrators to insist on a dress code that levels the playing field.

167

Do you as a teacher or coach wear certain brand-name shoes, and do you have students who are embarrassed that they are not that affluent? I heard of a coach who expected his athletes to wear a certain brand. I am wondering if he received his shoes free from that manufacturer. The school that ignores this problem cannot say that it is value neutral. It will be teaching that fashions have value and will be letting stand the notion that clothes make the person. Being value neutral is impossible.

To balance out this discussion which seems to favor the underdog, let's turn the tables for a moment. Students of that category who are there under whatever circumstances, also, have lessons to learn. It is important to their mental health to learn to live peacefully and effectively in an imperfect world. Learning to use anger constructively is more important than conquering the multiplication tables. If anger is rightly directed, the student will be free to learn the tables according to his ability. If we accept the apparent truth of that statement, then why is so much time spent on the tables and the emotional issue is sidestepped? Anger may well be the primary cause for full prisons, and sadly, it is an anger that could have begun or was perpetuated in a classroom.

Children from low-income or broken families, or who have learning disabilities, need assistance in directing their anger about what life has handed to them into efforts to prove their native abilities. When educators understand the right of these disadvantaged persons to be angry, then everything possible from an encouraging word to professional help must be given. Being given recognition that is based on their potential will go a long way to help make up for no father at home, or little money, or not having a higher IQ.

Students deserve recognition, the giving of which makes a statement that a person's potential isn't gradable, just what they do with it is. A larger school or richer district doesn't necessarily produce the best students. What happens in the interaction of teacher and student, taking into account the possibilities of good mental health, should be seen as a God-given opportunity to produce a responsible citizen.

We would not mean to say that equipment, new technology, comfortable surroundings aren't important. The problem is that to focus on the physical aspect of the setting leads us in the wrong direction. Those schools "who have it all" also receive criticism sometimes for not achieving acceptable goals. And some who do not have "it all" act as if they can't teach without all of it. There is a fundamental flaw in both situations. Both should have all the latest but not think that those surroundings alone will do the job. In the same way consolidation is not a cure all. Neither is the status quo sacrosanct. New theories need to be tried and old ones that fail discarded. Also, some old ones need to be kept or maybe even revived. We are so caught up in change that change itself has on occasion become our drumbeat. For the emotional health of students and teachers alike, it might help to have a few more interminables.

One of those timeless approaches is that of history. Considering the rewriting that is going on, one might question the "timeless" designation. In our mobile society with rapid change, and with the assault on moral standards in recent times, we are a people without anchors. History lessons can help us with that if they can be shown to have current import. I was never a good history student. I believe if local history had been part of our curriculum, I would have had more interest. In other words I would have been a better student had the history teacher started where we were, at home, and helped me put the past in a meaningful perspective.

The interest is for us all to make sense out of our present circumstances. We need more than the history lessons, this chapter today and that one tomorrow. Through it all we need a sense of where we fit into the last chapter; however, it has special import for this discussion of education. Emotional health is tied in with our feeling a part of something larger than ourselves. History facts may not do that alone, but the interpretation of history as

Merom College

being relevant to the moment does.

Sometimes just a historical site will serve to stimulate an interest in education. We did actually have one college within the bounds of our county, and the glory of yesteryear does not fade. In Merom, Indiana, we have a well-preserved college campus as a reminder of its service to education in the late 1800s and early 1900s. It is now under the auspices of the United Church of Christ as a conference center.[87] With or without further restoration, the majestic five-story structure can be seen for miles around, as a visible testimony to the county's historical pursuit of education for its citizens.

While putting the new roof on the Davis Place house, I gazed at this symbol of education less than three mile across the countryside and dreamed of learning experiences to come in a college somewhere. Even in its glory of yesteryear it stood as a witness and stimulus to the potential within me.

There are signs that we are doing things quite well in some areas. We do recognize that there is more to life than the three "Rs" and now have a broad spectrum of activity. Some believe we are getting too broad in that respect. Maybe back to basics would be better. Defining "basics" would be

---

[87] *The Tribune Star*, op.cit., "Sullivan County Today,"September 6, 1996, In 1996 it was announced that Historic Landmarks Foundation of Indiana had awarded the Merom Conference Center Inc. a $3,200 grant to study the feasibility of restoring the 1863 Union Christian College building.

our problem. Yet, what we are doing at this time, as well as for the past several years, is an expression of concern for the total person. There can be little emotional health without it.

Teaching about respect for women is an important improvement for both boys and girls. The world only appeared to be a "man's world," and that worked as long as men held the power in finance, in decision making, and were the only bread winners. Women have always carried their share of the load, and it seems right and just that children learn that the kind of work one does is not a guarantee of exalted status. It is hoped that teachers will follow through and act on the premise that work done well is due recognition rather than giving support based on the student's sex.

Today, males need support as they adjust to a world different from their father's or grandfather's. Teachers who do not understand this are adding to the emotional stress of males. Females need the continuing support to prepare for that which they are best suited. Equal treatment is hard to come by, whether in yesterday's world or in today's. The battle of the sexes will not be history unless both learn the lessons of respect and need for each other.

We see more and more help being given students who may not aspire to college studies. Sullivan, as mentioned, started a scholarship for

172

vocational educational students.88 This seems to be a recognition of the importance of supporting all students, and not just those who are gifted intellectually. What sense of worth is connected with the receipt of that scholarship! Whoever said it was better to work with your head than your hands? Since when does it not take both, working hand in hand?

And who does all things well? Those who can work well with their hands, so to speak, ought to be rewarded the same as those who do intellectual work. Try working with computers without your hands! What would the professor do without the plumber? So in the classroom the signals must be clear that it is okay and appreciated when you work at what you do best.

There is a special compliment to be given to any school district that has former students returning to become employees. Someone there did something right when they come back to teach in their home territory. Sure, they had to be taught the necessary basics. However, it seems they may have come back because something special happened to them. School must have been very rewarding and probably enjoyable despite test time.

Also, there must have been a significant event of the heart. That would have been an emotional experience that recalled some teacher going

---

88 *Sullivan Daily Times*, op.cit., June 9-15, 1986, A new scholarship trust fund for vocational education was established at Sullivan State Bank in 1986 by the wills of Reid and Nina Ross. At least two scholarships will go to Sullivan High students who will attend Ivy Tech or another technical college, according to trust officer Lorene Pigg.

beyond their duty and teaching them something over and beyond the textbook. My supposition is that the experience involved appreciation and commitment. When something life-transforming occurs, we tend to appreciate it and return the favor.

Teachers in Sullivan County must have done a great job, and so many of their students have returned to follow in that profession. And in doing so, they have given something back to the community that was so good to them. Whether here or elsewhere, and whether former students return or go elsewhere to teach, it is believed that they do so by the example of those who have given so much to them. Returning such a favor is good mental health.

The classroom is not a professional setting for mental health. As such, neither does the teacher need a degree in psychology nor psychiatry as we said at the beginning of this chapter. It is important that we here again state this position. Because teachers or administrators do not have that formal training, it doesn't follow that they are not practitioners in mental and emotional health. Everyday we all are practitioners as we handle our own emotional lives and as we respond to others around us. We do not think it is necessary to add another year of training to do the job required. Yes, a master's in counseling would make them a better teacher. Yet again, as we said, that is not necessary. You don't have to have a medical degree to know how to practice good nutrition, exercise, and hygiene.

For some, the extra training is not needed because we have so many experts upon whom they can rely. No one has a better feel of the emotional state of the students than the teacher. No one else is better qualified to deal with the everyday occasions of emotional distress than the teacher. That is to say that they are qualified if they meet one requirement. The one requirement is to always be a very human, caring person.

You will not be the teacher who didn't know that she had a special education student in your class until late into the school year. You will not be the teacher who didn't understand why that student wasn't making the grade. You will not be the teacher who didn't bother to consult with the student nor check with the administration. That teacher flunked and so did the student because she simply didn't care. A caring person will find ways to be acquainted with the pupils, especially those who exhibit a problem with the study or in behavior.

Most of what I think is required in the classroom in regard to this topic can be done by the educator with a heart. There will be sometimes when we feel inadequate to the task. That's OK; it is a step in the right direction. Then you will seek out the in-residence school counselor. Sometimes the counselor in consultation with you will work with the child. There will be times when more help is needed, and you have resources available to make the appropriate referral to social, medical, and sometimes religious services.

Not to follow this protocol, is to make a referral when all that student needed was a few encouraging words or a good listener, which should easily come from the caring heart. There is always detrimental labeling when a student is referred. If not by the teacher, then by other students. Referrals must be thoughtfully made, but only after the educator reaches out the hand and heart.

We still live in a society where emotional problems taint us. If what is being suggested here is too much to ask of the teacher, then I hope that teacher will consider another profession where dealing with emotional issues is less required. Always put yourself in the shoes of the student, and you will be adequate for most occasions. Nothing said here diminishes the work of a mental health specialist. What I am saying is that all of us have a role to play in the mental health of others and no one, professional or not, has a corner on caring and the ability to reach out to the hurting.

A teacher has a unique privilege to make a child's day with sometimes only a genuine smile and cheery "Hello." To such a teacher a disturbed student will likely come and tell more of their story. You have been at your best when that happens, and if needed by the student, you will not teach anything else effectively to them until it does happen. Then if referral seems advisable, do it. Until then, that student sees you as an open door to a better life. You blow it, saying in effect, I don't care, when you brush off the student in whatever way.

For your own emotional health, never feel alone. Know where to turn when the load gets heavy, and it does at times. Be on good terms with the others in your building so you will not hesitate to ask for assistance. Neither consider it shameful to make such requests. Maturity never means we always appear adequate. When you don't get help from one person, seek another.

Your charge as a teacher or administrator is too important not to find the help you need in order to help your students. Attend in-service training on the subject. If there is not one available, request one. I'm sure there will be others who have wished for the same. If necessary, go to a mental health professional yourself. Would you insist on that kid who gives you fits to get help, and not go yourself?

This chapter, my friends in education, has come from the heart. I hope it will encourage you to open up your heart that you may teach our children more effectively. Yes, tough love may be required at times, but it, too, must be from a caring heart. In this way you will help to make a gentler nation. In closing, it is appropriate that I dedicate this chapter to all those teachers and administrators who were my support and inspiration along the way, including a very few in spite of whom I succeeded anyway.[89] A final word...if there be

[89] Graysville Elementary and High School teachers of this author: Helen Willis, Laura Francis Lund, Mildred Lofton, Maurice Sakel, Carlos Watson, Homer Arnett, Irma Gray, Enid Monk, Maureen Medsker, Fleming, Smith, Kathleen Adams, Emmett Wagner, Ruth Pleasant, Leon LaDuke. Principals:John Holden, Ora Clayton

one student that you simply can't stand, please let him or her succeed anyway. When you can't do good, do no harm.

WOODMERE TO WOODLAWN

Chapter 5

"Humanitarianism needs no apology…Unless we…feel it toward all men without exception, we shall have lost the chief redeeming force in human history."—Ralph Barton Perry, American author and educator (1876-1957)[90]

Dear Dad,

This is one of the chapters that you are really helping me write. No, I know you are not really here, but I secured your medical records and in them I find answers to many questions that I raised in my first letter to you. So, in a strange sort of way, you are here now to help me sort out something of what happened to you during your long confinement.

I had wondered what you understood about your illness. We could only imagine how much thought you gave to your family. In this chapter we can now fill in many gaps in our knowledge of your world. We know more now about your relationship to those who attended your needs and treatment. Generally speaking, we

---

[90] *Terre Haute Tribune* op.cit., Thought for Today, March 2, 1998

179

know now that you generally had good care, and that is a relief to know.

We had often wondered about what good could come from this time you spent away from the rest of the world. In this chapter we want to share some thoughts about that experience. There are things to be learned by so many of us who have any contact with people who suffer as you did. Never too old to learn, you would say.

It is our hope that every reader will be able to see a life such as yours with a new perspective. When you worked on a house, you thought of your job as being something more than the materials and tools involved. You were building a house for a family and that put your labor in a new light. I hope we can all learn from your experience and come to see patients like you as human beings and more than a number on a chart. If that is accomplished, then this is another example of your life not having been lived in vain.

This letter needs to be brought to a close and get on with the examination of your inside story of those forty-seven years of confinement. I must admit before closing how difficult emotionally it was to work with this record. This brought me face to face with the reality of your everyday world. At times the tears came. At times there was relief and satisfaction. At times there was puzzlement. And at times there was amusement at some of your tricks. We will write about these times.

You might like to look over my shoulder while I write this chapter about your experience that was akin to Rip's "wilderness" of which we spoke in the first chapter. So here is our interpretation of your story in the "wilderness" of Evansville's Woodmere, of the shaded environs of Macanell, and Woodlawn of Sullivan.

So long for now,

Love, Gene

"No man has a right in America to treat any other man tolerantly; for tolerance is the assumption of superiority." — Wendell Willkie, American politician (1892-1944).

When I asked for one set of Dad's records, the medical records secretary inquired as to whether I would understand them or not. She continued by stating that some of the records are quite technical. It is true that every profession has its jargon that may or may not be easily understood. However, she seemed to be indicating that the professionals which she represented had some kind of insider knowledge that would not be comprehended by outsiders. Again that underlying assumption can be replicated in all professions by some of their practitioners. The accessing of records in this case was not traumatic, and I am grateful to those who did cooperate within a reasonable amount of time with only a little resistance.

This question of records, however, brings me to comment on another underlying assumption that has far more serious consequence. It is quite natural for any professional to think of themselves as the expert. The critical temptation for those rightful experts is not to be open to other viewpoints. Here you will read about one of those "other" approaches to our common interest, the opinion of the family of a patient.

Every professional can easily give examples of the lay person's inadequate and inappropriate response related to their loved one's care. This writer has worked with most professions related to this subject, and I do understand the frustration when lay persons do not understand what is being done. However, I have learned that all knowledge doesn't flow from our professional text books and that professional experience is not always the last word. Every research project is either to confirm, disprove, or expand our knowledge.

So this chapter is begun with a disclaimer that has already been stated earlier in this book. This writer might be considered as one of those lay persons with inadequate understanding by some standards. Technically, that is true when it comes to background and training. The difficulty here is that too often the professional doesn't want to eat at the same table, so to speak, with the laity. Worse yet, is the loss of appetite when the nonprofessional brings a dish to the table and the expert chooses not to partake. Sometimes that happens even if the lay person brings the dessert.

In this chapter a lay person brings something very special and unique. I come now with the special knowledge of a son who is responding to his father's illness. The hostages of Lebanon all experienced the same event; however, a commentator quoted by Terry Anderson, remarked about how different was their own story in their separate books.91 So this writer will try very hard to share with you something that is uniquely mine. While I may not know all there is to know about mental illness and the care of patients, I do

---

91 Anderson, Terry, CSpan, March 22, 1998

know something about being a family member, the son of a person confined in custodial treatment and care for forty-seven years.

I bring that uniqueness of experience to this table and hope that it is found to be nutritional. Any professional, at whatever level, that refuses at least to sample the aroma is not worthy to be a professional in this field. Does this make one more qualified than the other? No, it does makes us partners as healers or comforters. The professional is asked to expand his or her menu, and any family member of other patients is asked to make a special dish presentable and palatable, so that we together nourished may assist our patients and loved ones effectively.

In this particular chapter, this writer feels like the player up to bat. As that fast ball, the enormity of mental illness itself, comes rushing across the plate, we have several opportunities. I don't come to this plate expecting to strike out. I came with confidence that there will be some kind of hit, and, as in any game, we will know the score when the game is over.

You the reader will take your turn with the bat, too. Then I become the pitcher, and you can enhance your score as a more effective player. The worst thing I can do is to walk you, but, if I do, you can still make a run. It is hoped that regardless of the position we play, let us be a part of a team that participates as if for a charity. The winner will not be either of us with our recognized capabilities, but the beneficiaries will be those entangled with mental disabilities.

We start examining the medical record of my father with a word about the physical settings where was found some solace on his journey. He was an outdoors man, having lived his life in the countryside as was learned in the genealogy chapter and in the one about our early family life. Growing up without the comforts of air-conditioning, he knew where to find cool places of rest and meditation. The woods always served that purpose well. In our childhood days, we as a family would take long walks through the woods on a Sunday afternoon.

Woodmere

Dad found the woods of Woodmere, the large wooded front yard of Macanell, and the quiet setting of Woodland nursing home to be a place of peace. Woodmere sat way back in a grove hidden from the traffic of Lincoln Avenue at the east end of Evansville.

Macanell was a former county home for the indigent with a large front yard shaded by many trees. It was set on a hill overlooking the river bottoms in mid-Clay County. Likewise Woodlawn at Sullivan was off the busy Section Street at the north end of town. In so many entries in the record, notes were made evidencing his joy when out in either of those places of natural tranquility.

The records taken as a whole are comforting to this son. One of the recurring questions in a family member's mind relates to the quality of care that their loved one receives. It is hoped that mental health professionals will understand some of that anxiety that is felt by a family when they turn over care to strangers, albeit, those who are trained to do the job.

Dad on lawn at Macanell

I have learned this not only from my personal experience regarding my father but also as one who spent nearly forty years giving support to other families of nursing home patients. There are still too many horror stories that circulate, too many verifiable, of care in both mental institutions and nursing homes. Some of the issues with which we deal in this chapter will reflect some of those concerns. Just this week a social worker sensitive to this issue shared the fears expressed by a friend whose mother needed special care.

Initially, I must comment on the general care that I believe my father received. This is important, first, because it deserves being said. Secondly, it must be said lest the reader comes to believe by our dealing with certain

186

issues that our approach is only problem centered. To be sure, we will devote the bulk of this chapter on issues that we believe need to be addressed. If that were not our intention, then we might as well have expanded on the next paragraph and submitted it to the popular monthly digest. Such would not do justice to the lessons found in my father's and my family's experience.

It deserves to be said that I am satisfied and relieved by the record that I have reviewed. Those involved in his care who might have some trepidation about the records being made available to the family, need not be concerned. Certainly no law suits are contemplated. We only want to make a positive effort to improve the care of our mental patients, and lessons learned in the record will add to those who professionally work in this field as well as the families.

There were genuine attempts made to help him. These were made at all levels of his daily experience. He was given work which we shall describe later. There is no reason to believe he was grossly mistreated in any way. The psychiatric staff used various approaches common in the fifties, sixties, and seventies with which we will deal more specifically later. The social workers can be commended for some specific efforts such as talks in the woods where he was more vulnerable to sharing.

The nurses' notes reveal some real caring on the part of some, and that is appreciated. He received annual physicals either by RNs or the physicians. Regular checkups at the dentist were noted. There were chest X-rays and flu shots, regular blood work, treatment for colds, ears irrigated, EKGs, and daily vitals were taken. He was checked for anemia including bone marrow biopsy. Cholesterol and blood pressure were monitored. I have seen the medical needs of mental patients neglected, and I can say that was not the case here.

This son was only fifteen years old when my father was first admitted for treatment. Dad spent two months at Central State Hospital in Indianapolis, Indiana, from mid-December, 1944, to mid-February. That record is not included in this chapter nor is that time given any further note except in this paragraph. I had just received my permit to drive and, accompanied by my mother and Uncle Ollie, drove the old 1936 Chevy about a hundred mile to see my father.

The only other thing remembered so well about the trip was the stark brick buildings with their window bars and patients peering out like criminals. The sights and screams heard that day made a lasting impression on this young man. Dad would accompany us home on the next trip, and I remember wondering if the slight improvement noted would be lasting.

He would be improved for the next couple years and able to tackle some everyday chores regarding our livelihood. We had hogs and cows as we did in earlier times at the Bicknell Place as mentioned in the chapter on my childhood. Now there were twenty- five acres on which to grow crops, and they had to be productive for income and to pay the mortgage. Two happenings I remember quite well. We built a barn during that time. We looked around the community and finally found a barn that could be torn down and rebuilt. There were big timbers that had to be re-mortised to fit the new plan. Dad seemed to handle the plans and their execution quite well.

Barn at Davis Place

The final rebuilt product was about 30x40 ft. with a hayloft. The south end contained the stalls for six to eight milk cows that we had. Two-thirds of the remainder was made into pens for the brood sows and their pigs. There was a feed storage area and a place for old Snip, our riding horse. Dad approached the banker about a loan so he could buy gilts which would later be the mothers of little pigs to be sold at weaning time. "Sorry", the banker said, "I understand that you have been up to Central State, and I can't loan you any money."

That was the turning point in his recovery; now it would be downhill. No, that didn't make him ill, but it was a contributing factor. Maybe we have come a long way since then, and I would like to think that wouldn't happen in today's enlightened world. I suspect we do not have to look too far to find a recurrence of the banker's attitude. This barn will play an important role later when we write about community and church support in the chapter, "Kneeling to Dance."

The barn brings back other unpleasant memories that brought his stay at home to an end in June of 1948. He became physically violent with me one evening over a dispute about when the cows could be milked. He had become uncontrollable and violent, and we could no longer handle him at home. He had never done anything like this before. It was not in keeping with his old self having not been an abusive person by any standard.

The Davis Place house that Dad had remodeled for us. The child is a g-grandson, Paul, that he would never get to know. It was from this house that Dad was taken in 1948 to begin his forty-seven year confinement.

At this point we had to seek the help of the sheriff to place him in custody for the safety of himself and us. I remember that day well when he was placed in the Sullivan County jail until the court could get his papers processed for admission to Evansville State Hospital which we are referring to as Woodmere. Seeing him, a sick man, being led away by police officers was very disturbing; nonetheless, we tried to understand the necessity.

A recent study suggests that such involuntary commitments to a mental institution are not as necessary as was thought back then.92 There seemed to be no option to us. One who has been choked or otherwise physically threatened would quite normally think there was a need to isolate the offender, a mental patient or not. In specific cases involuntary commitments must be made, but carefully. As the article suggests, it is all too easy for one to be frightened of a mental patient just because he or she is a mental patient.

The May, 1998 edition of the *Archives of General Psychiatry,* the source for the news article, concludes that discharged patients who abuse alcohol or other drugs are five times as likely to commit acts of violence as people without substance abuse. Non-patients with substance abuse were three times as likely to commit violence. There must be safeguards built into involuntary commitments; however, violence from some mental patients is very real to those families who have experienced it.

Also to visit him in the jail was upsetting. It was understood that for his protection and ours there was no other way to deal with the situation. How difficult it was, however, to see him behind bars as were those accused of a crime. Even more disturbing was to find him all bloody the next day having beat his head against the wall. He had complained of a terrible headache which may have been the cause. He had been having these, and the family

---

92 *Terre Haute Tribune Star*, op.cit., May 15, 1998, "Fighting for Rights"

doctor made a call to examine him. Yet, he never had committed a crime worthy of jail and may have had enough understanding of the situation that he intentionally hit his head on the wall to stop more than a headache.

This is just one of many times when we will call attention to the human side of the equation, not just an issue of cleaning up a bloody mess but raising the question as to why he might have injured himself in the first place. A related current event that is receiving attention today is the ruling by the Indiana Supreme Court that sheriffs and jailers do not have blanket freedom from liability in the case of inmate suicide.[93]

Some communities now have other accommodations for those awaiting commitment, but in this locale officers of the law often are used if the patient does not go willingly to a hospital or mental health facility. The basic question is how do we view the mental patient and how can we best treat them like other patients when safety is not an issue. While officers are sometimes necessary, we must at least think of the patient as someone who has not committed a crime and whose remedy is not in just being

INDIANA OPERATOR'S LICENSE
BUREAU OF MOTOR VEHICLES   FEE $1.25
Date Issued 2/27/46   No. 272613   Expires: Feb. 28, 1948
NAME Clarence Gilbreath
ADDRESS R. # 2, Sullivan, Ind.
AGE 38 RACE SEX M EYES Brn WT. 180
HGT. 5-11 HAIR Black BIRTH DATE 11/22/07
RESTRICTIONS:
SIGNATURE:
VOID UNLESS STAMPED VALID ON BACK AND SIGNED BY LICENSEE IN INK

He had passed his driver's test after the Central State hospitalization. It expired four months before he left.

---

[93] *The Tribune Star*, op.,cit. March 10, 1998

locked up.

We must question how emergency crews sometimes handle a hostage situation where a mental patient is endangering other people's lives. We should make sure we do not contribute to the instability of the patient by increasing their stress and adding to the likelihood they will do the very thing we are trying to avoid.

As if it were yesterday, I can remember as a youth learning to spell and gain a little understanding of what dementia praecox and schizophrenia were. My father's symptoms then included being withdrawn, hostile if disturbed, lacking in energy to do common tasks, having hallucinations, being distrustful, fearful of being poisoned, and experiencing unreality. The symptoms were severe enough that both local doctors and the psychiatrist who examined him for commitment diagnosed him as schizophrenic quite readily. Within a week he was taken to Woodmere and would stay there for twenty-eight years before spending the remainder of his life in two nursing homes.

When Indiana decided to transfer their mental patients to more community based facilities, usually nursing homes, my father was placed in a nursing home in Clay County, Indiana. The record shows that the family was notified of an impending move but had no input as to where he would go or when. My mother's objections were overruled by the hospital administration. This was a decision brought about by a newly enacted law

193

and executed administratively with little, if any, regard for anything other than fulfilling a statute. In reference to his diagnosis, the transfer papers reveal that the patient was released void of the original diagnosis. Wow, wouldn't it be nice if all schizophrenic patients were cured by State edict!!!

The original diagnosis at Woodmere was "dementia praecox, schizophrenic reaction, catatonic type 295.20."[94] On my birthday, August 5, 1976, when he was transferred to Clay County, the diagnosis changed to

An enlarged photo of the right pose shows a very frightened man. It is hard not to think of these as mug shots. It is understood these were needed for identification.—He got within two mile of home once so the safety plan didn't work too well. The writer wonders if such pictures are still being taken. Why would it be necessary for mental patients and not for any other?

290.02 senile dementia and was consistently listed in the records henceforth as organic brain syndrome. Quite shockingly the record states that the patient was dismissed from Woodmere as being "returned to mental health."

This brings to mind what allegedly is happening currently in some for-profit mental facilities where patients are dismissed as improved or well on

---

[94] Giving respect to the privacy of the medical record and to persons who assisted in Dad's care, we will not use footnotes that might unfairly expose specific persons. The reader can be assured that references are based on actual material from the record. We respect the humanity of the workers as well as plead the same for the patients.

the day that their insurance runs out. Students who want to further examine this might want to investigate the law that dispersed these patients and to study how that was administratively handled. It is not within the scope of this book to do such research.

We desire here to raise legitimate questions that others may want to pursue. Was it necessary to change a diagnosis in order to meet the requirements of the law and move patients to other facilities? Were psychiatric categories renamed just at that particular juncture? Not likely, since major changes were not made in the Diagnostic and Statistical Manual of Mental Disorders until 1980 and again in 1987.[95]

Or can we describe this event as being mostly economically driven, or was it in response to the advocacy for community based care, or both? The records both before and after do not substantiate any claim that there had been any dramatic improvement to justify the change. The only one mentioned was that he had not tried to run away for some time. A new diagnostic symptom? State appointed administrators, naturally, were expected to follow their bosses' wishes, that is, the legislators. Later, attendants at both nursing homes would testify that he had to be watched in both spring and fall to prevent such an occurrence.

His "preoccupation with his delusions...hearing and answering voices...at times quarrelsome...would sit and brood" as an early description

---

[95] http://www.nvo.org/merck.htm

195

of his condition did not change drastically before 1976. By another decade he had became more quiet and less delusional, but this was not a change that could be construed as being "returned to mental health." The diagnosis changed to "organic brain syndrome, chronic eczemoid dermatitis, and hyperlipidemia" in Clay County.

At Sullivan and for his last two years of life, his diagnosis was recorded as being organic brain syndrome. Does Medicaid not cover patients with mental disorders that are not shown to have physical origins? A certain treatment modality that will be discussed later may be another possibility for the change in diagnosis. Laws that decide care for mental persons and the subsequent execution of those laws create confusion in the minds of family members. This story happened in a time when families were not considered partners in treatment as much as they sometimes are today. There will be more discussion of families who have to deal with regulations later when we broach this topic in the chapter, "Confidence and Cents."

The question of import here regards decision making relative to the treatment and placement of patients. I agree with the basic premise that patients would fare better closer to their communities. It is understood that financial support for their care be of concern to the state which in this case was footing the bill. However, it seems inappropriate for a legislature to have that much to say about the treatment of any patient. It seems that the circle of caregivers, professionals and family, comprise the group where treatment decisions must be made. Progress is all so slow. Didn't we hear about this involvement of the state in history of the late 1800s here in Indiana?96

The reader will immediately recognize that there are forces today such as insurance companies who dictate the parameters of medical treatment rather than the patient and his physician. So while the intent was acceptable, the implementation left something to be desired. If the state desires to involve itself again in such matters and be helpful, it would do well to see that there are equal rates of reimbursement for benefits for mental and physical disorders. Hopefully, that is the case by the time you read this. I suspect I am dreaming just like the reformers of old.

The inevitable conflict between institutional regimens and personal preferences and habits of the patient is an issue that emerged during this review of the medical records. It seems almost impossible for an institution to run its daily affairs in any other way than to have considerable regimentation. It appears just as unlikely that a patient, or any human being, can function well and happily if expected to do so without regard to their accustomed routines. Those active and well would have at least some minor feeling of discomfort if someone attempted to force us to do something out of the ordinary. There are those who are quite grouchy until they have their caffeine in the morning.

---

96 Boomhower, Ray E; King, Lucy Jane; Drenovasky, Rachel., op cit Agnew, op cit

Now take someone who is ill and in this case mentally ill and expect them to be congenial when asked to do something foreign to their accumulated experience, and we have invited trouble. Some routines must be done anyhow, but the concern here is that personnel may think less about how the patient feels and more about getting an assigned task completed. Throughout in this chapter, indeed the whole book, we are pleading on behalf of the patient for understanding on the part of personnel and family. We need an understanding that reflects respect for a patient as any other human being. That simple statement has profound implications.

What are some examples of this conflict in these records? We will elaborate on two of these, the use of tobacco and the intake of food. One of the greatest conflicts regards my father's use of tobacco, mainly chewing tobacco. He had this nasty practice from childhood. For forty-seven years those in charge of his care tried to convert him to abstinence. He was given the latest in drugs for his mental condition but never was there any medical attempt to help him break this habit.

Rather there was constant warfare between those who didn't like his habit and he who loved it or, in addiction parlance, needed it. The popular nicotine patches were not available early in his period of confinement so breaking the habit was not much of an option which left deprivation as the next best choice for personnel. Weren't some of these personnel addicted to tobacco?

Here is the conflict again. Granted his habit was unsightly and unclean by any standard. Attempts to control it always focused on that issue of cleanliness. He would get tobacco juice on the bed, on his clothes, and on the floor. Someone had to clean up after him, and that someone had less chores when the patient was careful with his chew. You see that the focus was on the institutional needs. This patient was a problem, and his use of the tobacco had to be controlled for whose benefit? The focus was not on adding pleasure to a man who had so few pleasures anyhow. Maybe only in an institution is it expected that a patient's pleasures take back seat to those of the nurse or attendant. It seems that no one noticed that his irritability and lack of cooperation on other matters coincided with a shortage of tobacco.

During his last years he became more careless, it appeared, and more restrictions were placed upon him such as only chewing in the smoking room. One nurse who is to be commended responded in a way that reflected some measure of understanding. She records that the messiness was the result of not being able to see well. When he was deprived of sufficient "Five Brothers" or "Red Man" chewing tobacco, he would find cigarette butts and chew them. Great pains were taken to prevent this. He was monitored closely to keep him from "stealing cigarette butts" and chewing them. Now he is viewed as a criminal? Surely not seriously, but yet the characterization in the record reflects a lack of understanding of the patient's need for nicotine. It seems so strange from a patient perspective that professional caregivers would consider deprivation an appropriate and only remedy.

Other conflicts between the needs of the institution and those of the patient help to raise the issue of whose needs should have priority. This becomes an increasing concern when economics has reduced staff and a bottom line is more likely to be one of profit rather than patient care. Visit any hospital today, and you will find numerous examples of institutional needs taking priority. What we are reporting here are not isolated events.

Sullivan Convalescent Home, in Sullivan, Indiana, about six mile from Dad's home. He knew he was close and more than once he tried to make the final run.

An illustration from the nursing homes is the routine matter of giving baths. How would you like to be getting your bath at 3:30 in the morning? Sure, the patient can go back to sleep later, and where do they have to go anyway? The caregivers have several patients, and in order to get the baths completed on a certain shift, such an unusual schedule appears necessary. However, on what basis can the institution defend such a schedule except on an economic one? Why can there not be more personnel? Maybe we should ask the owners.

The other area of conflict involves something more than economics or time. Are the patient's wishes always first when it comes to food? Yes, if we mean that all is done that can be done to provide the nutrition needed by the patient. In this case, there is no question about acceptable nutritional menus for the patient. The review of the dietitian's records reveals balanced meals and sincere efforts to provide for the patient.

Dad was always eating too much or not enough, seldom keeping his weight stable, according to the reports. In the first half of his institutional life there was a constant battle to keep him from being overweight. This involved some very strict diets and the administration of dexedrine. On a couple of occasions he moved to a different ward, more like an infirmary, to accomplish the purpose of weight reduction. He worked in the dining hall for many years, and periodically he was removed from that job as a means of weight control.

Given the fact that weight and health are related, one still becomes curious as to why the obsession to keep his weight so close to the mark. I bet any overweight people today would wish they were not sent to Evansville for weight reduction! Hopefully, other potential causes of the weight gain were explored. It is not obvious from the record that that was the case. The combining of anti-psychotic medications, his sedentary lifestyle, availability of food in the dining room, and the questionable use of high blood pressure medications might and should have been considered. We

201

would not have wanted his physical health to have been endangered by obesity; however, in this case one gets the impression that an insistence on ideal weight was detrimental to the comfort and contentment of the patient. We are seeking a balance here between the implementation of institutional orders and the patient's human right.

Under what circumstances should either calorie reduction or supplemental feeding be the prerogative of the patient? Was a mental patient capable of saying, "Yes" or "No" to either of these and having that wish respected? This patient appears to have had that capacity regarding food most of the time. It is important to say that the effort of personnel to encourage a normal intake of nourishment is appreciated. No family would be happy for their loved one's eating habits to be ignored.

This writer has seen cases where the tray has been placed before a patient with no assistance given and later removed without the patient eating. I have also known families who went each day to assist their loved one with eating to ensure adequate nourishment. This happened because there was not sufficient help to feed the patient, so the administration said. Such cannot be condoned. Thankfully, that was not the situation with my father. He was capable of feeding himself, but the amount he ate tended to be dictated by someone other than himself.

A review of the charts indicates that the persons in charge felt obligated to make that choice for him, a responsible obligation if the patient could not indicate his own wishes. Those who recorded the incidents were very defensive about their efforts. It seemed as if it were necessary to report that they had done all they could and to note his lack of cooperation. He was the bad guy when he would refuse help with his meal or not eat what they thought he should. "He does not like to be told what to do" was a frequent entry about this as well as other issues. Never did it dawn on the assistant that the corollary of that statement is "I like to tell him what he has to do."

Such reporting is understood as a defensive act on the part of the institution and such can be defended in this litigious society. The issue here is that the patient was not given the opportunity to choose either to eat or not eat and how much. We would like that opportunity ourselves, would we not? Who of us have said that we were not hungry or didn't want much to eat? We would resent those who would choose to cram it down our throats or to deny us the privilege of eating too much. Mealtime should not be a war zone, and if it is, the patient should win.

Normal encouragement to eat or normal discouragement not to eat too much is one thing as those relate to the duties of personnel. However, we believe, as we interpreted the record, that respect for the patient's personal right on many occasions was violated. The plea to caregivers here is that you relate to the patient in ways in which you would want to be treated. Those who cannot pass that test should seek other employment.

Here again we plead for mental patients to be treated as human beings who happen to be in custodial care through no fault of their own. It would seem to be good treatment for a mental patient to be allowed opportunities to exercise some autonomy. In an institutional setting such chances are rare enough. The record indicates that often personnel take the "Father knows best" attitude, and this is to say that it is not often appropriate when it comes to such personal matters as another's appetite.

We cite the opening statement of Ralph Barton Perry once again, "Humanitarianism needs no apology…Unless we…feel it toward all men without exception, we shall have lost the chief redeeming force in human history." Mental patients are one of us whether in an institution or out, and they need every redeeming force that the best of our own humanity can muster. We have quoted O. W. Holmes in another chapter, and it bears repeating here. "The true essentials of a feast are only fun and feed."

Mental patients deserve to have a meal that is interpreted as something beyond the physical intake of food; in fact, a little fun would enhance rehabilitation better than conflict. Sara Eckel in a local newspaper column sums up what I am attempting to say here. She states, "What you chose to eat or drink or inhale has absolutely nothing to do with how good a person you are."[97] Eating too much (who says how much) or refusing a meal or half

---

[97] *Tribune Star*, op.cit., March 20, 1998 saraeum@aol.com

of it is not a character issue and should not be translated into such by those who feed our patients.

Quotes from the record and from our own experience with him are interesting because they reveal something about Dad's behavior and thought processes. We have no medical record for about the first ten years except a few admission records. Given that lack of information for a very critical time, we can only make some inferences from the record at hand and from the family's own observations during this period.

During that time there was little or no communication with him. A visit was merely time spent together in physical proximity without any meaningful conversation. Uncommunicative, yes; catatonic, no. The words he uttered were usually related to his own inner world. Such questions posed by him such as, "Did you get your ticket?" could not be explained by him. He didn't know where the ticket would take him or what bus he might be riding. "I'll tell you where you need to go...you need to talk to this government guy, and he will help you."

The most troubling comment from him in those early days was, "I don't know you. You are not my son. Shhhh, don't tell anybody here...I don't want them to know who you are." We were not family members, he claimed, and yet in a strange sort of way he sometimes made us think that he knew the real truth. He would become agitated when we spoke of the relationship, and later on I decided it was better to converse as with a friend and not as a son with his father. That was always very painful emotionally. It would be in his latter years before he would speak openly about his family that he once knew, but the many intervening years blocked his recognition of his offspring.

On the flyleaf of a 1970 book on schizophrenia there appears this dark tornado cloud out of the sky and on it are printed all sorts of descriptive terms regarding the disease. Underneath are written these words, "No matter what you call it, it's hell on earth."[98] Seeing and hearing his distress, we could not conclude anything else. Not having a key to open his door was like hell to the family, also. If the patient is in a hell, then wouldn't it be better to give a measure of comfort, a cup of cold water, if you will, and not fan the flames? We will come back to this subject.

A long time nurse would indicate some change after those first ten years. In late 1966 she wrote, "Patient's attitude and conduct much improved over first contacts with him." She does not elaborate on those early years, but from here on we get the fuller picture of his behavior and feelings. The one recorded request that expressed his need was for his "Five Brothers" or "Red Man." He seems to be able to express his needs for such physical desires for the remainder of his confinement. Expressing any emotional needs however are not so obvious. He didn't "talk unless spoken

---

[98] Pfeiffer, C.C, et.al., *THE SCHIZOPHRENIAS, YOURS AND MINE,* The Professional Committee of the Schizophrenia Foundation of New Jersey, Pyramid Communications, Inc., 919 Third Avenue, New York, NY 10022, USA, 1970

to......very much a loner...doesn't socialize...very suspicious and seclusive...nothing to say to other patients...making no complaints...speaks few words...likes to stay in his room by himself..."

Dad at our car in Evansville. He was wanting to go home with us. It was so difficult to tell him that he couldn't.

Two other sides of his personality were noted including a positive one. In 1975 a nurse writes in the record that "he had a dry sense of humor." Another wrote that "he was at times witty.'" It is good to know that amid his inner turmoil and external circumstances he could on occasions muster some humor. He was "clean, cooperative, and quiet" as well as polite and causing no trouble. Seemed contented, friendly, and pleasant. Being so quiet he seldom made complaints. Such were the positive comments written during the time of which we have records. One also will smile as the record is read when he goes to great lengths to avoid taking his medication. Maybe some personnel are upset because their mentally ill patient could outwit them.

There was another side of his personality that cropped up not as often but no less dramatically. One of the attendants coupled stubborn with being witty. Such stubbornness requires a second look. That character trait might not have been related only to his illness. He was known to have that long before he became ill. Many people are stubborn and not considered mentally ill, thank goodness.

We call people stubborn when what we want conflicts with what they want. And often such labeling was done when institutional or personnel preferences clashed with his desires. At times he was aggressive. He would "become combative when reprimanded." Does an attendant ever wonder before reprimanding if that is an advisable course of action and if the problem was of such import? Whether it was true in any instance with my father does not negate the issue here of appropriate action with a patient.

Let's approach this from another angle. I suspect that this patient given his condition and the setting was at times very defiant and obstinate. We should not overlook the fact that the mentally healthy are sometimes this way including those who work with the mentally ill. There is also another form of stubbornness that makes such situations more volatile. Authoritarianism is a trait of some personnel that contributes enormously to the conflict. The reader may ask why I am always turning the attention from the patient to personnel. Just maybe I am defending my father, right or wrong? Believe that if you will, and most likely staff will be defensive, but let's not loose sight of who is sick here and who isn't.

Workers with these patients, or any patients anywhere anytime, need to examine their attitude toward those for whom they have some responsibility. If you see yourself as being the boss when relating to a patient, then you can expect defensive reactions from many patients. Dad was one of those. He "did not like to be told what to do." We tend to think that is a description of the patient and that is partially true. The entry was made to characterize the patient.

But what does it say about the caregiver? Would he have accepted suggestions if someone was "telling him what to do?" We think of "telling" as ordering and "asking" as negotiating. Is there something wrong with approaching a patient with the "asking" frame of mind? If that rubs the caregiver the wrong way, maybe there is an issue of being the boss when one was intended to be an assistant or partner in the healing process.

Raising this issue of the mental attitude of the staff brings us to discuss further some entries in the record expressed more blatantly. Here we want to give a specific example of staff persons' attitudes that affected the patient's response. During the period of about 1964 to 1975 we see in the record several times both good and bad assessments of the patient that appear to evoke good and bad reaction by the patient.

One worker was consistently negative about the patient's person and behavior. He "is quite lazy and spends a lot of time sitting around." When we visit the question of medication, we will see possible reasons for the lethargy. Chronic depression alone is sufficient reason for Dad's appearance of being "lazy." When we talk about his work schedule, we will see also abundant evidence to the contrary.

The other worker who reported quite often alongside the negative attendant entered completely the opposite opinion. Which of the two were the most accurate in their assessments is not the issue. Either one could have had unhealthy psychological motivations for presenting the patient in either light. Neither is it necessary to explore those here. We simply want to make the point that caregivers bring their own emotions to the ward which may make for healthy or unhealthy interchanges with those entrusted to their care.

A potential improvement of this issue of the relationship of patient and caretaker can be found in better preparation for the task. That would include an on-the-job effort to understand more about the patient. It is believed by this writer that the above person with negative remarks knew little about the nature of the patient's disease and his treatment. It seems important that workers be evaluated psychologically and that such training be ongoing. A supervisor could have seen the same red flag as did I and given the worker additional training.

With the proper assistance she might have become the very one that put a smile on my Dad's face rather than to cause him to be "sullen and uncommunicative." She surely would have been willing to see that his sweater "that smells awful" got to the cleaners or that his need for a new one be shared with his family. She might have been helped to understand her own anger that he would "not help on the ward." One would wonder if he did not "hide out in the basement" not to keep from going to work but to avoid this attendant. More adequate screening and training are needed at all levels of the medical delivery service to avoid this kind of situation.

Knowing something about the patient's family would also help to understand the patient. This is going a second mile on the part of some but a highly desirable goal. In this case the social worker attempted to fulfill this role seeking to bring the family into the treatment plan during the first decade. After we were not so available, one social worker made this entry, "No interested relatives."

Sorry, but it seems that there was a non-interested social worker instead. This lack of help from the social worker for about another two decades seems strange. Was there no way to contact the family other than face to face encounters? A new era opened when Dad was transferred to Clay County. One important factor was the patient's closer proximity to his family and therefore more frequent contacts. From 1976 on, the family was personally known by some workers which relationship inevitably was an advantage.

In the early years it appears that what knowledge the social worker had was not shared or maybe ignored by other caregivers. The social worker's accomplishments at both Clay County and Sullivan were commendable. The record reflects many calls to the family for various reasons; unlike at Woodmere, the workers took the initiative and maintained contact with the family.

The lack of understanding of the family situation is expressed by comments in the record about mail and about personal visits from family members. Often in the record someone makes comments about

Mom and Mary visited more often.

the patient having no family support. One expression of this regards the receipt of mail. Early in his illness we often found him carrying letters in his pocket which I had sent. They had not been opened, and he seemed not to understand their source. However, in retrospect, they must have had some value to him since he carried them around. That supposition makes me sorry that I did not send more. However, at the time it seemed that if he was not reading them, there was no point in sending so many.

A worker states in 1971 that he "occasionally gets letters but will not claim them says they are for another Gilbreath, not him." We did send cards however on special occasions. A partnership with families surely would have helped us in the relationship, one that we wanted to be better. This was one of those many times when we simply did not understand what was best to do and were not given any assistance. A good social worker will help in such uncharted territory.

There were also mixed feelings about personal visits. During the first

four years of his illness I lived close enough to visit him often. This was the period when most of the Electro Convulsive Therapy was being administered. These were very difficult times to visit. He had often just had a treatment and was most certainly always in

In all his confusion as to who we were, there was one telltale bit of evidence that tells the real story. This billfold was carried in his pocket all of the forty-seven years. And in it was the picture of Mom when she was nineteen not long before their marriage.

physical and mental disarray. There came a time when I had to visit less frequently in order to maintain my own emotional stability.

Later when I had moved upstate and was attending seminary in Evanston, Illinois, there were fewer visits. Visits were only about twice a year on the average for me during his last 24 years at Evansville. My mother visited more often, but those were difficult trips. She often needed someone to take her in the early years. Later on, when she had a better car, she worked in Illinois, had health problems, and didn't get to go visit very often.

My brothers were in the army in this period and unable to visit. My sister lived much of this time in northern Indiana and Illinois. She couldn't make the trip often either with four small children and on limited income. Attendants on both wards G and H at Evansville reported to the Clay County home that his family never visited him. Maybe that was their assessment, and the lack of visitation had nothing to do with our love but more with unavoidable circumstances that were not understood by the staff.

Later, when he was moved to Clay County and to Sullivan County, all of us could visit more, and when we didn't the staff recorded their awareness of acceptable health-related reasons. Again this is good reason why community based treatment is preferred and why the work of an active, caring social worker is so vital to ensure family participation in a patient's welfare.

Work was used as therapy during the Woodmere event. Although the records are scant for the first decade, there are references to Dad being involved in work from as early as 1954. The Chores were performed in the laundry, in housekeeping, in the dining room, and on the ward. The later is not spelled out so we do not know the nature of those duties. Also, we know little about the other jobs. During the time when he worked in the laundry, we supplied shoes much more often because in the process he got his shoes wet.

He told us that he would set the table in the dining room and help clean up after the meal. Contrary to a few entries that indicate he "was lazy" and would "hide out to keep from going to work," his work record is quite impressive for a mental patient with his diagnosis. Often he would tell us during a visit when it was time to go to work and get up and leave. We had the impression that he liked his work, and entries about that experience indicate that also.

He was a good worker in his pre-illness life, punctual, proficient and reliable. Punctuality must be seen differently than when he was at home. Here he did not have a watch so he would lose track of time. "Pt works in housekeeping and does a fairly good job. Doesn't show up for work until real late sometimes for he likes to walk around on grounds." Given the fact that he didn't know what time it was and his enjoyment of the outdoors, one can understand why he didn't show up on time on occasions. This is another time when this patient, or any patient, is not much different than any of the rest of us given like circumstances. Another time he was found in the basement resting but got up and went to work willingly after the attendant reminded him.

As has been said earlier, he liked his job in the dining room, maybe because there was the opportunity to eat more. He is reported to sometimes

215

just stay there all day. At least it was preferable to the ward that he didn't like so well. Maybe it was not that he liked work so much but a lesser of two evils. However, the record indicates that he really liked his job. When he had been taken from that job in an effort to reduce his weight, he was very unhappy. Comments were made by the nurses that he appeared so happy and content when he was put back on that job. He would leave the ward at 5:45 a.m. to go to the dining room. That would be quite early for many of you readers. He worked from 6 a.m. to 2 p.m. each day except Thursday.

Sounds like a regular job except for the lack of pay. His was an inner reward of feeling better having something to do, being useful as in earlier life, and just maybe a respite from staring in space or thinking irrational thoughts. Here was another effort on the part of the hospital to deal constructively with his illness by giving him an outlet, routine, and reason for being. Or was it just that the state needed the help?

One must wonder how much more he might have improved if there had been more emphasis placed on a work experience at Clay County. I suspect he would have been delighted to have followed a handy man around the property. When other activities did not interest him, being able to use his occupational skills might well have caught his attention. However, we must remember that a nursing home is not a psychiatric institution where one would expect the caregivers to be better trained in psychiatric matters.

216

As we move this discussion to treatment modalities, the reader is reminded that this writer is not a pharmacist or a doctor. During most of Dad's treatment days, we, the family, operated as others of that period, namely, trusting that the doctors knew best and being confident that the medical procedures were appropriate. Now as I read the medical record at the close of the Twentieth Century, I approach the subject quite differently.

Although troubling and threatening to some physicians, we are now entering a new day when a partnership between a doctor and a patient and the family is expected, appropriate, and hopefully increasingly welcomed. I now review Dad's medical treatment record and in doing so encourage any family member of a mental patient to insist on being an informed participant in their loved one's treatment. For this reviewer to be wrong at some point should be just acceptable as a doctor being wrong on occasion.

At various times, not in any chronological order, Dad received the following treatments and medications: Thorazine, Electro Convulsive Therapy, Benemid, Navane, Hydergine, Dextro amphetamine, Atropine comas, insulin coma, Haldol, Apresoline, Serpasil, Normodyne, Lopid, PeriColase, Feosal, antibiotics, and analgesics, and salves or sprays for rashes. The administration of these brings us to comment about therapies such as ECTs and Atropine comas, use of antipsychotic drugs, and medications with more general applications. We will discuss experimentation, use of medicine as a behavioral control, and the

217

monitoring of usage. We note here initially that the family had no knowledge of some of the conditions for which he was treated.

Let's begin with the application of medications to general conditions. We have noted that it appears that non-mental conditions were generally treated appropriately. Dad had some recurring complaints, and those were not uncommon to the general population. It is comforting to know that these conditions which could have added to his mental anguish were not ignored.

All the information is not available; therefore, it may be unfair to raise some questions about the use of medications for two conditions. Medications were given for both high blood pressure and cholesterol. Based on what records are available, one must raise questions about the treatment for these at particular times. The record shows that on occasions neither were high enough to justify the dosage given.

While this writer is not a physician or pharmacist, the general public is often knowledgeable enough to know what is considered normal or abnormal readings. This happened at two different settings both at the hospital and at a nursing home. One doesn't have to think very long about such events when it is all too common today for physicians not to conduct adequate review of medications for such common conditions. That is a serious oversight with any patient, in fact, one that can lead to dire consequences if the patient has not chosen to be educated about both the condition and the treatment.

218

In keeping with our advocacy approach, it seems that such circumstances are compounded when the patient has mental illness. Anyone might have a problem recognizing warning signs and then communicating those to the doctor. How much more so if the patient has cognitive and communication deficits. We are not accusing anyone here of gross neglect, but we are unequivocally raising a flag on behalf of those who are so incapacitated to be unable to defend themselves against such inadequate medical review.

A further complication here is that my father refused medications on occasions, and the record later revealed him to have been correct. No, he didn't have the education of a modern day patient, and maybe he just incidentally happened to refuse at the right time. Once he was transferred at the state hospital from one ward to another, the record states, "because he refused to take his blood pressure medication." My, what a rationale! That was sometime in the spring, and the two medications were discontinued— one by May 9 and another by May 14.

Just maybe there was some reason for the necessity of treatment and that necessity was short-lived. Or it could have been from one of the other medications such as dexedrine given for what they called obesity or Haldol for agitation.[99] Increasingly, caution must be taken regarding drug interactions. The person on the street can now check with his pharmacist,

---

[99] http://www.mental health.com/fr30.html

but that is not generally possible for confined mental patients. Anyone who listens to the TV or reads the newspaper is aware of the serious problem of drug interactions and overdose anywhere within the medical field where medications are distributed.

There is an example of a physician prescribing medication without apparent justification. The doctor thought that Dad should have a mental examination in order to determine if Haldol would help Dad's "behavioral problems." These are described in the record as "Some confusion at times, chews cigarette butts and spits on bed linens and floor." Because the attendants were tired of the messes (an assumption based on their own reports), then the doctor should be Mr. Fix-it and give the man Haldol to keep him from spitting. Doctors are human, too, but what was this doctor succumbing to this day?

He went ahead and prescribed the Haldol expecting the social worker's exam of his mental status to confirm his action. Did he not believe Haldol was an answer to the described problem? The Haldol was prescribed on October 16, before the exam, and discontinued on January 15 after the results of the exam on November 8 did not support his action. At least he made a correction, albeit, not until his next monthly visit. So Dad was mistakenly on Haldol for two months.

Such use of medication as well as the decision making process to do so is faulty to say the least. A serious problem for nursing homes particularly is what appears to be a lack of accountability of attending personnel. The only recourse for family members is to be informed and alert to such possibilities. Nurses and other personnel could, if rightly trained and so motivated, assess such happenings appropriately if they are on the side of the patient as opposed to the side of the physician or institution.

Other treatments were atropine coma and electro convulsive therapy. We were unaware of atropine coma being used until we read the medical record. Information about the use of atropine for anesthesia or for an antidote to nerve agent poisoning is quite accessible. However, articles about atropine coma are scant and then mostly in non-English. It was a treatment, quite like the electro shock treatments, that received little attention in the record. We were told that the earlier the records, the more scanty the reports would be. Given the fact that Dad's first few years of records are not available, we have so little to go on.

Let's talk about the atropine comas first. We do not know how many were given or if they were in conjunction with the electro shock treatments. Our best conclusions, however, can be drawn from a paper provided by Harold D. Lynch, M.D. and Milton H. Anderson, M.D. former physicians at Woodmere. According to their report, extending from 1954 to 1975, 3000 patients at the State Hospital (Woodmere), Clearview Psychiatric Hospital, and the Psychiatric Unit at Welborn Baptist Hospital received these therapies. The patients received from six to twenty comas each.

Since Dad was admitted in 1948 and had received many of his electro shock therapies by 1953, he may not have been one of those treated by Dr. Anderson. We simply do not know if he received combined treatments but likely so since that was their recommendation. These physicians report that with schizophrenic patients, the combination of atropine coma and electrosleep (sounds more palatable than electro convulsive therapy or electro shock!) is more effective than either alone. These physicians in 1975 believed atropine coma and/or electro shock to be effective and that their lack of popularity in 1975 was due to the emergence of a wide range of psychotropic drugs.[100]

So why was Dad included in these treatments? Maybe he was not responsive to the more conventional treatments. Yet the record indicates that electro shock and apparently atropine coma were used early on which fact suggests that other conventional methods were not tried or were ruled out given his condition. It should be noted that another treatment called insulin coma was used as indicated by one brief reference. The article by Lynch and Anderson, plus an article in 1958 by Gordon Forrer, suggests that insulin coma was generally rejected in favor of atropine coma because the latter was safer.[101]

---

[100] Lynch, Harold D., M.D. and Anderson, Milton H., M.D., "Atropine Coma Therapy in Psychiatry: Clinical Observations Over a 20-year Period and A Review of the Literature," *Diseases of the Nervous System*, Vol 36, No. 12, December, 1975, pp 648-652

[101] Forrer, Gordon R.,M.D., and Miller, Jacob J., M.D., "Atropine Coma: A Somatic Therapy in Psychiatry," *American Journal of Psychiatry*, 1958, Vol. 115, No. 5, pp 455-458

One might conclude then that my father probably received insulin coma, electro shock, and atropine coma in that order and sometimes simultaneously. How much good did either do? In later years he was better, but were these remedies the cause of the improvement? There is no available record that would help us answer that question. Both articles state that atropine was recommended because it put the patient in a temporary position to receive group or individual talk therapy. However, it appears that schizophrenia patients were very unlikely to be talkative even after the coma therapy. Since schizophrenia patients were not considered then to be responsive to psychotherapy, one wonders why they were considered to be good candidates for the treatment.

That brings us to comment about experimentation. It is quite obvious that such did take place in such settings. We all acknowledge that experimentation is the basis for progress. However, when one reads records such as these, the question arises as to controls. Who decided that a treatment was indicated and on what basis was that decided? We just noted that some patients appear to have not been good candidates.

Where was the accountability? In this case the family were not aware of the coma activity. Certainly patient consent was out of the question. The court gave consent for admission and treatment, but did that mean the judge was approving a particular treatment? Obviously not, which left the matter to the physician's judgment. Or was it also the judgment of a pharmaceutical

223

company who wanted clinical trials? The physostigmine that was used as an antidote for the atropine was provided as a courtesy of its manufacturer.[102] This is not necessarily bad, but it does raise a red flag about who is doing what to whom for what reasons. While we can't answer that in respect to this case, it is important that the public be aware of such issues, that families be educated watchdogs in such matters, and that there be professional and legal guidelines.

It appears that much progress has been made in this area of concern; however, it is no time to become complacent. The treatment of my father was left to someone else, and that might have been an acceptable protocol during this past century. However, the thrust of this book is a concern that responsibility for mental patients encompass the family, the public, and even the patient, not the mental health professionals exclusively.

In this evaluation of treatment one more consideration must be shared. Dad received by our count as many as twenty-one electro shock treatments. He received these at a time when those were the acceptable remedy to the illness. The question here is in regard to a dangerous tendency, just as prevalent today, to see some treatment modality as a cure-all. The medical profession is quick to criticize unproven approaches such as alternative ones and yet participates in a system that is at times quite unscientific itself.

---

[102] Ibid., p 457

This history is a good example of how remedies come and go and how they are so quickly laid aside for the next panacea.

Finding something better is our way of life. We do not drive Model Ts today. We must search always for a better method and that will involve experimentation. The problem is with those who forget the larger picture, prescribing the same medication or procedure indiscriminately, or fail to let go when a modality is shown to be not the Godsend it was thought to be. Or a further tricky component is the vested interest of researchers, providers, and drug manufacturers. Insulin, atropine comas, and the state hospital approach went by the wayside while ECT is dying a more slow death. The saga will continue as this and that psychotropic drug is superseded by another wonder therapy.

It is shocking (yes, to use an ECT term) to think about how many so called treatments are actually dangerous. Dangerous is defined here as more than a question of mortality rates. Such is no less a concern today when drug reactions rate so highly on the list of causes of death, a less publicized fact. ECT remains controversial so we will not enter into that argument as to its appropriateness in any particular case today. We do want to say here that it may have not been the right treatment for my father. There is evidence in this case that it might have been detrimental. We admit we cannot be certain of that.

There now seems to be some explanation of his not claiming us as family members. Maybe his tachycardia can now be explained and his high blood pressure. He probably was transferred to another ward to keep his pressure under control after the atropine comas were administered. Not knowing the time and place even forty-five years later and yet having little snippets of knowledge of the past might be due to the ECT treatments. There are several experts who would agree, and here we will cite one reference about the ill effects of electro shock.

To help resolve questions surrounding the use of ECT, the National Institutes of Health in conjunction with the National Institute of Mental Health convened a Consensus Development Conference on Electro Convulsive Therapy on June 10-12, 1985.[103] While many studies indicate ECTs are helpful with some forms of severe depression, acute mania, and some forms of schizophrenia in the short term, there have not been adequate studies as of 1985 to verify long term positive outcomes.

A study in 1977 by John M. Friedburg reveals the same and catalogs the adverse effects of which my father suffered.[104] While my qualifications to make comments may be questioned, no one can challenge my concern

---

[103] Electro convulsive Therapy. NIH Consent Statement Online 1985 Jun 10-12; 5 (11): 1-23.

[104] John M.Friedberg, M.D., "Shock Treatment, Brain Damage, and Memory Loss: A Neurological Perspective," *American Journal of Psychiatry* 134:9, September 1977. pp:1010-1013. (http://www.idiom.com/~drjohn/amjpsych.html)

that our mental patients be treated responsibly and their intrinsic worth should be seen as something more than one number in a clinical study.

The panel is concerned that the use of ECT be decided on an individual basis. Financial pressures of the institution or staff convenience should play no role in the decision to administer ECT. For such a consideration to be voiced in this Conference indicates the potential for ill-conceived treatment that this writer suspected. One has to be suspicious (a schizophrenic term!) that 3000 patients in Evansville in a twenty year period were treated. That's close to two new patients a weekday, and these patients were treated six to twenty times.[105] One might think that the Evansville area must have a lot of mental illness, but the rate probably is no higher there than anywhere else. Certainly, they had enough of a concentration of patients, whether chosen properly or not, to bolster their clinical studies. Further, it is disconcerting to think that so many of these patients were captive and had no choice.

We have attempted to highlight some mental health issues that are worthy of consideration on all levels of delivery. It is hoped that this will not be seen as just a history of one patient in a time too far removed from 2000 AD to be of any consequence. Mental health is too vast a subject and there is still too little known about causes and treatments for any of us to travel this major thoroughfare as if we are the only vehicle on the highway. That is

[105] Lynch, et.al., op.cit.

227

to say we should respect the other driver so we can all arrive at our common destination.

In the history which has been described above, the family would have been walking along this same highway that was clearly marked "No Pedestrians Allowed." This is not the slogan in my advocacy platform. The highway belongs to all who desire to assist in the treatment of the mentally ill. Who knows, in the future someone in a yet undersigned vehicle, may pull up alongside of us. Give that vehicle the same road courtesy that you have expected for yourself.

Specifically, we have asked that we develop a partnership in this healing and comforting process that includes the human rights of the patient and the full involvement of their families. It is felt that we have a long way to go on this issue. So whether you are one of the involved professionals, a patient, family member, or responsible friend, there is surely something here for us to digest. There are still plenty of turf wars among professionals that are very detrimental to the delivery of services. Ways must be found to lessen these and to incorporate ideas from what professionals all too often feel are unlikely sources of remedies, the non-trained laity.

From the researcher to the attendants, from legislators to the person on the street, from administrators to office secretaries, from the highest to the lowest, let us all be in word and deed advocates for the mentally ill. There will be no better preparation for the day when any one of us or our families

228

may well become one needing the kind of service for which we plead. Let us make the patient our highest priority above our search for our own emotional and economic gratifications. Make it a safe ride on this highway so that we will all find ourselves on time and well-prepared to do a good day's work for the mentally ill.

CONFIDENCE AND CENTS

CHAPTER 6

"The word 'impossible' is peculiar because if you examine it closely, you'll find that most of it is 'possible.'" Anonymous

Dear Dad,

In my last chapter, I explored your experience of confinement from a medical point of view. I learned a lot, and it was so difficult to attempt to put myself in your shoes. We remember that old Rip slept through it all, but that was not so in your case. Now I am faced with a similar situation trying to understand what it was like for Mom while you were gone so many years. We can safely assume that both of you spent some sleepless nights while you were apart.

Probably neither one of us can come close to appreciating what Mom endured. It was not needful for you to worry about food and shelter. From what we have already said, there were other things that did greatly concern you, and you felt many stresses that we even yet do not understand.

However, Mom's worries were about fulfilling the basic needs for everyday survival. For sure, she had many others, but these basic needs exhausted so much of her energy. Making ends meet was her primary objective. In your earlier days of marriage you knew what that meant, and now she was left alone to keep body and soul together for the children and then for herself.

On your better days you felt sorry that you weren't there to help her. Your illness, not of your choosing, wasn't anything you could help. Yet I'm sure you would have if you could. You wrote through a volunteer that you felt you were needed at home. The fact remained that Mom was left to keep things going. At times surely she felt cheated that there was not a helpmate. Dad, if she ever felt sorry for herself, no one knew it. She met the challenge, one that looked impossible, facing it with confidence.

In this chapter we want to explore something of her childhood and youthful days. It was those experiences that gave her confidence that her task was possible, courage to face the obstacles, and determination not to throw in the towel. Most of all, Dad, we will show by using her voluminous records how she turned cents into dollars.

You should know she didn't get rich by any means, but she kept the bills paid including the retiring of the farm debt. Now she is back at a low financial ebb, living on her Social Security check, but she is holding her head high for making the impossible possible.

I had originally thought that this chapter would be named, "Faith and Cents" because it was the coupling of religious faith and cents that carried her through. Yet personal confidence is something she developed early in life, and it is important here to note how that played a significant role in her life. Her religious faith deserves more discussion, and we will give it just due in the following chapter, "Kneeling to Dance."

Dad, you would have been proud of your wife. While you used to be angry at her for her part in seeing that you got treatment, now you can sit with her, as it were, on the front steps in the cool of the evening as in better days long ago. Now you will hear her tell of her long and arduous day that turned into years and years, an experience of faithfulness and demonstrated love for you and for your family.

She is a little apprehensive about this chapter devoted to her, one who kept her feelings quite close to herself and who has an aversion to the limelight. She was always, like you, willing to help others, and we pray that she will be compensated by knowing that this may help another spouse who might be left alone for whatever reasons.

Rest in peace, Dad. Mom will in time find her deserved rest, too.

Bye, Gene

"Life is a grindstone. Whether it grinds you down

or polishes you up, it is up to you" Source unknown

We used to have a grindstone at our house. It had a large grinding wheel that was operated by pedals as one sat on the seat. As smaller children we sometimes thought of it as a play toy. With nothing to grind, we would sit there and pedal away. That was kids' stuff, and in such revelry there was no thought of it having anything to do with life. If Dad wanted to sharpen the ax or hand sickle, we often would volunteer to do the pedaling. Never did we think that Dad's thoughts were in the grown-up world while ours were in playland.

When we were just a little older and big enough to swing the ax, then we began to know the importance of the grinding. Also, we learned that there was a right way and a wrong way to hold the tool that was to be sharpened. Not understanding that, we were most likely to grind down the tool rather than polish it up and put a keen edge on it.

While Mom didn't do the sharpening, she came to know the meaning of letting the grindstone do its best thing for her. She learned that life is a grindstone, and remembering experiences of childhood and youth, she resolved that it would polish her up and not grind her down.

My mother, Fleda Helen, was another of the multitude of coal miners' daughters. Who knows, she might have made the charts. She could sing as well as the celebrity. But in our family's book, she did make our charts, and

234

her songs still reverberate in our minds. Fleda is a very unusual name. She doesn't know the source of it. She was born November 27, 1909, just two years and five days younger than Dad. At this juncture of time she is almost ninety-three telling me to hurry up and write this so she can read it.

Recently I received an email from a friend entitled, "How do you spend your dash?" It sets the stage for what I want to say about the span of my mother's life.

"I read of a man who stood to speak at the funeral of a friend. He referred to the dates on her tombstone from the beginning to the end. He noted that first came her date of birth and spoke the following date with tears, but he said what mattered most of all was the dash between those years. (I900 - I970)

For that dash represents all the time that she spent alive on earth...And now only those who loved her know what that little line is worth. For it matters not, how much we own; the cars...the house...the cash, what matters is how we live and love and

how we spend our dash. So think about this
long and hard...

Are there things you'd like to change? For
you never know how much time is left, that
can still be rearranged. If we could just slow
down enough to consider what's true and
real, And always try to understand how
other people feel. And be less quick to
anger, and show appreciation more and
love the people in our lives like we've never
loved before.

If we treat each other with respect, and
more often wear a smile...remembering
that this special dash might only last a little
while. So, when your eulogy's being read
With your life's actions to rehash...Would
you be proud of the things they say about
how you spent your dash?"[106]

Imagine this agrarian scene of a farmer plowing his field with horses and
walking plow. They saw the birds following the team and plow, descending

---

[106] Source unknown

to grab a worm as the soil was overturned. Every round made the area larger where corn or beans could later be planted. Here were two preschoolers, Mom almost three and her brother Vernia about five, standing on the rail fence taking in the key attraction of the day.

Certainly this is a page out of yesterday as Mom describes these early days of her life in her notes written in January of 1996.[107] No doubt at that age, she was not thinking about that scene having any symbolic significance for her later life. She was not aware of how a land was being laid off and what the turned-over soil of life would produce for her during the ninety-some years to come. She did not think that she would experience nearly a century of plowing, planting, cultivating, and harvesting seasons before she herself would rest beneath the country sod.

At this point in time her parents were renters, and they would move three times. This would be the first lesson in change and adjustment. From age three she experienced such change as she recalls the move into Sullivan by horses and a big wagon. Stability was found within the family circle as she, being the oldest daughter of this third family of her Dad's, found her place in the family scheme.

She recalls helping sister Lillian learn to walk, with Mama on one side and herself on the other. This house in town was a three- room one located

---

[107] Gilbreath, Fleda Helen Riggle, "Memorable Notes in the Life of Fleda Helen Riggle Gilbreath," unpublished.

just three houses south of the present Frakes Street, just north of the present American Legion. Here she was learning early to help others and being content with less than the best in housing. These lessons would serve her well later in life.

And more family lessons in life would be acquired as she started to school at the McKee School at the north edge of Sullivan where a carpet store now operates. As we wrote in the chapter about education, here was a student going to school with a piece of home life with her. In this case a beautiful one. Mom tells it this way:

> "Sometimes the snows were so deep, dad had to walk us to school. My dad was a coal miner and he and 2 other miners sometimes walked up Section Street passed the McKee school on their way to work. And sometimes walked with the school children on their way home from work; which to me was a thrill to have my dad walk home with us kids. Sometimes he drove the horse and buggy to work. Horse and buggy rides were one great pleasure to me as a kid."[108]

---

[108] ibid, p. 3

That is a beautiful story not only to show family solidarity and support but revealing childhood fun and contentment. She relates more about their mode of transportation. In her own words, here is more of the story:

"Horse and buggy, horse and carriage, and sleigh rides. The spring wagon in the fall, wheels off, and put on sled runners...was our transportation through Depot Town (Eastern Sullivan along the railroad tracks) to Grandpa and Grandma Riggles house at 324 Orndorf Street. (It) was so much fun riding in the sleigh, straw in the bed, the blankets to wrap in, snow flying from horse hoofs back in your face. Then on Saturday nights (in the warmer seasons), we went downtown (by) horse and carriage to visit and shop. Our groceries were mostly bought in Depot Town (where for) advertisements (the merchant) gave caps to customers. I always wore a cap...(they were) like what we call stocking caps today. They had a long top and a ball on the end.

239

You wrapped the long part around your
neck like a scarf today."[109]

Horses were the usual mode of transportation, but the children in the State Street neighborhood developed another method for playtime. Mom tells this story:

"We had our play wagon and sleds. We
drove our dogs...Ours was Jack, a medium
size yellow dog and Bob (was) a bobtailed
black dog that belonged to Bill and Howard
Wright...who lived 2 houses south of us.
The boys had harness for their dogs. We
hitched them to our play wagon and drove
them around like horses. We had a lot of
runaways and wrecks. (And another
pastime related to transportation) was to
run to wave at the train crews as the trains
run past our house."[110]

So far Mom has learned the joy of creativity, to work with others, to be daring, how to purchase necessities, how to have fun, to do what is necessary to achieve, to observe productivity, to guard her own health, and

---

[109] Ibid
[110] Ibid, p 4

to make the most of school. These will be experiences from which she will develop coping skills for a difficult life ahead.

From State Street the family moved to the country about a mile and a half northeast of Mt. Tabor Methodist Episcopal Church and in the midst of some oil fields. The family traded places with Mom's G-uncle David and G-aunt Cindy Chastain, and this was the first time for home ownership. The Chastains had lived in a house with one large room and a lean-to kitchen plus a large

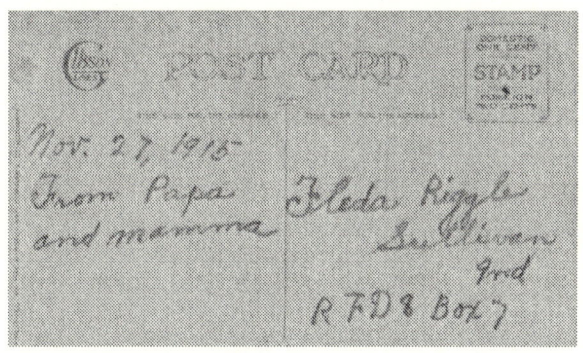

There wasn't money for much of a birthday celebration. The family had this tradition of giving a postcard. Mom saved several of them.

porch on the front. They lived in this house with their eight children. The barn was larger than the house. What a comedown, Mom thought. Yet here she as a teenager learned many more valuable lessons.

Was the house really a comedown? At first, the house seemed small and inadequate. However, they made do. They had two folding beds that made out at night and were folded up during the day making nice pieces of furniture. A metal cot with sides that would fold down also did double duty. A gas grate sat in the east end of the living room and was fueled by free gas from the oil fields. A fireplace with a mantel was a focal point also providing

241

more heat and fueled by coal picked by the coal mining dad. There was a kerosene cook stove in the kitchen as well as the small coal stove in the middle of the floor for heat.

Not much attraction here except what Mom first thought was a comedown, turned out to be a home. She learned that a home is not the physical appointments of a house but those relationships which bound her family of seven together. When we later lived in a two room house, as we have previously described, Mom knew what to do with that comedown; she would make it a home.

When we moved in 1944 to a partially remodeled house, Mom once again made it into a home. It would be several years before she was able to put in new ceilings and decorate the walls, covering up Dad's unfinished plastered walls, a project cut short by his illness. Mom kept her goal for improvements in mind and abided her time until there was money. She learned this patience and more back at the Chastain house turned home.

The family, then too, looked forward to remodeling and expanding their quarters. My grandfather hired Charles Milam of Sullivan to add two rooms to the house. So another lesson, ideas about how a house can become a home and, also, how a house can be made more physically appealing and comfortable as well as be properly maintained.

An expanded house enhanced Mom's ability to relate to her friends. Now a teenager, she was interested in the boys. Mr. Milam had two sons who came with him often to work. Mom says she thinks they came more to see her and her sister Lillian.

Friendship with her girl friends was greatly enriched. Now friends made at school such as Jewell McKinley, Catherine Thompson, Frances Moore, Bonnie Malone, Thelma Huff, Pansy Barrick, Wallene Johnson, Helen Hayes, as well as neighbors, Martha and Thelma Daniels and Geneva Robertson, could visit or have a sleep-over. Before these newfound friends, she considered the move to Graysville School "devastating" after having attended the smaller McKee school. Learning that friends are there for you will prove to be a great support in the turbulent years to come. Some of these like Jewell and Wallene would remain best friends for a lifetime.

She had here in childhood and youthful days learned how to relate and would find new friends wherever she was, including the fifteen years she worked away in another city. Even now at her apartment she has a new set of friends since all of that original gang are gone. One other friend must be noted during those teen years, that of Dad, the kid who walked by her house each day to tend the farm adjoining the Riggles, the one who would remain a silent friend and companion of the heart for life.

Just four more lessons need to be highlighted. One has to do with illness. When Dad became ill, Mom had already seen much of illness earlier in life. Strangely, she had seen what the aftermath of the flu could do, as it would be with Dad's initial illness. Her mother, Ena, and sister Amelia suffered prolonged lung problems after having the flu at the Sullivan house. Both Drs. Maple and Briggs told Grandpa that he had to get them out in the country. The smoke from all the coal and wood-burning stoves and fireplaces in a concentrated population was recognized as a detriment to healing by these doctors very early in the century.

The Chastain property was the place where they could be outdoors a great deal getting lots of sunshine, fresh vegetables, and milk. Living on twenty acres, they had a big garden, chickens and cows, as well as a pear and apple orchard. Who knows how much the thick, brown medicine they took for years may have helped. While Vernia didn't have the flu, he had his own remedy for good health. He would gulp down whole eggs which made my mother's stomach turn, she says, just to think of it.

Mom would be frustrated later seeing that there was no medicine or change of scenery that would reverse Dad's illness. Mom experienced tragedies in these youthful days. The most devastating was one which was quite common in Sullivan County in the heyday of coal mining. Mom writes about it nearly seventy years later and she tells it briefly this way:

> "Sadly my dad didn't get to enjoy the addition to the house...he died September 19, 1927. His body lay in state in the front room of the new rooms. I was 17. That year in April the school at Graysville (had)

burned. So we were at home from school when Vernia and Rollie Pirtle came from the mine about 9-10am and told us of our dad's sudden death by slate fall that morning. At that time, wake and funerals were very common to be at the house. (So) dad's body lay in state in the living room of the new addition. The funeral was at the Mt. Tabor Church."111

There is something to be learned in all circumstances of life; even good can come from them. Mom further describes the modest lifestyle of the family. Miners' families knew well how uncertain the next paycheck was. When work was available, they made a fair living. When strikes or shutdowns occurred, they needed the help of other family members, of their union, and ofttimes of the state. Mom had told me earlier of Grandpa taking bacon grease sandwiches in his lunch pail. The paths out back of the house and to the outhouse were "paved" with the ashes and cinders from the stoves. "They made such a good sidewalk and were cheap," Mom related.

Rabbits were to be had for the hunting, and Mom and Grandpa did some of that taking the beagle, "Spot," with them. Meat was scarce

---

111 Ibid, p 7

sometimes, but relationships formed during hunting excursions were memorable. The family didn't own a car until the oldest son, Vernia, was old enough to drive. Before that, rides to town by horse and carriage to see a movie provided a double feature as they rode home under a starry sky. Other stories of simple pleasures, not requiring much money, indicate the lifestyle of a family who knew how to make do with very little.

How much more so as the Great Depression gripped the country and then Mom and Dad tried to make ends meet as a married couple with three little mouths to feed. All this and more taught Mom how to make cents count. A penny saved was a penny earned. Now we don't bother to pick up a penny. Her experience set the stage for coping with many years of deprivation. She could, and did, handle it because she had been there before. She gained skills that with confidence she could make the cents go around.

We mentioned early in this chapter about the fun that the Riggle family experienced. Let's expand on that story. The father liked to sing which his daughter believes he could do well having a beautiful voice. He played a flute, harmonica, and Jew's harp. The family were entertained very often by her father's music. By this outpouring of music my mother was encouraged to sing and she enjoyed trying to play the flute. We will come back to this later as we see how she applied music in her everyday good and bad times during her married life.

Sadly, there is one talent she gave up early and did not develop. She liked to go out close to the oil pump house not far from the barn and sit on a corner post where she could view the oil field sites and so much of nature. There she sat quietly and sketched the scenes that thrilled her heart. She kept many of those, and they were stored in a trunk which stayed in her family home until it burned in 1940.

A drawing of a bird, of reindeer, and of crayfish, grasshoppers, and fish remain. This was another option that she might have used had she had time beyond keeping body and soul together. Music and art are great tension relievers, pulling us out of ourselves, renewing us, and giving us peace. Thankfully Mom learned these early in life, and they were options for her as she faced many years of hardship.

Mom learned how to "spend her dash," applying the lessons of life, and making a success of what was handed to her. We will now see how these principles played out during Dad's long confinement and her years of single motherhood and being a surviving spouse. As we proceed we will see how blessed she was to have been somewhat prepared for the unseen.

Dad's years were heart-rending, but so were Mom's. We do not mean to compare them, just to say that both of them experienced a life that words fail to describe. Hopefully, the sharing of their story will encourage others to proceed with confidence. There will be a way through your personal hell when you apply the resources at hand, especially those within you embedded long ago for such a time as now.

The "confidence and cents" saga for the time period of Dad's confinement really started before his illness. As has been indicated, Mom and Dad were among the millions of victims of the Great Depression. The Gilbreath family had lost one hundred and twenty acres of farm and pasture land as well as three productive oil wells. That loss was no small one for that time. Now add on several years of barely paying the rent and sometimes not succeeding at that.

With that history one would think that all the enthusiasm for starting over might have vanished. Who would want to try to buy a place of their own? Mom and Dad did. They took advantage of the same method that took the Gilbreath farm in the first place. There was a twenty-five acre farm with an old house on it that had been sold for delinquent taxes, not much different in principle than a delinquent mortgage.

John and Henrietta Davis had lost the farm because they couldn't pay the $128.84 taxes due. For a hundred dollars down and a hundred a year, the place would be ours. However, where would they find a hundred dollars for the down payment? They sold an old cow for fifty dollars and took a personal loan for the other fifty with the Baldridge and Stewart Loan Company in Farmersburg and made the deal with the Wabash Federal

Savings and Loan Association of Terre Haute in 1941.[112] This Association had become the owner of the property after acquiring it from the original purchaser; thus, two parties had already capitalized on the misfortune of the Davis family.

By 1944 they had paid all but $487.28 to Wabash Federal. Times had been better, and Dad had had wartime employment. The WPA days of employment were now over. All along their plan was to get a loan from the Sullivan County Common School Fund because of the low interest rate of four percent rather than the six percent. Dad was getting ill, and Mom was getting nervous. Was this to be another foreclosure? Yes, if Dad wouldn't do the necessary paper work with the county auditor, James McGarvey.

Mr. McGarvey, sensing the situation, worked with Dad at Mom's encouragement to get the loan processed. Here a county official was sensitive and caring as opposed to the man at the bank who didn't want to make a small loan to one who had been mentally ill. So the loan was approved on October 21, 1944, for twelve hundred dollars with annual payments of eighty-eight dollars plus interest on the unpaid balance.

Thus Mom performed her first critical intervention in this period of Dad's inability to mentally function adequately. Just in time, too, because he would

---

[112] Information for these numerous financial transactions are taken from my mother's records kept over these many years. Records tell a story and their potential value should be considered by anyone. We will not footnote any further financial transactions. Only our interpretations of these bona fide records may be questioned.

be committed to Central State Hospital in December for an almost three months stay. (This stay is not counted in the forty-seven year record. Actually, Dad was ill over fifty years.) Fresh in Mom's mind are the agonies of years of physical deprivation during childhood and early adulthood. Now she is determined that what was rightly hers would not be taken from her and her family. She tackles the first crises with confidence and cents.

By now the basic remodeling had been done on the Davis Place, and we had moved in. Mom describes that experience this way: "If we hadn't of done that (secured the School Fund mortgage), I don't know how I could have managed. Because the Mutual Federal would have foreclosed and I don't know where we would have gone. Anyway it was a roof over our head and we 'existed,' the same as we always had done through the Depression. Rev. McCord (our Methodist pastor at the time) said one time, 'The Lord keeps us as poor as it takes to keep us inline.' So I guess it had to be that way. Rough road

The Davis Place house that Dad remodeled into this four room bungalow. This is as it looked several years later after some improvements.

anyway."[113] But instead of resignation, there was determination to make this deal work.

Rough road, yes, for there were more financial backsets to come. Would the Common School Fund foreclose when the eighty-eight dollar payment was not there each year? "No," said Harold "Bootjack" Reynolds the auditor who succeeded McGarvey, "as long as you pay a dollar or five dollars." Therefore, until 1953 when an oil lease with the Texas Oil Company was signed for one hundred twenty-five dollars, Mom paid only what she could. The amount paid would had been very little because Dad left in 1948 having been some incapacitated for most of the previous four years.

There was no income until Mom went to work after Dad's departure except some milk sold, an occasional voucher from the township trustee for food, a few dollars from the unproductive soil of the twenty-five acres, and a few dollars earned at odd jobs by us children. Now it would seem that there was still confidence but the cents were not turning into sufficient dollars. Let's pause in this discussion of financial occurrences to introduce another demand on Mom's resilience, that of court appearances.

The day that Dad was taken by the sheriff to Central State Hospital was a difficult day for me as I have previously described. That depiction did not do justice to my emotional disturbance. Also, words are inadequate to tell

---

[113] Gilbreath, Fleda, op.cit., p 20

the story of Mom's inner turmoil over seeing her husband taken away. As we have said, he had been uncontrollable, and so it was a relief to have someone take over for us. You will remember that back in the forties, the common person was not informed of what such a transfer really meant. What would they do to him? What was this illness anyway? Would we be able to face the public now since many felt it best to hide such illnesses? Mom and all of us would wonder when he would come back. Would he get well? We had more hope when he went to Central State than when he left for Woodmere.

So doubts about recovery began to rise when he was taken the second time, and yet Mom expected him to recover during those first two or three years. Those two different days when he was taken away were very sad days. The relief that something might be done for him was overshadowed by the confusion over the meaning of it all. Maybe Mom expressed it best when sometime after Dad was gone, she said, "There are some things worse than death."

Those days of his departure were days of sorrow and grief. Those days would turn into forty-seven years of silent grief for closure could not come until he made that final journey home and was laid to rest. Only then did a struggle begun so long ago end for him and for his loved ones. The emotional stresses of those years made it "The Long Journey Home," an alternative title considered for this book.

A few days before Dad left for Central State, Mom experienced the first of several court appearances. Each appearance would be for different reasons and would involve various levels of stress. Surely, the first was stressful for two reasons. She had not had to appear before a judge before, and, secondly, she was overwhelmed by her own inner turmoil as so inadequately described above. There was only one complete committal hearing done. When he was committed to Evansville Woodmere, the Judge acted privately on the basis of Dad's history and new evidence of a relapse. My uncle Ollie signed the first committal papers, and Mom signed the second ones.

The application for an Insanity Inquest included information about a person's place and date of birth, residence, nationality, place of parents' birth, education, occupation, estate value, history of the indication of insanity, physical history, family history (physical and cause of death), personal lifestyle questions like alcohol, drug addiction (for parents and grandparents as well), the findings of three physicians, and the order for committal by the judge.[114]

An order to perform sterilization could have been given, but it wasn't. The three physicians all came to the jail the same day. Mom and Uncle Ollie had taken Dad to a psychiatrist in Terre Haute several days before, and the

---

[114] Application for Insanity Inquest, dated and signed, December 16, 1944, Sullivan Circuit Court, Sullivan, IN.

diagnosis was schizophrenia and treatment was recommended. The psychiatrist's report was made a part of the court record and duly considered by Judge Walter Wood. Dad's appearance before the Judge also served to convince the Judge of the necessity of a committal.

It is easy with hindsight to think how necessary it was to have the court involved. To have a committal against one's will is surely a serious matter, and one would not want it to happen just because some person wanted a person committed. Even the mentally ill have legal rights, and these should by all means be protected. Having said that, it is also important to note how emotionally wrenching it is for a family member to experience such a procedure as a necessary means to treatment. It is one thing to sit in a doctor's office and hear that your spouse needs to be hospitalized. It is quite another thing to hear the same verdict being given by a Judge.

The whole atmosphere in the court room is not the most conducive place to be making health decisions. So we are saying, while necessary, the court appearance for the purposes of committal is not a nonchalant and untroubled happening in the life of a spouse. Later on in this chapter we will read about another court appearance that was probably more upsetting for my mother in some ways than this one.

Bill joined the Army Nov. 2, 1948. Married Rejean Wilson Jan. 4, 1952.

There was one bittersweet development that helped her out financially. I was the oldest and had had some summer work on the David Huff Farm, and my sow and pigs had been sold. I shared those dollars with the family because at this point we needed to eat and have clothes to wear. Much

more will be said about this period when we write about the wonderful community and church support. I left for Taylor University in northeast Indiana and worked there in the dining hall for tuition. My brother Bill joined the Army, and my sister married Butch Huff, the next door neighbor, and they moved to the north part of the state.

Gene and Stella married August 28, 1949.

Mom was left with her youngest son, Tommy, who was still in school and only twelve when Dad left in 1948. Now there were two mouths to feed

and not five. A Sullivan businessman remarked to Mom that we all left at a bad time; "abandoned her," he said actually. Those words reinforced her feeling that we had done just that. How much we all are unaware of the influence of our words when speaking to anyone already burdened. None of us were able to do much in the way of support. My work didn't pay the tuition. Sister

Mary married Charles "Butch" Huff January 30, 1949

255

Mary was starting a family, and Bill sent his allotment check of twenty dollars a month. She was pretty much on her own and yet with fewer groceries and clothes to buy.

On balance she was some better off, but it still was that "rough road" in every respect. Even if it looks to this son as a break for her, her recent statement about it reveals how much she felt abandoned by those who had no choice but to move on. This was probably the worst emotionally-stressful period of her life. Dad's illness before he left, the vacancy afterwards,

The youngest, Tom, was 12 years of age when Dad left for Woodmere.

and the continual financial strain, and a young son to provide for with, at least, the necessities of life. The Texas Oil Company lease was a break, for only one year, but would there be others? She thought so in spite of the fact that the School Fund was about to be dissolved, and with that confidence she sought another source of funding.

That source of revenue would be primarily from three sources, a job or jobs, farm income, and other loans to save the farm and maintain the house.

First, transportation and the job. If you

One of her first bills was this delinquent tax due bill for the farm and house. $30.16 was a great lot of money for her at this time.

256

have a job, you need transportation. Our last car had been a 1936 Chevy. It had always been a chore to keep it going, and it is a wonder it lasted as long as it did since many repairs were made by my brother and me. It must have quit for good about 1946, and from then on we relied on neighbors, the Ferrees, and others for transportation. When Mom got her first job after Dad left, she needed a car. Her son-in-law, Butch, found one in South Bend, an old Pontiac, for fifty dollars and brought it to her.

By August she was on her first job at the Bus Station on the Northeast corner of the Sullivan Square. There she waited tables for fifteen dollars a week. After three months she was fired. Sure, she hated to lose the job but would not let that defeat her. Another employee had taken Mom's tip money and put it in the jukebox. Mom had learned long ago how to take care of herself and to protect herself. She complained to the management, and being the new one on the crew and of another generation, she was the one to leave.

The Graysville School cooks 1951-1956: L-R Mabel Setzer, Ninas Kasinger, and Fleda Gilbreath, all three widowed and in need of work.

She soon found other jobs doing housekeeping chores. The Walkers of the Index Store, a five and ten notion business

257

frequented by all Sullivan Countians, was one of those places. Another employer was the Melvin Custers who owned and operated the Marathon Service Center on old US 41 in the midst of town. Melvin and Gladys had two children so Mom also did a lot of baby sitting. These jobs lasted for six years, and this house work was done for fifty cents an hour.

In 1951 she started a second job working at the school cafeteria for $38.40 for a two-week pay period. Now she could give my kid brother more money for school expenses including those needed for basketball. He became captain of the team, and Mom with understandable pride tried to do the best she could for him through his high school days. Mom had been given this cafeteria job by Earl "Buddy" McElwain, who had been our driver for most of our school career. She was part of a team that consisted of three ladies who needed assistance like Mom. She had learned how to have good working relationships with others and found these jobs to be rewarding not only for the financial gain but for the opportunity to make friends and enjoy the companionship of others.

This cafeteria job lasted until 1956 when she moved beyond the local scene and sought employment away from home. At the time she sought another job, a new trustee was wanting her to divide her time and her meager pay with a new employee for whom the trustee was wanting to provide work. Mom was sympathetic to the woman's need for a job but did not agree that splitting the meager income would be of much value to either one of them. Later we will return to this theme of employment to support herself and keep the property she and Dad had purchased.

The second source of income during the first twenty-seven years of Dad's absence was the farm. The soil of these twenty-five acres was very unproductive when the farm was purchased so the yield was always meager. Sometimes a five or ten acre field was used for pasture for the cows, horse, and the hogs. One year Dad had succeeded in raising five acres of tomatoes for the canning factory at Terre Haute. That produced about as much income as would a crop of corn or beans, and it was a project requiring family assistance.

One year in an effort to build up the soil, Dad planted soybeans and turned them under. One could see the difference right to a row when next year's crop came up. However, since his illness came on so soon after the purchase, he had little time to enrich the soil as he might have done had he remained well. Another half acre was used for a garden for several years after the place was bought.

In the first years when we had livestock, most of the grain produced was used to feed the cows, hogs, horse, and chickens. The average net income from the farm, using years 1959-62 and 1963-74 for which there are reliable records, was only five hundred and sixty-nine dollars. Surely, with that average, no one could think that Mom became rich off of the farm. It wouldn't have bought her groceries if she had been unable to work at other

259

jobs. It did not meet the continual mortgage payments due each year needed to pay off the loans required for maintenance and improvements on the house and transportation costs.

Would a judge later rule that half of that average income was accrued equity as an estate of Dad's since he and Mom had originally purchased the land together? Lily Tomlin, an American comedian, said it best, "We're all in this together - by ourselves."[115] And so it was for Mom on the farm; however, the state would consider it togetherness when in reality it was Mom alone.

Beside the jobs and the farm, Mom relied on loans to have money to complete special projects. Loans were a way of life for her from the time they bought the farm in 1941 until she paid off her last loan related to it in 1975 at sixty-five years of age. The third loan would be the smallest one for one hundred twenty-five dollars in July, 1950. The loan was taken out with Fidelity Loan Company at one and a half percent interest per month, the highest interest rate she would pay. While this was a small loan, it was for a very important project.

In 1950 Mom would experience electricity for the first time in her home. Kerosene lamps had been the order of the day. Now each room would have a ceiling light and a receptacle on each wall. Also, she could get a toaster and a hot plate. She could dream about one day getting an electric washer

---

[115] Reference unknown

when the old gas-powered Maytag would quit running. First things first, though, so it wasn't long until she found a used refrigerator to replace the old icebox. Best of all would be the day when there was indoor plumbing made possible by an electrical pump.

A small loan? Nearly fifty years later it is difficult to comprehend what such improvements meant to her. The only time now when we really appreciate living in an electrical world is during a power failure. So she finally had transportation, and now she had electricity. Even though the new power system came later than most in our country side, it was received with gratitude and, of course, the payments of eleven dollars a month for the loan and now a new utility bill. Also, thanks would go to son, Bill, who not only was serving his country but had sent his allotment check home, and Mom used it for collateral for this loan.

The Texas Oil Company lease mentioned earlier was the third occasion to go back to court, the first two being related to the commitments of Dad to the hospitals at Indianapolis and Evansville. This trip to court would be the first of three in order to deal with guardianship questions. Since this involved a legality regarding the land, a guardian had to be appointed to protect Dad's interests.

Murry Frakes, a trusted and competent neighbor, would be appointed and remain the guardian until 1975, making regular reports to the court as ordered. You will remember that the Frakes family lived next door to us at

261

Grandma Gilbreath's Place on State Road 154. Actually, they now lived about a quarter of a mile across the field from Mom. It had been Murry who did the wiring of the house in 1950. He would approve of other loans to make improvements on the property. He was a carpenter, electrician, and farmer by trade and had good advice when it was solicited.

We will remember that Mom had already experienced several remodeling jobs in her childhood or youth, as well as the major one from the tornado damage in 1935. In May of 1956 another one thousand dollar loan was obtained from the School Fund to pay off the balance of the 1944 loan, to liquidate tax debt, and to make more improvements. This project involved a new bath and running water to the kitchen. Finally after a six-year wait, her dream of indoor plumbing and running water was realized.

The improvements came at just the time when she felt it necessary to seek better employment and that meant being away from home. At that time I was pastor of two small churches near the state line close to Danville, Illinois. If she could find a job there, she could stay at our house for the next two years. She found work at a sewing factory called the Opelika Manufacturing Corporation in Danville. The first several weeks were very difficult.

She had done sewing all her life. She says she doesn't remember not sewing. Her mother had done it before her, making most all the clothes for the family. They had the old treadle sewing machine, a fascination to a

262

youngster, so much so that Mom tried as a child to see how it worked. She learned it quite naturally having watched and then practiced.

Also, she had been using that talent to sew for her children, husband, and mother-in-law. However, such skills did not help any on this job. These were factory machines that operated much differently than the old treadle ones. Her confidence wavered a little here as she struggled to make the company quota, but at last she succeeded. Her tenure there was for fifteen years making from about one dollar and fifty cents an hour to almost two dollars.

These were Mom's friends at the Snowers, the sewing factory, at Danville, Illinois. L-R Mary Bratton Sterling, Estella Schendel, Lucille Clemmons (with whom Mom stayed some of the time), Mary ?, Naomi Smally (1st cousin of Butch Huff), and Fleda Gilbreath. This were her support group during the work week. The car to the left was Mom's first new one, the 1952 Chevrolet.

While money was important during these years, there were other significant issues. I was transferred to another area, and Mom found apartments for her weekday stays. She rented an apartment for twenty dollars a month for six years at the home of a retired minister and wife, the Knights, in Perrysville where we had lived. For nine years she lived in Danville where she paid thirty-five dollars a month.

During these fifteen years she was away from old friends although she made some new ones. The farm and her Sullivan County home always demanded her attention. Being able to maintain the home was the chief reason for seeking better employment. This was part of her determination to preserve and enhance what she and Dad had begun.

At forty-seven years of age she was introduced to factory work, a different routine than she had ever experienced before. Life previously was filled with varied responsibilities which were never monotonous. So while she made more money than ever before, the new experience of factory work, being alone and away from friends, and still being concerned about the home front made these years difficult ones. Among the most stressful aspects of this stay was carrying the silent burden of Dad's absence and his inability to share the responsibilities, an inescapable strain regardless of where she worked.

Mom traveled home every weekend if weather permitted, about a hundred mile each way, and attended to the home maintenance and worshipped in her home church. To make this drive more trouble free, she purchased her first new car, a 1962 Chevrolet purchased at Cayuga, Indiana, near her weekday abode. Her practical outlook on life is reflected in her choice of this low priced car. This new one was replaced by another new one, a 1964 Chevrolet Biscayne purchased at Walter's Chevrolet in Farmersburg. Another used car, a Ford Fairlane, would also provide her the necessary and reliable transportation between Danville and Sullivan.

Her third new car was a 1974 Ford Maverick which she bought with net income from the purchase and sale of her mother's property. The next used one was a 1981 Olds which she still drove around town at ninety years of age. The significance of these car deals is found in her need to have transportation to work and to oversee the home property. Also, we note that these cars were not top line vehicles, even the new ones. Any pleasure, such as a new or good used car, was paid for out of her own hard-earned cents. Again, we will later see that an attempt by the state to recoup expenses for Dad's care was quite inappropriate from Mom's perspective.

During this fifteen year period, several necessary repairs and improvements were made to the Sullivan County property. These would necessitate more loans and more responsibilities for regular payments. Mom was the sole caretaker, and she would do all she could to make sure that maintenance was provided. During these years she put all the money she could into this maintenance and improvements.

Her records show no frills or unnecessary expenditures. She didn't drink, smoke, attend the movies, go to the beauty shop regularly, buy expensive clothes, nor eat the best cuts of meat. She paid the rent, the utilities, insurance on the house, car, and her medical, and Dad's one-thousand-dollar life policy, his canteen fund at the hospital and his clothes, her medical and dentist bills, her church contribution, and the rest for loan payments.

The loans enabled several projects. In 1960 there was a loan for one thousand one hundred eighty-nine dollars to pay off the old loan and to repair the foundation under the house. A furnace, the first central heating, was installed in 1964, and the house was further insulated.

Another loan in 1965 for two thousand dollars paid off the School Fund loan and a bank loan leaving about eight hundred seventy-five dollars for more repairs in 1966. Those improvements included new ceilings, siding and insulation, rebuilding of windows, and painting. Here are enough modest and necessary improvements to demonstrate that Mom through her own initiative, ingenuity, and resolve kept the property in good repair and did it conservatively.

In 1970 Mom quit her job in Danville and returned home. She received employment as a cook at the Miller's Manor Nursing Home in Sullivan. She worked there for about four years until she developed heart problems in 1974 that necessitated her retirement from that job. This was not only a time of coming home but also finding new avenues for income. With as many loans as she had paid off giving her excellent credit, why not try acquiring some other real estate?

Her mother died in 1970, leaving Mom as the administratrix for her Sullivan home on Beech Street. You guessed it, Mom borrowed six thousand dollars and paid off some debts, did more to her home, and paid thirty-two hundred dollars for my grandmother's home. The house was rented for two years to my uncle and his wife.

Another loan was secured, and the property next door was purchased for nine hundred dollars. That house was torn down, much of it by Mom and some grandchildren. After Mom's brother, Vernia, and wife Oleta moved out, there was an opportunity to sell the two properties for seven thousand dollars. The net gain paid off the indebtedness, and the profit was transformed into the new 1974 Maverick.

By now Mom was realizing her physical limitations and thought she would like to move to town. There had been many routine jobs such as pump repair, a new water heater, yard mowing, sewer work, and many more in the last ten years to keep the Davis Place up to par. A carport was added in 1974, that being the largest outlay at about seven hundred dollars. Again we should note that she was paying insurance, buying clothes for Dad, and contributing to his canteen fund on a regular basis, and paying on loans from her income. Increased farm produce prices for this period would help, but these came too late to help with the expenses during the difficult years.

The critical change would come as Mom finally decided, given health and age, that she should move to town. She would begin procedures in

267

1975 to trade the farm for a place in Sullivan owned by her grandson, Kenneth. This started a series of events in which the State of Indiana Department of Mental Health demanded payment of $63,765.36 for Dad's care while at Woodmere. This was an amount many times greater than the appraised value of the property which Mom alone had struggled to save and maintain. Not having been notified of such a lien by 1975, she proceeded to do what seemed to be right for her health and well-being.

The trading of the properties demanded a series of legalities. So she was back to court to get herself appointed as guardian. Murry had decided not to continue. While such a move could not have been done at the first guardianship appointment, such a move was now legally permissible, and she was appointed Dad's guardian in June, 1975. The Judge of the Sullivan Circuit Court at the same time gave the authorization for the guardian to trade real estate. This was done only after legal research was done, preparing and accounting for the former guardianship, appraising both properties, and all other necessary details of the transfer.

Mom gained ten thousand dollars from the transfer which was evenly divided between paying off her last loan and making necessary improvements to the new property. These included some new carpet, storm windows, new pump and furnace, paint, roofing repairs, refrigerator, and other smaller items. All these were completed in the following year and a half and exhausted the funds.

At last she was settled in and reasonably comfortable in her new location. This modest home was large enough to have her family in for special occasions such as Christmas gatherings. While not able to do heavy work as at the nursing home, she enjoyed serving weekday lunches to her daughter and family who were in the plumbing business nearby. I was reconstructing an old log cabin not far away and did often drop in, too, and enjoyed the time with Mom and other family members. Also, my youngest brother was often there as an employee of the same business.

Mom liked to cook, and my sister made sure there was something in the pantry for the weekday lunches. She was a good cook and found it very difficult to enjoy the food at nursing homes where she would be a few times before her death. Mom had taken her Social Security in 1973, and the less than one hundred fifty dollars a month wasn't enough to pay all the bills. Determined to do all she could for herself, she did laundry for a local doctor's office. Would you believe that this relative calm in her life was about to cease?

On August 5 (my birthday), 1976, Dad was transferred to the Clay County rest home called Macanell. This event has been described in the chapter about Dad's medical care. Here, however, the story takes on a different hue. Mom was notified of the impending change. She objected because Dad had run away several times, and this would put him much closer to home. The old fears of him returning home unannounced, as he

269

had almost accomplished more than once, understandably erupted. That fear is understandable to us as a family but not so well understood by the state.

The hospital officials assured Mom that he had not attempted to run away for some time, and anyhow the state had decreed that the patients would be moved out for community-based care. We have discussed the pros and cons of that in the last chapter as a hindsight reflection. At that point in time it was not hindsight for my mother. The hospital could not give a date for the transfer and subsequently notified her after the fact. This episode shook her confidence no small amount.

Runaways did continue to be attempted, but soon Mom had more disturbing news to consider. The state would no longer be responsible for his care. This was now a private matter, and the spouse was the one responsible. Aahha! Now he has been decreed well (which he wasn't) and now his care was up to Mom. She had worked to make sure she was not a burden on society and was now settled with a roof over her head in a secure and modest location. But how was she to pay for his care on the meager income just mentioned? So it was back to seeking legal advice once more.

She decided, after encouragement by a local attorney, that divorce was part of the answer. What a difficult decision for a woman who didn't believe in it on religious grounds and who had not entertained the thought for all these thirty years. It was true that there was no marriage in any respect except in the heart. Finally she did what many others have done when the state has so interfered in private affairs and made such a choice inevitable. The bottom line had always been for these many years to save the farm and to secure herself for her declining years.

Terrible as it seemed, she decided she had no choice but to get the divorce to protect what she had so struggled to gain. The divorce never lessened her visits to see my Dad, nor the money spent for clothes or the canteen fund. This was a legal issue and in her mind one on paper only. When Dad died, her name appeared as his wife, as it should have, because in her heart he was still her husband.

She was advised that she could transfer Dad's half of the property to herself, giving her complete control of the property. In order to do that, she needed to resign as guardian and have my sister appointed. That was done in 1978, and my sister by the authority granted by the Judge produced a guardian's deed that made my mother sole owner of the property. Given the history of who paid the bills and her commitment to that task, the judge decreed that such a transfer was appropriate.

Now she could legally file for Medicaid in Clay County for Dad's expenses. She did that, and as is routine, the Department of Public Welfare of the county did their investigation as to his qualifications for support. The investigation included, as it should have, all these aforementioned transactions for the preceding thirty years. The Department concluded that

271

all those steps were legal and legitimate and were not impediments to granting care for Dad. All this activity came to a conclusion at the proper time. On the day the court procedures were finalized, Mom received a certification of assistance from Clay County Welfare. What a sigh of relief when she knew that the bill would now be paid by Medicaid.

The reader should note that all legal steps were taken as advised by the attorneys and approved by the judge for the transfer of property or sometimes for the securing of a loan. Please note that this lady who had no training in such matters was relying on the legal profession to steer her right. What neither the attorneys, judges, nor Mom knew was that the State of Indiana's Department of Mental Health had filed a lien against the Sullivan property on January 18, 1977, for Dad's care at Woodmere for $63,725.36. The lien had not been discovered during the Medicaid investigation.

At that time the law in Indiana allowed a lien to be placed on property without the notification of the owner. The amount was enough shock in itself, but Mom had believed that she was exempt from such assessment. She had notices from the Department at various stages of Dad's confinement that relieved her of any responsibility. No such notice had been given since the Acts 1971, Public Law 221, had been passed.

References from two different communications reveal the problem. One in 1951 simply states that Mom was exempt from paying the ten dollar per week maintenance fee. The latest one in 1970 spells out that only Mom,

272

personally, was exempt from payment and not Dad nor any other relative who might be legally responsible. To confuse the issue further, the notice of lien states specifically that Mom is a responsible relative. A state senatorial investigation found that she was fully released from any previous obligation. It should be noted that the existing state law of 1951 stated that a husband, wife, father, mother, or adult children were severally liable for maintenance payment.

Two issues here make this case difficult. When one is told they are not liable, then they tend to think and act as if it is true. If communications are lax on the true import of not being liable, the state's responsibility, then one can easily misconstrue the law. Further if attorneys and judges interpret the law differently than would a state official, then there isn't clarity as to the ramifications of the law. So one issue is the question of clarity and communication regarding the law, a state responsibility in both the construction of the law and in its communication of a department's official policy.

The other issue is the natural response of a family member, in this case, my mother. We have spent a significant portion of this chapter showing how she worked to save and improve this property. In fact and feeling she owned this property, a fact that no average citizen would deny. Had she been given her day in court with a trial by jury, as was requested rather than just a hearing, we can surmise that a jury would have ruled in her favor. From her

273

perspective she had earned the right to the assets and the right to exchange those for more adequate accommodations given her age and health.

Was she expected to go on welfare in order to satisfy the lien? How else did the state expect this to be played out? The reimbursement director of the Department indicated that no sale of property was being required to satisfy the lien. Mom had only to not make any transaction that would require a clear title. That would mean that she could not trade properties. Now if that isn't affecting her assets, then what is?

You are free from the obligation, the state would argue, but do not do anything with that which you rightfully own or you will see just how free you are not. Also, one would have to question what would have happened had she chosen not to trade. At her death, one would assume the state would have taken the property in its entirety given its low value and not have acknowledged the one-half that, according to them, belonged to Mom.

So what does this lady do who does not take "No" for an answer when she is sure of her grounds? She commenced her defense and with her usual confidence. She left no stone unturned. The assistance of the Director of the Vigo County Mental Health Association was sought. Mom went to the library and read the Public Laws that had been sited. She writes to her governmental representatives both federal and state. She consults the array of judges, attorneys, and other authorities who have previously assisted with her case.

There are exchanges of letters with the State Mental Health Department. She states her case over and over attempting to show that she alone had saved and maintained the property. The Clay County Department of Public Welfare was convinced of the veracity of her claim, but the state maintained their position that the lien was legitimate. It defies any logic, but they somehow believed that they could collect that amount from Dad's interest in the property.

The record showed that Dad had only contributed a total of one hundred dollars very early-on based on a marital fifty-fifty division. As we have indicated, not even both properties together could have satisfied that lien. Why the state never accepted the former transactions as being both legitimate and legally binding is somewhat a mystery.

One has to conclude that the law stated they were entitled to make the claim, and make it they would in face of a loss. Political appointees sometimes have a way of protecting their careers by showcasing their authority. No other explanation makes any sense in this case. Mom's confidence and cents made sense in this case but the state would have to take her to court to prove it.

The state's case was built upon my mother's fraudulent activity, they alleged, which served to delay and defraud creditors, specifically the State Department of Mental Health. There were no other creditors at her door and never had been except right in the beginning as we explained, ones she

275

took care of as she could. One wonders why they did not sue the various attorneys and judges who were party to her fraud. How ridiculous, yes, of course. I suspect they did not dare, given the expertise available to refute their claim. Numerous attempts were made to negotiate with both the Attorney General's office and the Reimbursement office of the Department. While there were occasional overtures, never did the state alter their first demand.

So Mom found herself before the judge in a hearing and without a trial by jury. There she was humiliated by the state's prosecutor who was determined to win the case at all costs. A typical action by attorneys who know they don't have a case. This included personal attacks on my mother's character and reputation. A jury of her peers would have been outraged. The suffering of this spouse had been enough. Mom still held her head high and awaited the judge's ruling.

That ruling came on November 10, 1980. The judge found that the guardian's deed that transferred the property to Mom was invalid and unenforceable and that the lien was good and valid. The judge ruled that my mother had contributed forty-four hundred dollars towards Dad's half interest. What was that judge thinking? Mom had secured more in loans than that amount and paid them off. The appraised value of the property was fourteen thousand and eight hundred dollars, indicating that Dad's half was worth seven thousand and four hundred dollars. Since Mom had only contributed forty-four hundred to his half, that left, according to the judge's convoluted calculations, Mom owing the state three thousand dollars plus court costs. Over a period of time, the debt was finally paid, unfair as it was.

Many questions will always remain. It isn't clear how the judge arrived at such neat figures. The chances of that constellation of figures are astronomical, and quite unbelievable given her efforts through the thirty-two years. The notice of lien itself was faulty giving one land description and giving another address. The lien was "Johnny come lately" in 1977 since the properties had been traded in 1975 without such encumbrance.

Also the bill presented by the state lacks credibility. Twelve summarized entries accounted for the total. Maybe that was all that was needed given only a few changes in the rates directed by law. It was obviously prepared after the fact; no running total had ever been shared with Mom.

There was one glaring omission in the accounting. The law stated that patients during part of this time were to be paid for their services. No such accounting is given. You will remember that we have discussed the importance of work for these patients and that Dad was always happier when engaged in some meaningful work schedule. His medical record is clear that he worked most of the time and several hours a day having one day off each week. Just for fun, let's say he worked for twenty-five cents an hour, four hours a day, for 300 days of the year. In twenty-eight years, he should have been credited with eighty-four hundred dollars.

277

Further the state had by law discretionary powers regarding adjusting claims and were by law not to be arbitrary. The last entry of charges covers a period including from August 5 to November 5, a period of time when he was not at Woodmere, having been transferred to Clay County. That amounts to an almost three thousand dollar mistake in bookkeeping. There are other issues which we will forego, all of which indicate that justice was not done. Nothing said here indicates lack of appreciation for the services given to Dad through so many years. We have already spoken of this and restate it.

However, given the circumstances of this case, all documented, we believe the state inflicted an unnecessary burden on one who by all accounts had played by the rules and contributed all she could toward Dad's welfare as well as her obligation to the state. In speaking with Mom just a few days ago and mentioning these issues, she said, "That is all water over the dam." So now with confidence she did the right thing, obeying the court's interpretation of the law, she puts it behind her and goes on to the next challenge. That challenge in some ways hasn't changed. Her battle is still to remain independent as she confronts failing health and the desire to remain on her own.

Mom continued doing the laundry for the doctor and selling her Studio Girl products well into her eighties. During the last half of the 1980s, she faithfully visited me with her goodies in hand thirty mile away while I was

278

confined. In the early and mid nineties she made the trip west of Sullivan to do the same for my sister who is crippled with rheumatoid arthritis. During this same period she would make sure her friends had groceries, or they would take a ride out into the countryside or around town. These later years were still productive and rewarding yet being quite different than the preceding thirty and more years.

We said that she paid off her last loan related to the farm in 1975, but that would not be her last. This lady remained mentally keen and could not turn down another opportunity to make another dollar. The necessity of a cash flow to meet her personal needs hadn't gone away. When her brother and his wife died in 1982 and their home on Court Street was eventually due for foreclosure, the veteran of loan making with good credit was back in the harness. She borrowed five thousand dollars and made the purchase.

My brother, Tom, and Mom remodeled it and rented it to a lady for ten years. She was an excellent renter, and Mom profited from this transaction by a sale for eleven thousand dollars. Mom knew that sometime she probably would have to give up the home purchased in 1975 and go to an apartment so there was a need for reserve. She was so grateful for this profitable adventure that she expressed it this way, "So really God has been good to me. I've always said if one door was closed, God always opened a better one for me."

In April, 1991, she had foot surgery and that finalized a decision to move to my sister's apartment building. There was only one more real estate transaction that of selling her home to my brother after he had rented it for over a year. He then bought it on contract for fifteen thousand dollars in 1992 and refinanced it through a bank in August, 1995. Now there was money to pay the rent at the apartment.

Now Mom and daughter, Mary, in a new relationship, one of mutual benefit, in the apartment business. (Mary standing over Mom's left shoulder).

However, Mom didn't just sit in the apartment and write a check for rent

Mom at Mary's apartment building at 11 N. State Street. This is her last car, '81 Olds, still drivable in 2003. The author used it to transport her to Terre Haute where she stayed with us during recuperation from her cataract surgeries in 2002. An excellent driver she was and quit on her own before a bad accident.

money each month. Soon after she moved to the apartment, she was given the opportunity to work out some of the rent. How would this lady do that? You could easily and correctly call her the apartment manager. My sister did the interviews with potential renters, and Mom handled many of the responsibilities of a manager. She collected the rent and deposited the funds for several years while still able to get to the bank.

Renters knocked on her door with their complaints. If repairs were to be done, the various service people scheduled with Mom and got the necessary keys from her. When adjustments for heat were needed, she was the lady to do the regulating. The laundry room across the hall was monitored as well as the parking places. More recently she couldn't navigate the many stairs so other family members did investigations whenever they were indicated. It was not until 2001 that she was replaced as manager, or as the family jokingly says, "Fired, at 92 years old! Age discrimination!"

So it is with great pleasure, admiration, and love that I close this chapter about my mother who has been confident and adequate to the task for the forty-seven years of Dad's confinement, as well as several years before. In a very small and inadequate way we have shed light on her life's "dash." This is really the short

The five of us, Mary, Bill, Mom on front row and Tom and Gene standing, a rare gathering in the last five years of her life. Gathered at Christmas time at Tom's beside the genealogy screen that her grandaughter, Sue, had compiled of Mom's family line. Mom had almost completed the sorting of pictures for each of us. She needed only 3 or 4 more days to complete the task before her death.

281

version of the "dash" having not explored so much of her inner thoughts and feelings out of respect for her privacy.

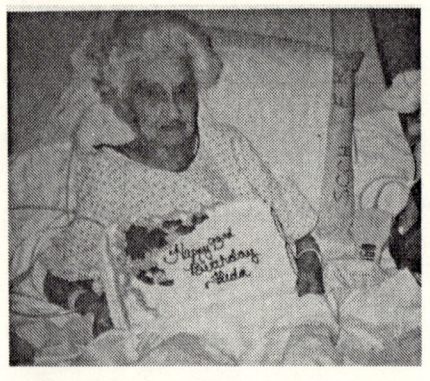

Celebrating her 93rd birthday in her next to last trip to the hospital, November, 27, 2002, holding the cake so lovingly provided by her ex-daughter-in-law, Joan Campbell Gilbreath.

Since this book has the theme of mental health, it is hoped that her life is a testimony that emotional health can be enhanced in difficult circumstances. Whatever leadership role we play, it is important to understand how critical early training is as a foundation for an effective life. It is likewise crucial that we have acceptable and meaningful goals which we pursue with confidence. Further, her life suggests to us that we learn how to handle setbacks gracefully and with renewed determination to begin again. Another component for mental health is having a cause in which you wholeheartedly believe and for which you will give your life. Mom's story illustrates all of these. One important ingredient in her life, her religious faith, will be discussed more fully in the next chapter.

Among Mom's papers are several poems that gave her inspiration and courage for these years. One, simple and yet profound, expresses something of the driving power behind this lady who succeeded in accomplishing her goal against great odds.

You Tell on Yourself

> "You tell on yourself by the friends you keep,
>
> By the very manner in which you speak,
>
> By the way you employ your leisure time,
>
> By the use you make of nickel and dime.
>
> You tell on yourself by the things you wear,
>
> By the things you think, the burdens you bear.
>
> By the kind of things at which you laugh,
>
> And the life you reap, whether wheat or chaff.
>
> You tell what you are by the way you walk,
>
> By the things of which you delight to talk,
>
> By the manner in which you bear defeat,
>
> By so simple a thing as the way you eat."[116]

On January 20, 2003, Mom passed away at ninety-three. She had been in the hospital and nursing home for about six weeks and, with her usual determination, was planning to return to her apartment on the very day of her death. By the way, she had read all of this book up through this chapter,

---

[116] Source unknown

Gene Gilbreath

made a few corrections, mother-like, and was pleased. In my "Final Tribute"

you will see her making her final contribution to this work.

KNEELING TO DANCE

Chapter 7

"Some seek bread; and some seek wealth and ease; and some seek fame, but all are seeking rest." - Frederick Langbridge, English clergyman and author (1849-1922).

Dear Dad,

We come to the closing chapter of this attempt to make sense out of your many years of incapacitation. I am not so sure that I have done justice to such a complex subject. It has been enlightening to me to take the time to consider in this form what you must have experienced.

While helpful to me, my writing falls short of understanding your life away from your family. That fact is humbling because we all need to recognize that the understanding of mental illness and its treatment is far from perfection. Hopefully, we will all continue the search for preventive and curative measures. Dad, if writing about your emotional and mental turmoil helps someone, lay or professional, to do a better job in this cause, then I will feel compensated for this effort.

285

But, Dad, there is one aspect of our experience that we have only alluded to so far. Being last does not make it of lesser importance. Church, you remember, was such a vital part of our life. I wonder how much you were able, in your mental state, to draw upon the strength and comfort of our faith. It was comforting to me when you acknowledged your faith in the Great Shepherd on the day before you died.

I will not try to argue here in this chapter about the existence of God. This chapter is not meant to prove anything but to be just a sharing of our story as has been true throughout this book. I will try to leave behind my professional training in religion, inasmuch as that might be possible.

Here I want to only tell our story of the importance of believing in something, someone, beyond ourselves. In the above quote Frederick Langbridge reminds us that we all proceed with our life with some focus or purpose. We will acknowledge our need for such centering and hopefully help the readers to see how our choice of focus served us well.

Now, Dad, having come this far and put on paper my interpretation of the events of your and our lives, I now forever "let you go" and let you rest in that home where no mental illness can strike. We just pray that this illumination of our experience will serve to strengthen, encourage, and guide other individuals and families who must endure this kind of illness and hardship. If that happens, Dad, your life and times will not have been lived in vain.

My, how time passes so quickly, and we have so much to do for the cause of mental health. We leave you with great appreciation for what you have taught us all through your suffering.

Thanks be to God, Dad, for you!

Love, Gene

"Your faithfulness extends to every generation, like the earth you created; it endures by your decree, for everything serves your plans." Psalms 119:91 The Living Bible Version

"Intellect alone is a dry and rattling thing." — Ilka Chase, American - author, actress, humorist (1905-1978).

"I believe that man will not merely endure: he will prevail. He is immortal, not because he alone among creatures has an inexhaustible voice, but because he has a soul, a spirit capable of compassion and sacrifice and endurance." — William Faulkner, American author (1897-1962).

"We do not become free by refusing to acknowledge something above us, but by respecting something above us." —Goethe

Many, many famous people from all walks of life have left some kind of personal testimony to the importance of faith. We could easily fill a chapter with those kinds of quotes. What an impressive display that would be. In fact, many a book has been written about what others have said about this or that topic. Many good books have been so written. Such writings show that the author is well read and knows the topic very well. Such anthologies have their rightful place in literary circles.

Our approach or method here is different. We want simply to share how we survived this ordeal that lasted nearly a half century. Sometimes those celebrating a hundred years of life are asked by friends and reporters the secret to their longevity. Maybe you have asked, too, how we as a family managed to cope with a husband and father afflicted with mental illness for so very long.

First, we have already hinted at some ways, but further elaboration is very important since herein we find some critical ingredients for mental health. These "roads to travel" require a conscious decision on our part. Too often mental health is something we take for granted, like breathing. Only a little thought encourages us to take conscious steps to enhance that breathing capability. For instance, when we go to a restaurant, we quite deliberately ask for a table in a nonsmoking area. To reply to the hostess that it doesn't matter is a decision to ignore what we have learned is best for healthy pulmonary function. Improved mental health dictates that we take advantage of what we have learned and apply them to our daily living.

So here we share some of what to us were steps to take to assist in our own survival; physical, mental and spiritual. These in no way were "miracle" pills that took away all the pain. However, sources of strength, comfort, and direction they definitely were. We harbored no unrealistic expectation of Dad's recovery, especially after the first two or three years. Even when we had hope early on, we knew we had to move on with living without him. There were cows to milk and hogs to feed. There was planting time and then harvest, seasons demanding action, if we were to physically and emotionally survive.

Once when I was a youth, my employer, David Huff, helped me to realize a better way to deal with such an impossible situation. I was attempting a religious fast that day. Somehow from my various church associations, I had gotten the idea that if we prayed hard enough, had faith enough, or fast long enough, God would honor that effort giving to us what we asked.

My, what arrogance on my part that I could demand that of God. I learned that I would not be special by God removing Dad's affliction but I was special by receiving His help in coping with that which I could not change. More later about what I think living by faith means. For now as it was then, I learned that one best handle life's difficult times by working within the midst of those troubles rather than seeking their magical disappearance. This approach fits best as one of our coping skills. Religion is misguided when it encourages us to seek miracles that are not in keeping with the reality of the situation. There is a fine line between

The Mt. Tabor Methodist Episcopal Church built in 1871. It had its beginnings as early as 1851 in a log church just west of this one in the old cemetery. This is the place where we discovered the importance of faith.

accepting what is inevitable and yet not giving up hope.

Was that approach easy to accomplish? Did I do that in a week or a month or a year? No. I was in my first year of college when Dad left for Woodmere to begin his forty-seven year journey in confinement. I worried, as the eldest, about my mother and my siblings. Should I go home and delay my schooling? Mother in her take-action approach would suggest I stay in school. I thank her now for that long-range view. That decision would not be an easy one for me. A psychology professor at school helped me through some very difficult days. Even one little chat with him put me on the road of which I speak. Worry, he suggested, if I must for a short period, but understanding that such action changed nothing.

Worry, if you insist as a result of previous conditioning, for just a little while and get on with what had to be done. In that case, it was working in the dining hall for 25 cents an hour to help pay my tuition. In that case I was also concentrating on my studies to fulfill my career objectives. Just recently I discovered that my mother did feel abandoned by my not being there, and later on by the leaving of her other two oldest children. Yet Mom did as I am suggesting here, put her hand to the plow and plowed ahead for her sake, Dad's, and for the kid brother left at home. However, her love for us never wavered. Please note here that we are talking about how we as a family coped and not how Dad coped. However, one must not assume that mentally ill persons cannot follow some of this same advice. Only those who are psychotic can be expected to assist not as much in their own recovery and adjustment.

One of the earliest things we did for ourselves was to seek medical advice. It didn't take our beloved family doctor, James B. Maple, long to see something was radically wrong with my father. In his quiet and efficient way, he took the history and first concluded that Dad was suffering from inflammation around the lining of the brain. Indeed that was a most likely diagnosis given the history of the flu with high temperature. One cannot say that he would not have avoided all those years confined had he lived many years later and benefited from modern antibiotic treatment. Playing that game now of "What might have been" serves no helpful purpose at this point in time, nor for our mental health.

It is instructive, however, to realize that when one is faced with a serious medical problem, it is well to secure some advice from the experts. As a child I had appendicitis, and we didn't know what to do. The surgeon, Dr. Irvin Scott, did know and saved my life since the appendix was ready to rupture.

It serves us well to know when to admit our lack of knowledge and seek the input of others. After your reading of the chapter about Dad's medical record, you realize that I have a few quarrels with the delivery of medicine at many levels. Did that keep me from choosing to have prostate cancer surgery last spring? No. Why?

Simply put, I knew the urologist knew more than I did about urology and had an abundance of experience far exceeding mine. I knew so little that he had to draw me pictures. We get along best in life if we know when to ask for assistance. Such is not my easiest task to accomplish. I'll manage this ok myself, thank you. I often pay the price for such arrogance. I suspect my mother also paid a dear price for acting on the same idea of managing the problem herself. She accomplished the task, as we have seen, but nonetheless, it might have been much easier to have reached out for help in more ways and more often.

Medical experts are not the only ones we can turn to for expertise. Some of us learn the hard way that we should have called a plumber. So whatever assistance might make our life more productive and rewarding, it would be best to reach out for a helping hand. That helping hand might be a professional or maybe just a friend or family member. In time here we will see our need to reach out to "someone" beyond our human existence.

So early-on as I learned there were some things I must do to make this situation manageable for me, education became part of my strategy. The more we know about a problem the more manageable it will be become. All through life, that philosophy has served me well. While my majors were sociology, theology, and counseling, psychology always presented me with new insights as to how to make life more meaningful, productive, and rewarding in spite of what life set before me. Whenever faced with any

293

problem, there is always something more we can learn about that issue. We are in an age when knowledge is so accessible, and we cheat ourselves by not taking advantage of every learning opportunity. Education is one way we can do something to equip ourselves in the midst of the fray.

The reader may be wondering to herself/himself if this is really a chapter on religious faith. I assure you that this writer thinks it is. My faith tells me that I am to do all I can for myself and that God is with us in that process, too. I believe that God gave me talents and mental ability to use and that my first obligation to myself and to my God (Your God, as perceived by you, might be different) is to be productive by the full exercise of those gifts.

So recognizing your legitimate question about this being a religious chapter, we thank you for asking, and please read on. One more comment before we continue discussing what we can do to help ourselves. Religion is hardly a subject set apart from other aspects of life. It permeates all we do or it cannot be characterized as faith. So while I am talking about what appear to be non-religious matters, we are in fact feeling faith's impact in all we say and do. For example, here in this paragraph we make a religious assertion when we speak of using our talents as a coping mechanism. It is a good mental health approach to see life as a whole, integrated, connected, and as we will be suggesting here, having a guiding light to show us the way.

As we hinted in the paragraphs on seeking professional advice, our help might be also in a trusted friend, a colleague, a partner who has suffered, too, or a spouse. As we indicated, professionals have their rightful place. Yet, we are not limited to those with special expertise, but we hopefully will know when to seek what from whom. Supportive relationships is the operative phrase here. None of us can go it alone without suffering unpleasant consequences.

In our society today we experience far too many disconnects. We began this book with the subject of laying off a land. Since we are from a rural, agricultural background, we use also this analogy. When one goes to the grocery store and buys any product for the table, it is so easy to get home, prepare the food, and devour it without much, if any, consideration for the source of that food. We know money does not grow on trees, but so many are so disconnected to aspects of farming that they have no idea how the food chain begins.

As we are disconnected from that reality, we also sadly walled ourselves off from each other in daily life. It seems to be a little of heaven if we have a few wooded acres where we can hide away. It is one thing to seek necessary relaxation from a hectic day, but it is quite another to disconnect from those who we could not live without. We could ask why our day was so hectic; what goals of our lives took us down that road.

Let's not pick on those who have the means to provide such respite. We can live next door on a crowded street or in an apartment and seldom say a "Hello" to a neighbor. Now with the security measures as follow-up of Nine Eleven, we are even encouraged to be suspicious of our neighbors and we're almost asked as government policy to spy upon them. There are mental illnesses, such as schizophrenia, that have paranoia as a symptom. Shall we all become "schizophrenic," paranoid?

We are about to become a mentally ill nation, focusing on our physical security alone. The terrorists are delighted! No one can affect our feelings unless allowed. More than ever in today's insecure world, we need supportive relationships just when we are avoiding them the most. Could it be that an effective deterrent to terrorism is to get better acquainted with your neighbor, not less? Now putting it that way, we begin to feel the resistance to tear down our fences and make friends; hesitant, aren't we?

It is not our purpose here to share a list of effective ways to be a supportive person. We only intend to make the point here that supportive relationships are vital to those who want to make the most out of their life and circumstances. We encourage the reader to search out persons whom they can trust, whom they can lean on when necessary. Given our humanity we will fail sometimes and pick the wrong one. Maybe that is best said with an old saying, "It is best to have loved and lost than never to have loved." Reach out; worthwhile living depends on it.

One way to reach out in a rewarding way is to be the first one to speak. The best way to find a friend who will be there when we need them is to befriend another. In other words, take the initiative. If we wait for someone to make the first move, it may not happen, and we just deepen our perceived notion that no one cares anyhow. Making such a move is good mental and emotional exercise. It puts us in charge of a situation which we are wishing to change. It doesn't always work and in that case, we just have another opportunity to do some more exercise. We emphasize physical exercise so much. Let's put a new focus on the mental and emotional and find new thrills in our human relationships.

One specific way to open up relationship doors is by assisting others. Surely there is, at least, a short list of people around us who could use a little assistance. Even small kindnesses are appreciated by the majority of people. We will not take the time nor space here to make a long list of ways to help another. Why not list several for yourself? Why not use your own mental faculties and devise your own list? That would be a list with which you are comfortable and one that matches your talents. I respect your ability to do that, but I suspect you still might have some hesitation.

Privacy is a real question to consider. Sure we would want and should respect the privacy of others. However, it needs to be said that some who appear not to be interested are the very ones whose day would be made better by a kindness from another human being. Some people have been

297

hurt deeply by relationships that went sour. They are afraid to become vulnerable again, understandably so. We need not invade others' privacy to let them know that they are worth a valuable moment of someone's time.

The main issue here for our emotional well-being, especially if we are burdened ourselves with some problem, is to focus on others rather than on ourselves. Thinking of others and finding positive ways to lend a hand to another, friend or stranger, is good medicine. It might be well in many cases, where no physical reason contraindicates, for the doctor to prescribe such rather than the newest version of a tranquilizer. Although I am not a physician, this workable remedy sounds like a good suggestion. No high pharmacy bill will be given, either.

This is a matter of reaching out beyond ourselves, legitimately meeting a need of another sufferer and getting high return for our own well-being in the process. We do that knowing that whomever we help is just another fellow pilgrim along the way. To assist another with a condescending attitude will spoil our good return. Never do we know when we, too, will need a friend. That same person that we helped might not be the one to be there for us, but having the right attitude puts us in line to receive a lift from someone along the way.

Just this very day, this came true. My grandson and I love to fish. Once when I was incapacitated for a long period, two fishermen shared their bluegill catch. Now both of them are not able to go fishing. We shared our

298

fish with them this past summer. They were grateful. End of subject, I thought. I looked out to check the weather awhile ago and found a package on our patio. One of the recipients had left it, in Santa fashion, sometime this afternoon. We are not what you call close friends, but we all do belong to a group who need each other and who will return the favors when and if they are able. Shortly here, we are going to learn more about that kind of group who were our support and comfort during the difficult days.

There comes a time for all of us when reaching out to others, being knowledgeable about ourselves, seeking the help of the experts, isn't quite enough. We live as if there is a remedy for everything, a pill to be dispensed, a fad that surely will perfect us, and even mighty power to blow away our enemies. Some of what we did as a family during those years of Dad's absence worked for us, and so I suggested above some of the key sources of strength. During those days we found no perfect solutions, no short-cuts, no magic sources for our aid. Such did not exist, and despite appearances today of all we have going for us, coping is a chore, and there are times, many times, when we are at our wits end.

These were things we could do, emphasizing here things to do, action. There will be times in life when doing is not sufficient and we are left with being. We are such a culture of action that we are at a loss to know what to do when action leaves us shortchanged. Dad's life seemed worthless to most people. In fact, in some sense to me, also. I have spent a lot of time

299

and energy attempting to make sense out of his life. We have wanted to show the reader that even a person lacking in a contribution to our work-a-day world can have a reason for being.

This is a faith statement on my part. It is something I believe very deeply. It may not be your conclusion to this half century of Dad's confinement, but it is mine. It has not always been mine. My thoughts on the subject only changed when I realized that by sharing his story, his life and being could be redeemed. There would be no book without my decision to share this faith that everyone is a segment of the ages and has his/her place in that great scheme. And only you, each reader, can decide for yourself whether my action, by faith, has placed a legitimate value upon my Dad's life.

We believe this so strongly that in the beginning of this book, we have dubbed my father Rip Van Winkle II. While Dad did not regain all his mental faculties, he has now come out of his long slumber of over forty-seven years in an unexpected way, posthumously. Now he provides us with the setting by which he can, though us, make a contribution to mental health. This was not even a dream ten years ago before his death. This is an example of how we can and must remain open to life's unexpected turns. These possibilities take on a spiritual meaning, that is, something far beyond us, bringing events of this nature to fruition.

It is when we view the total picture that we get a glimpse of the potential. We began the story with an overview of his ancestry. Far more than dates and times, we noted that such a view back in time aids us in our understanding of ourselves. We looked back, also, at the good times when we were a normal family in rural Sullivan County. Far more than childhood stories common to so many of us, we wrote about childhood as a critical stage for mental health.

Far more than reminiscing about school activities, we had the opportunity to see how elementary and high school can be the place where we develop coping skills with the aid of caring teachers and administrators. Far more than just reading lots of medical charts, we saw how the medical community complex holds the key to healing of the body and mind not by technology alone.

Far more than relating how one single mother made ends meet, we were amazed at my mother's confidence and strength and noted how her early life prepared her for success. And now, far more than "preaching" our own brand of the Christian faith, we are attempting to show how one needs a focus far beyond themselves, one that works by faith for the long haul. You may not be a follower of the Christian faith; you need not be to understand our human limitations and have a view of something beyond ourselves. Always in this Twentieth Century long story, mental health is the issue—For Pete's sake and mine and yours.

301

Gene Gilbreath

Before I tell you about our involvement in a church, let me share what I believe is the inspiration and motivation for all the action potentials mentioned above in this chapter. Without question many groups are good at physical and psychiatric healing, education, charity or social work, and spiritual searching, all wonderful activities that make our human existence bearable and productive. We applaud all these efforts. We do not seek to raise one in status above the other.

It takes all of the above to make life worthwhile, assisting each other as we mentioned before, each contributing to our well-being. Regardless of how each of these disciplines appear to be segregated, there is one common thread that inspires and motivates. Laying aside the selfish monetary interest of some individuals in any discipline, these are bound together by a common source of inspiration. It matters not what you call the forces at work in our world, but simply stated there are good and bad. The bad is a corruption of what was meant to be good. The "good" is what holds us together. It motivates and inspires to do that which is beneficial to us all.

The source of the good is our Creator. Granted some will argue otherwise. This, however, is not an argument here; it is a statement of faith that has served us well. Until we kneel to that Source far beyond our comprehension, we will not dance the life of caring that we were destined to perform. That Source beyond our own capabilities is our inspiration and motivation for all our action potentials. Have you noticed how many

302

astronauts are verbal about that-which-seems-beyond them as they take in the sights of an unfathomable universe?

At this point in the writing Columbia was lost with its seven crew members. What a tragedy in every aspect even for the whole world. It is my faith that such events, while not caused by my God, are the kind of happenings that have something profound to teach us. What is to be learned here? It is a thought that follows the very kind of effort of which I have just been writing.

There is nothing wrong with our efforts to improve ourselves and to do so on what appears to be our own intelligence, initiative, and strength. We have just been suggesting we do that as a starting point to devise coping skills for the rough places in life. In my religious faith we can do that for ourselves and others by using the talents God gave to us to use for just such occasions.

What goes wrong then? Martin Luther King said, "Our scientific power has outrun our spiritual power. We have guided missiles and misguided men."[117] What goes wrong is that we do succeed and in that success we displace gratitude for Someone's assistance with our own pride of accomplishment. Pride of accomplishment is a good and appropriate feeling providing we know how we got the job done. No one does anything alone. Think about it. We can do nothing without building upon the gifts of others.

---

[117] *Tribune-Star*, "Cryptoquote," May 1, 2000

303

Gene Gilbreath

To make this clearer, what would you have accomplished if someone and Someone had not taught you how to nurse, suckle, or swallow? Contrary to our prideful nature, we can do nothing alone. Maybe the larger sin is our arrogant attempt to do it all alone.

Much is being made of the feeling of family within the NASA community. That expression is impressive. There is no doubt among that whole complex that no one does anything alone. No shuttle goes up without the laying on of hands of anyone who ever had any thought of its potential or made any contribution toward the liftoff. Now we know, too, that no shuttle comes down safely without that same assistance of that family, seen and unseen, living or dead. God bless that sense of community responsibility within NASA. My, what a contrast with the way Congress operates and what national goals and purposes for the greater good are thwarted by such partisanship and self-serving.

However, despite the accomplishments in outer space and for our national good, something went wrong. Something went wrong also with the Challenger and as well with other tragedies within the history of the program. I am not suggesting that we will ever do it perfectly. As long as human beings are in charge, it won't be without terrible setbacks. Regardless of who makes a religion out of our secular efforts, we will always be indebted to someone before us and to Someone beyond us.

304

Have you noticed Who we turned to for comfort and strength? I wonder if those who desire to have one nation but not under God notice how we reach out to Someone in these times of national tragedy. Do they really believe that our human efforts alone will avoid further mistakes? One would think that if that belief in human ability alone is valid, then we should not have made these mistakes that sent Columbia to its death. It has been years since we suffered the Challenger destruction also with its crew. It has been years since we have known about a potential tile cause or maybe more recently ignored other flaws. We are so good at learning from our mistakes, aren't we?

Ok, what is the point if we are going to have mistakes, even tragic ones? Our human mistake is that we ourselves believe, we ourselves, can fix most anything. The mantra now is, "We will fix this." This is admirable but deadly. We should fix it, yes, but with whose help? When will we learn that we were not here in the beginning of the universe and that we will be long gone before the end of it? The unfathomable universe denies our exaltation of self. Our confidence needs to be tempered with a little humility. We thought we would find Osama ben Laden, too, didn't we?

The needed ingredient in this mix for space exploration, world problems, or for solutions within our own lives is to know our limitations and to then lean on the unfathomable resource of the Creator. The Creator made us and the whole universe and is available for guidance, strength, and comfort, as we find our way in space or personally. A statement of faith? Sure, but will we find any better security elsewhere or bright stars to lead us? The record of humanity alone does not reveal much lasting improvement for humankind. Wars used to be more localized, and now we are almost into WWIII. Our hearts are just as evil as ever toward our each other in this earthly existence.

Even if you cannot subscribe to a personal God concerned with our affairs, are there not "tablets of stone" in the universe which point us to a way of life as it ought to be? Are there not "laws" that you didn't make, that you can't change, and ones with which you have to deal? Is the "survival of the fittest" the first and only precept for our guidance? It seems to be the basis for much of our activity as humans. Just what if you turn out some day to be less than the fittest? Would that be fair? You would prefer that the law didn't apply. So you see that allowing yourself to be duped into believing and acting that way with your neighbor, or with another nation, will not be justice for all.

"Survival of the fittest" is quite all right until you get sick. Then somehow you come to believe that the sick should have medical care at reasonable cost, right? Insurance company CEOs will feel differently if they become mentally ill and discover that their policies to save money were unfair. Pharmaceutical CEOs will feel differently if, by some fate, they fall to the level of the poor who cannot afford their expensive medications. A "tablet of stone" of the universe indicates the unfairness of the rise of medical costs far above any other commodity and less than adequate coverage for millions. Some day soon we will discover that the medical complex, with its high costs promoted by our worship, is not a god afterall. It enhances our emotional life to understand that death will come to all regardless of how many surgeries, pills, and even makeovers.

"Survival of the fittest" is acceptable to you unless there is a stock market collapse, and then you will be in favor of charities that run soup kitchens. Only the well and secure think one should leave their life savings to the unpredictable stock market. "Survival of the fittest" is great for the investor unless the CEO of the company gets millions and the investor loses his pension. Then one sees that the haves and the have-nots have so much in common. The universe teaches an obvious lesson that hasn't soaked in yet. We are in this together; we occupy the same space. Good is meant for all or meant for none!

Let us state the issue another way. As we have made a god of our own ability as suggested earlier, we have also made a god of technology. I am using technology right now and enjoying it fully. Technology is God's gift to human kind. What would we have accomplished if it were not for the dependable forces and resources of the universe? We would not have technology unless we lived in a universe that made it possible. I am not suggesting we not have nor that we do not improve our technology.

307

Technology is not so much our gift to ourselves as it is a gift built into the scheme of things. We would not have discoved it had it not been there!

Given what we know about the universe, the gift of it to us, shouldn't we all have the ability to share in the same advances of technology? How would sharing our abundance reduce some cause for terrorism? Are not terrorists the have-nots? Shall we deliberately keep some nations underdeveloped? Radical thinking? Yes, humankind has always thought God's message that we all are His children was radical.

Since this is a book on mental health, let us think about that field for a moment. At one time in history, the mentally ill were thought to be possessed by some demon. We had rudimentary technology that found ways to produce apparatuses that were called restraints. We locked them up and threw away the key. Now we have technology that is better at diagnosis, and thus we find some illnesses to be caused by physical disorders and not, as thought, from hysteria, nerves, or anxiety. History shows how the medical profession in every generation has had some catch-all term to use when they did not know the answers.

Some of those disorders are now treatable with pharmaceutical technology. Others are also controlled, restrained if you will, by the same branch of technology. Our mistake is to believe that any technology is a cure-all in its designated application. Again, we are saying that we must be careful about thinking that alone we can conquer any frontier or that we alone should get rich from providing help for the mentally ill. When pharmaceuticals make sure of their representation in the State Mental Health Agency, is it because they care so much? Or does it have a little something to do with making sure the return is high enough for CEOs and investors? Is there not some "law" of fairness for just gain?

Am I suggesting in any way that religion can always be the guiding force in our human activity? No! Religion, as such, has a history of making the same kind of mistakes that I have referred to above. It made those mistakes, critical ones, because we too often mistook our own human conclusions to be "gospel." We have yet to know God's will fully and so we are cautioned to realize again how mistaken we can be as we are quick to tell how life should be. It is hard for us to understand that the same God is God of both sides in any war.

The faith that will sustain the universe and prevent it from being destroyed by us is a God bigger than any practice of any religion expressed by its human constituents. Brother faced brother in our own Civil War, and brother, like it or not, faces brother in any war. Good religion dictates that universal truth of our relationship to each other, a recognition that our enemies are kinfolk, like it or not. It is hard to understand how any group can mow their enemies down in the name of their religion. Well, maybe not so difficult since the real issue is power disguised as religion. This goes for Muslims and Christians alike.

Take race for instance. The color of no people is their ticket to heaven. How often religion has been used to keep certain peoples in their place. How often governmental systems have elevated some races and keep others subservient. But it is a question of more than race. It happens to all levels of the disenfranchised. How often we use an attitude of superiority to deal with the poor, the hungry, and the sick. All of these expressions of people's inhumanity to other people reveal someone's misdirected notion of their own superiority over others. It says so much about us and nothing about the God of the universe who seeks the best for all His children. Without some standard above all of us, this planet and the next is in grave trouble and will self-destruct.

My own faith, Christianity, with its various disparate groupings, ranks among those who should take notice that none of us exemplify the whole truth in our treatment of others and of our environment. We have made our mistakes and will continue to do so. Does this mean that there is something that discredits our faith beyond repair? No more so than saying the space program is invalid and beyond correction. Can we discredit the Muslim faith because certain extremists accept terrorism as the answer to their problems?

One of our answers to our personal or world problems is to admit our lack of perfection, look beyond our provincial knowledge, and strive to work within the framework of the best that we can conceive. Those of our faith who back one political party or another surely must always acknowlege gross imperfections on either side.

Just maybe, some will say, we will keep learning so much about the universe that we will have explained it all and then have no need of this God to whom you refer. That is something like saying you can explain your mother and dad away. The comment about no need of God is based on the idea that God only exists within the framework of what is unexplained. I just read today the news story about the NASA probe now a million mile out in space that took a picture of the universe in its infancy. That does nothing to lessen my belief. In fact, it does just the opposite. The more I know for sure about what I saw as a child gazing into the heavens in our front yard back on the Bicknell Place, the more I believe that there has to be a Designer out there!

Everyone should be a part of a group who seek to fulfill this dream of a better world, one beyond what we have and one that challenges our own selfish desires, one that comforts and strengthens us for difficult days and gives us an encompassing purpose. We need a group with the highest ideals so that we are never left alone to our own devices. So understanding our imperfections, let me tell you something about our participation in a supportive group that we called the Mt. Tabor church. You may find the same support within a large church if it is designed for small group quality time of participation.

It was a small group, yet part of a larger fellowship, and a part of the community. We were a small rural congregation numbering under fifty most of my childhood and youth days. During those times there were five churches on the same charge, that is, under the supervision of the same pastor. These other churches were also considered small, some with more or less people involved. While limited in the type of activities a small group can provide, one positive characteristic stands out. It is, all too simplistic for some, the caring and supportive atmosphere provided to our family. We were never a stranger there. You are most likely to feel welcome in a group if the members of that group understand, as we have said, their own imperfections. Support is most likely forthcoming if others get to know you.

The title to this chapter has a special origin. Early in our church experience we knelt to pray at the services. There were no kneeling benches as in the Catholic churches. We knelt at the pew seat. Theologically speaking we were in keeping with our faith. To talk to God one should humble oneself. Humility is another word that could have been used above in our discussion of looking beyond ourselves to Someone greater. We came to see that kneeling is a symbolic act of humility. So in time, the practice of the physical bowing of the knee was discontinued but never the spirit behind the practice. To find help we believed we should kneel, and if not physically, then certainly in the heart and mind acknowledging our dependence on our Creator. So "Kneeling to Dance" is a way of saying that

312

if we are to be joyous over-comers in the midst of life's hardships, we need to use our strengths, bow to our limitations, and trust God who is the Source of our strength and direction.

The fellowship of that small congregation gave us support similar to that of NASA. In word and in deed they were there for us. The critic points out that NASA is not a "spiritual" group, that is, it is categorized more accurately as a "secular" group. On the surface, it seems that the point is well taken. For one thing, certainly, it is a group driven by a worthwhile purpose. It is a group who know their need of each other. It is also a group, who understand that they are dealing with something far greater than themselves. In some respects I believe that their motivation for assisting each other in this difficult time is grounded in the personal religious faith of many of its members. We hear the term "faith-based." Faith-based people reach out to others. We were a part of such a fellowship.

Nothing is completely secular if the members thereof believe and practice some expression of their personal religious faith. So it is completely impossible for us to keep religion and our public life separate. A faith that is at the core of a person's being cannot be kept private. A person's life cannot be compartmentalized. This is a mental health issue again. We are one person, a whole person, just one person, and not two. We are not one person this morning before work and another at work.

313

Granted, we try keeping one hand private, but it is not healthy nor without serious consequences mentally and emotionally. Such division cannot long endure. This does not mean, though, that we can impose our own brand of religion upon another. If our faith really works, we will treat other approaches with respect. Caring can operate without imposition and should in America where we need the right balance between the freedom of speech and religion. What God says is Truth, but what I interpret God to say could be wrong.

Another way that the association of religion and the remainder of life comes together is the subject of several studies lately. We will not bother to reference the various studies here except to footnote one.[118] They make the news each time a new study is done that shows that one's faith has a lot to do with their physical health. Sincere religion usually affects lifestyle because the Books of the major religions usually speak, I think, of the stewardship of the body. Religion also tends to cause people to think differently about life, about purpose, and how we achieve our goals. That difference helps people to approach life with less stress and conflict.

A life with less stress, one that has a noble purpose, one that disciplines the physical body, and one that understands its place in the universe, is one that will be healthier. Would not then the person of faith find it imperative to

---

[118] Koenig, Dr. Harold, Dir. of Duke University Center for the Study of Religion/Spirituality and Health, associate professor of Psychiatry, assistant professor of Medicine, Duke University Medical School.

quit smoking or stop over-eating? Those are just two applications of how the relationship of religion and physical health are intertwined. We point out that mental health is enriched by the religion based lifestyle.

For years some in the psychiatric related professions have been skeptical about any positive influence of religion. I suspect that part of that problem has been the aversion of that worker to religion personally. It is not unheard of nor uncommon for those who treat people's emotional ills to approach a problem from their own perspective and viewpoint. Our very human nature makes that likely. Another contributing factor in discrediting religion is what these counselors have seen in their treatment experience as displayed by psychotics.

Yes, psychotics make the headlines when in that state they sometimes believe God told them to do some horrible act. One does not proceed to discredit all religion just because a deranged person thought they heard God speak. There is absolutely no comparison of that state of affairs with what average people experience within any congregation, whether Jewish, Christian, Muslim, or whatever. The logic of those few who hold the whole accountable for the few is faulty, to say the least. We were people who were trying to make sense out of life's rough places and knew we could not do it alone given the gravity and magnitude of the situation. We chose the church as our best bet.

So the people of our faith-based group were there for us in specific ways. Their faith was their motivation that caused them to put their arms around us and support us with encouragement and prayer. They went beyond the emotional support and helped us with our physical needs, too. It was announced one Sunday that there was a needy family in the community. We were to bring to bring food items for their pantry the next Sunday. We had very little to share but took some canned goods, most likely home canned ones, and placed them as did others at the chancel rail. When the service had ended the pastor announced who the recipients were. It was the Gilbreaths! That small congregation had shared so sacrificially, and we went home with enough groceries to last over a month.

Sunday after Sunday we gathered there with this group of friends. Children and adults alike were part of classes that learned more about their faith and what they believed was expected of them as followers of Christ. The Bible was studied which gave the basis for why we were to express love to those around us. We listened to sermons which also inspired us and taught us about our faith. We learned that while we were a small group in the Midwest, we were to share in the burdens of humankind all around the world.

The founder of our Methodist denomination was John Wesley who believed that "the world was our parish." We were to save all we could to be able to give all we could. Such a concern for all peoples world-wide and

316

adequately grounded in the Holy Bible was sufficient to inspire us to care about and act with compassion towards all peoples. We found joy and satisfaction in adhering to our creed. Far more, we found emotional compensation in the living out of the faith as it pertained to helping others.

Mom expressed her satisfaction in those ways, too, and in one other. Mom was a whistler. She used it in two different ways. She could make a loud, shrill whistle with different fingers strategically placed in her mouth. One we were sure to recognize was the whistle with one little finger in her mouth. Since we kids wandered over a two mile range, you can imagine why she used that one. We could pretend not to hear, but unless we had evidence that we were actually too far out of reach, we had no excuse for not heading for home. I learned to whistle about as loudly with two fingers but just couldn't make the one finger work.

Rev. Lennis Donaldson, pastor of the Graysville Circuit of five churches, the daughters, Virgiline and Gloria, and wife Helen. Lennis pastored those churches from 1943-1947.

So in time, I could answer her if we were within range.

Her second kind of whistling was the common teeth-tongue-lip maneuver. This one she used to express her joy in her faith. During our years at home, she whistled gospel tunes. It was not unusual for her to do this most of the day as she worked. Whether doing the laundry, cleaning house, or cooking a meal, the songs poured forth. Looking back on those days makes me wonder how she could be so happy under the circumstances of those days. Dad was still home then, and housework was drudgery, hard work. She managed the day with this music of the heart. Needless to say, it made the day for the whole household more enjoyable.

On another occasion, the church and community rallied to assist us. This time it was the community joined in with the church providing us with the necessities of life. We will say more about the community involvement in a little while. We lived in the middle of three Methodist churches, each two mile or less away. The event occurred on a Thanksgiving Day. Again, we were not thinking about any such happening. Our pastor and family, the Donaldsons, invited us to their home for Thanksgiving dinner. We gladly accepted given the shortage of money and a cupboard almost bare.

When we returned to our home, the Davis Place, we were not aware of anything different until we entered the house. The kitchen was a room about 12x14 ft. The large table was loaded; it could hold no more. There was barely walking room around the table. Items were stacked along each wall as high as they could be stacked. More stuff overflowed onto the back porch and into the living room. One can only imagine the feelings of surprise, shock, disbelief, and then gratitude. Those feelings lessened not for an hour or two as we sorted through the items. We were experiencing the love of a church and community. Carl Menniger said, "Love cures people—both those who give and the ones who receive it."119

Many had names on them and many did not. I can remember one offering from people that I hardly knew. They lived farther away than others, and we had little contact with them. I will always remember their names, Herb Christy and wife. It was touching in that they were of neither of our church fellowships. Tears often flowed as we continued the task of sorting out this love offering, articles from those from whom we would have expected and from those on expected and from those on

Graysville Church, 2 mile to our west, where I attended youth meetings and Sunday evening services. The third church near us was Providence two mile south of us where I attended mid-week prayer and Bible study services. On special occasions I attended the other two churches, Kingsley and Union Chapel. Each provided more small group experience of which we have spoken.

the fringe of our community. Cash was certainly needed, and it was often stuck in with other items or just in an envelope by itself.

We had come home about three o'clock. The minister had not seemed to be in any hurry to take us back home. He was deliberately giving people time to bring their offering to the house. With sorting yet to be done, Bill and

---

119 *Tribune-Star*, op.cit., "Cryptoquote" June 24, 1997, King Features Syndicate, Inc.

I left that chore with Mom and Mary. Bill and I went to the barn to do the evening chores of feeding and milking, and Tom went to feed the chickens and gather eggs. We had had enough excitement for the day, but there was more to come.

On opening the barn door, there were many bushels of corn in one big pile. Old Snip, the horse, the hogs, and the seven cows were happy with the prospect of more to feed upon. And certainly two boys were happy with this additional gift. Now we could keep the stock longer, especially the cows who were producing a little milk to sell. Also, to keep the hogs was good news since we would want to butcher at least one of them.

So now with the milking done, we went into the hayloft to toss down the remainder of what hay was left. There we found many, many additional bales of hay. What good news we had to share with the remainder of the family as we returned to the house. What heartfelt gratitude we felt for all this love offering from neighbors and friends. We slept well that night knowing now that all would be well for awhile longer. George Elliston wrote, "How beautiful a day can be when kindness touches it."[120]

Now a word about the community support. Some of them were close neighbors, others two mile and more away. They knew us for lots of reasons. Some were old neighbors when we lived at the other four places not far away or neighbors of Mom in her young days. Some were our

---

[120] Ibid. June 23, 1997

teachers in our school. Most of the people we knew by our participation in the other two churches and by my attending other denominations in neighborhoods close by. Other people we knew since Dad did lots of odds jobs around the area, helping local farmers who needed help and doing carpenter or common labor jobs. Some of the contributors were people he worked with on the WPA. The community had lots in common giving people a motivation to help. See Appendix I for a list of neighbors and friends who helped out in so many ways, not only on this special occasion but at many other times.

We have mentioned some negatives about that period regarding how people tended to shun mental illness victims and the reluctance of the banker who refused a loan. However, this

The Mt. Tabor Church being torn down in 1984 after a Christmas Sunday de-consecration service in 1983. Mom's son-in-law, Butch Huff, and crew are doing the work. Butch was the first to be buried in the new cemetery where the church stood.

great outpouring of support on this Thanksgiving Day overshadowed those isolated events. We could charge feed bills and grocery bills, the sellers knowing of the risk. We were allowed a few gallons of gas on the rationing sticker of friends who help us to have the fuel to go see Dad. We were

321

loaned farming equipment—what a risk in the hands of inexperienced boys! We boys were given odd jobs to do. And on many other occasions money was slipped into our hands or food items given to us.

The critic will say I am prejudiced, but let that be as it may, it seems to me that almost all of those actions were faith-based. To be sure there may

be some community support now for families of the mentally ill which does not appear at first glance to have that kind of basis. Even these less obvious motivations came from people who believed in something, if not Someone, beyond themselves. The point is that families and sufferers themselves need the support of the whole community.

Mom and Gene at Mary's with the bridge in the background, one built of lumber from the church, and still served as a form of support as Sue walked across it to help her mother, Mary, in her declining years.

Maybe it is volunteer work now within a local Mental Health organization, or local United Way, or involvement in legislative action, or just being a friend, all and more ways indicate our understanding of the need for community assistance.

Now someone asks, "Didn't your church close in 1983?" What does that say about anything lasting? In fact, did not the other church south of you,

Providence, where you attended weekly prayer services close long before that? And is not the third church, Graysville, where you attended Sunday evening services and youth meetings, is it not close to the same fate? You used the right word in those queries, "fate." Yes, that might be considered the fate of those church buildings but not of the church. Those are only physical manifestations of our faith and never the heart of it.

The faith lives on in a multitude of ways. Mom left that place and became a member of the Sullivan United Methodist Church serving there as her energy allowed at that stage of her life. She had supported the Mt. Tabor Church with the "widow's mite" for several years, still tithing her meager income, and then

The ladies from Sullivan United Methodist Church who did not forget one of their members in her need. They extended that love to her family by providing a dinner following her funeral. Thanks to Norma Mason and all who provided on that occasion. Churches demonstrate their care or they are not the church.

holding yard sales regularly. Why? Mom believed in God and His love for us all. She is at peace from her struggles of life, and I can think of her singing lustily in God's Presence as she did in the same spot many years ago. The God of the universe of which we have spoken will surely encompass her.

And now she rests with Dad, with her daughter, Mary and husband, Butch, and g-grandson, Jeff where the old church stood.

The support of Mom's new church was evidenced likewise. She received part of the altar bouquet many Sundays while confined during the last years. People from the church visited her and called on the phone. One group of ladies who visited bringing flowers included Evelyn Kent, Beverly Blair, Hazel Martin (another Mt. Tabor ex-member), Billie Markee, and Dorothy Burns. Some brought her food from the various activities of the church. Mom stayed active as she could being Prayer Chain captain even sometimes from her hospital bed. Why, again? We believe God's love for us makes us want to share it.

The church, its people and fellowship, was the good news in our lives. Others may chose some other avenue for solace, strength, and support, but this worked for us. We thought of it as a wise choice. We believed it to be a good choice. There were no delusions as to how it would help us. On occasion it fails because human beings make up any local group. Yet, compared with other options, the church served us well over the long haul.

We highly recommend it to those who want to choose the higher road to finding satisfaction in life that can be lived abundantly. For us, we found kneeling before our God, that is, acknowledging our limitations before the Father of the Universe, to be our source of a lasting joy that would make us dance even when we did not feel like dancing.

With this story that has spanned a century, we know now of more certainty that our God is the God of all generations. From gazing at the stars in childhood to the space age technology that took us to the moon, to the many space probes that have circled some distant planets, and someday now to Mars, we acknowledge the gift of the universe for our domain.

"Your faithfulness extends to every generation, like the earth you created; it endures by your decree, for everything serves your plans." Psalms 119:91 The Living Bible Version

Washington Irving, the well known author we quoted in the first chapter, said, "Love is never lost. If not reciprocated it will flow back and purify the heart." Dad's love seemed lost to us. It so often did not appear to be reciprocated. What we know now "purifies" our hearts, and we are at peace with that which we did not at first understand.

Thank you, Dear Reader, for "listening" to this story, in the name of Pete and all persons now affected by mental illness and those who will be, while you still have time to make a difference.

FINAL TRIBUTE TO PETE

Dad enjoying the peach cobbler that I had taken to him a couple days before he died. He could now see what he was eating after the cataract surgery. Thanks to the thoughtful caregiver who finally realized that his inability to see was his reason for making a mess from his tobacco spit. At last now, he is better understood and his story will aid others to more fully understand and care for others who become mentally ill.

REST IN PEACE, DAD

FINAL TRIBUTE TO FLEDA

This writer spent all day Wednesday, November 13, 2002, with his mother for the purpose of sorting out some more pictures that might be used for this book. She was not feeling well at all but insisted on staying in the kitchen after lunch to help sort. This was her last effort in assisting with the book. Early the next morning she was taken to the hospital. She spent two weeks there and then three weeks at the nursing home before her daughter, Mary's, death. She spent three more weeks at the nursing home before returning to the hospital for her final two days. Still determined to live to the fullest, she had planned to go back to the apartment on the day of her death on January 20, 2002. Was it the lack of medical care, of assigning the ninety-three year old to death, or was it God's time to go? Some day, like with Dad, we may solve that question, at least to our satisfaction.

REST IN PEACE, MOM

LINGERING QUESTIONS

"Nothing worth doing is completed in our lifetime; therefore, we must be saved by hope." Reinhold Niebuhr, American theologian (1892-1971)

We raised the question in one section of the Prologue Trilogy about the status of mental health in 2048. We chose that date since the first psychiatric hospital was built in Indiana in 1848 and Dad entered Woodmere, Evansville State Hospital in 1948. Counting the exact months, he actually was in his 48th year of confinement.

As Mr. Niebuhr reminds us, "Nothing worth doing is completed in a lifetime." That being the case, we have some lingering questions that come to mind from our experience of writing this book. I won't be around come 2048 so I hope that between now and then the following questions and many others will find solutions. A German proverb says, "Begin to weave and God will give you the thread." Begin now to "weave" and may the resulting mosaic be more beautiful than imaginable, displayed for all to see, for the sake of the mentally ill.

Question: Psychotropic drugs. How can we avoid using them inappropriately for restraints?

Question: Influence of Pharmaceutical companies. How can this be regulated? Sure, they are the ones who make the drugs, but is not a high ranking pharmaceutical company executive becoming the director of a state mental health agency, regardless of qualifications, a little too cozy a relationship?

Question: Experimental treatment. Who oversees such treatment? The pharmaceutical company who wants to sell the product and often provides it free? Will patients and family be informed and necessarily give consent?

Question: Qualifications for personnel who provide direct care. Will nurses, attendants, and any other assistants be better trained? Will they undergo psychiatric examination to qualify?

Question: Technology. Will we come to balance personal caring, respect, and understanding with the technology that we will develop?

Question: Principal leadership. Will an administrator of a State institution be chosen by his/her peers rather than a political appointment? Will that administrator spend any time personally with patients, enough to better know and understand their needs?

Question: Commitments. Will commitments continue to be more voluntary? Will non-mental health personnel be better trained in cases of non-voluntary commitments and hostage situations?

Question: Community based care. Will nursing homes, administrators, primary care givers, social workers, activity directors and dietitians be more qualified to care for mental patients than they have been since the inception of community care?

Question: Will there be a way to quantify quality care so that a provider of care has to balance adequate care with profits?

Question: Legislatures. What will their role be? How can they dictate fiscal matters and not interfere with the technical care by physicians and other care givers?

Question: Public Education. Will we develop better ways to educate the public on understanding the needs of mental patients and how to assist in their re-entry into society?

Question: Local County Mental Health Associations. Could we find adequate support and design to have an active MHA is every county? The need for more committed and dedicated lay and non-professional volunteers.

The answers will not be "Cheaper by the Dozen."[121]

---

[121] Obviouly a borrowed phrase, thanks to those better known Gilbreaths

APPENDIX I

THE MT. TABOR EXPANDED COMMUNITY

ABOUT 1929-1950 AS RECALLED BY AUTHOR

LOcations are only approximate
Not a complete listing

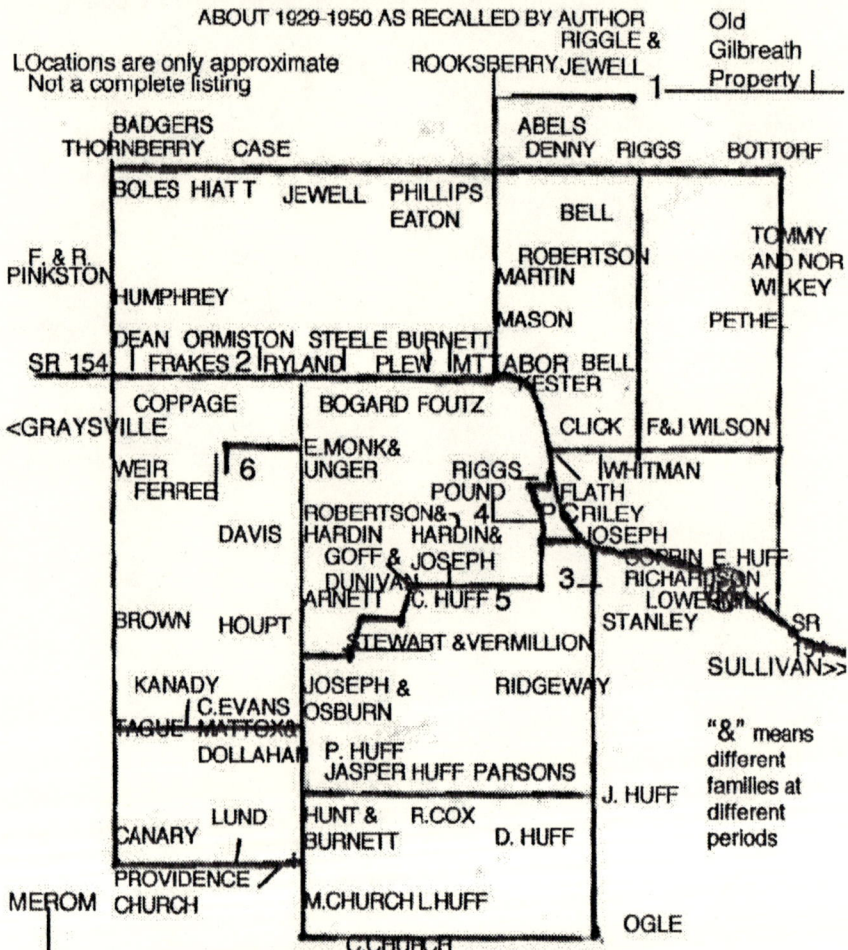

PLACES WE LIVED DURING CHILDHOOD
1 Grandma Riggle's where the author was born. 2 Grandma Gilbreath's (Ormiston) on St. Rd. 154. 3 The Kelley Place 4 The Homer Ray Place west of Poplar Cemetery (PC) 5 The Bicknell Place. 6 The Davis Place

IN MEMORY AND HONOR OF CHURCH AND COMMUNITY SUPPORT MY APOLOGIES TO ANY I FORGOT DURING MY "SENIOR MOMENTS"

APPENDIX II

MT. TABOR CEMETERY

Located in Turman Township, Sullivan County, Indiana, five mile west of
Sullivan on St. Rd. 154

BIBLIOGRAPHY

Anderson, Pearl D., "Country Boy", printed in the "Woodland News", Sullivan Convalescent Center, Vol 9, No 26, June, 1997

Anderson, Terry, CSpan, March 22, 1998

AnRebecca, Ph.D.<AHREF="/PNDI/PND/public/archive/1999/toc-0199.html">Physician's News Digest</a>, January 1999. & copy; 1998 Physician's News Digest, Inc

Application for insanity Inquest, dated and signed, December 16, 1944, Sullivan Circuit Court, Sullivan, IN.

Archives of Indiana United Methodism, The, Depauw University, Greencastle, IN 46135, Church Survey

Bell, Virgil, interviewed at 97 years of age.

Boothe, Dorothy

Boomhower, Ray E; King, Lucy Jane; Drenovsky, Rachael L. "Traces", a Publication of Indiana and Midwestern History" Spring 2001, Volume Thirteen, Number Two, (ISSN 1040-788X), Indiana Historical Society, 420 West Ohio Street, Indianapolis, IN 46202-3269

Court Records, Various, Sullivan County, IN, Court House

Electro convulsive Therapy, NIH Consent Statement Online 1985 Jun 10-12; 5(11): 1-23.

Farmers' Directory of Sullivan County, Indiana, 1896

Forrer, Gordon R., M.D., and Miller, Jacob J., M.D., "Atropine Coma: A Somatic Therapy in Psychiatry," American Journal of Psychiatry, 1958, Vol. 115, No. 5, pp 455-458

Friedberg, John M. M.D., "Shock Treatment, Brain Damage, and Memory Loss: A Neurological Perspective," American Journal of Psychiatry 134:9, September 1977, pp: 1010-1013. (http://www.idiom.com/~drjohn/amjpsych.html)

Koenig, Dr. Harold, Dir. of Duke University Center for the Study of Religion/Spirituality and Health, associate professor of Psychiatry, assistant professor of Medicine, Duke University Medical School.

Galbraith, Edwin A.S., "Early Scottish Kingdoms and the Galbraith Clan", printed in the Red Tower, a quarterly publication of the Clan Galbraith Association of North America, Vol VI, No 1, Fall 1984

Gilbreath, Clarence Homer, "Collection of Letters to my Family", 1929-1940

Gilbreath, Elmer C, GILBREATH, GALBREATH, GALBRAITH, publisher not known

Gilbreath, Gene, compiler of John Thomas Riggle Family Group Sheet

Gilbreath, Gene, Personal Recollections of Family History

Gilbreath, Fleda H. Riggle, "Memorable Notes in the Life of Fleda Helen Riggle Gilbreath", January,1996

HANDY BOOK FOR GENEALOGISTS, THE, Seventh Edition, The Everton Publishers, Inc, P.O. Box 368, Logan Utah 84321

Harrison Burns, *Indiana Statutes,* (Indianapolis:Bolbbs-Merrill Company, 1955), p. 375

Hasler, Janice and Metzger, Joanna, correspondence and interviews variously

HOLY BIBLE, The, The Living Bible Version.

Http://www.mental health.com/fr30.html

Http://www.nvo.org/merck.htm

Lynch, Harold D., M.D. and Anderson, Milton H., M.D., "Atropine Coma Therapy in Psychiatry: Clinical Observations Over a 20-year Period and A Review of the Literature," Diseases of the Nervous System, Vol 36, No. 12, December, 1975, pp 648-652

Marriage License Abstracts, Vermilion Co, IL, on November 18, 1865

Modern Maturity, AARP, 601 E St NW, Washington, DC 20049, article by Ken Wibecan, Nov-Dec. 1996

"Petition for Letters of Administration", Vermilion Co, IL, June 7, 1872

Pfeiffer, C.C, et.al., THE SCHIZOPHRENIAS, YOURS AND MINE, The Professional Committee of the Schizophrenia Foundation of New Jersey, Pyramid Communications, Inc., 919 Third Avenue, New York, NY 10022, USA, 1970

Paterson, Barbara, "Culcreuch Castle, a Synopsis of its History and Construction" Red Tower, Vol XVI, No 3, Summer 1995, p. 46
People's Home Library, The Culinary section, The R C Barnum Company, Cleveland, OH 1919, P 122

Placement of District Schools in Turman Township, Sullivan County, Indiana, The, Jeanette A. Watson, July, 1964.

Prochnow, Herbert V., A Treasure Chest of Quotations

Riggle, Charles, Jr., Danville, IL, data provided January, 1997

Rigle, John, Probate Box #29, Warren County, Indiana, Case filed August, 1849

Sapp, George G., personal correspondence with this writer, July 26, 1995

Schmidt, Jo Ann Brant, submitter, Western Warren County, Indiana Cemeteries, Vol II

Schuller, Robert, Dr., Hour of Power, The, Channel 10 TV, Terre Haute, IN, March 1997

Sullivan County Historical Society

Sullivan County Public Library, Genealogy Section

SULLIVAN COUNTY 175TH ANNIVERSARY HISTORY BOOK, Turner Publishing Company, P.O. Box 3101, Paducah, KY 42002-3101, 1991

Sullivan County, IN Marriages 10-106

Sullivan County, IN, Marriage records, Bk 16, p. 443

Sullivan Daily Times, The, 115 W. Jackson St, Sullivan, IN.

Tribune Star, The Terre Haute, P O Box 149, Terre Haute, IN 47808

U.S. Department of Health and Human Services, Substance Abuse and Mental Health Services Administration, Center for Mental Health Services, CARING FOR EVERY CHILD'S MENTAL HEALTH: Communities Together. Internet http://www.infoseek.mentalhealth. April 1997

Gene Gilbreath

Vermilion County, IL, Marriage Abstracts

Warren County Marriage Records, reported by County Historians, Mr. and Mrs. Walter Salts, West Lebanon, Indiana

Witham, W. Tasker, Living American Literature, Stephen Daye Press, New York, 1947

Wolfe, Thomas J., HISTORY OF SULLIVAN COUNTY, INDIANA, The Lewis Publishing Company, New York, 1909, Vol II, p. 399

ABOUT THE AUTHOR

Mr. Gilbreath is looking at the picture of the first psychiatric hospital of Indiana, Central State, as it was known in 1944 when his father was a patient there.

Mr. Gilbreath is a native of rural Sullivan County, Indiana. His early education was in the Graysville Consolidated School. He attended Taylor University, 1948-1949. In 1952 he received a BA degree in Sociology and Bible Studies from Evansville College, Evansville, Indiana. His Master's in Divinity was granted by Garrett Biblical Institute, Evanston, IL. In 1959. In 1978 Mr. Gilbreath earned a Master's in Counseling from Indiana State University, Terre Haute, IN. He served as Pastor of United Methodist

Churches in southern Indiana for over thirty-five years before taking disability in 1984. He is married to the former Stella Foutz of Sullivan County. They have two adult children and six grandchildren.

Printed in the United States
1350000004B/43-168